D0457896

THE FALLEN

THE FALLEN

A True Story of American POWs and Japanese Wartime Atrocities

Marc Landas

John Wiley & Sons, Inc.

This book is printed on acid-free paper. ♾

Published by John Wiley & Sons, Inc., Hoboken, New Jersey
Published simultaneously in Canada

All photographs are courtesy the National Archives at College Park, College Park, Md.

For general information about our other products and services, please contact our Customer Care Department within the United States at (800) 762-2974, outside the United States at (317) 572-3993 or fax (317) 572-4002.

Wiley also publishes its books in a variety of electronic formats. Some content that appears in print may not be available in electronic books. For more information about Wiley products, visit our web site at www.wiley.com.

Library of Congress Cataloging-in-Publication Data:

Landas, Marc, date.
The Fallen : a true story of American POWs and Japanese Wartime atrocities / Marc Landas.
p. cm.
Includes bibliographical references and index.
ISBN 0-471 - 42119-7
1. Watkins, Marvin S. 2. Bomber pilots—United States—Biography. 3. World War, 1939–1945—Prisoners and prisons, Japanese. 4. World War, 1939–1945—Aerial operations, American. 5. Prisoner of war—Japan—Biography. 6. War crime trials—Japan. I. Title.
D790.L258 2004
940.54'7252'092—dc22 2003023269

Printed in the United States of America

10 9 8 7 6 5 4 3 2 1

For my parents, Nora and Magno

Contents

Acknowledgments

There is a saying we've all heard: "You can't judge a book by its cover." And while it is generally applied to people's outward appearances, I feel that the truism holds even when taken a bit more literally. When you pick up this book and read the cover, you will see a title, subtitle, and other information pertinent to the book. You will also see a single name, and to that sole name you attribute the work. However, to a degree, the cover misleads because there were more hands responsible for the birth of *The Fallen* than my own. If we were sitting in the movies, the list of end credits would indicate as much. So let the credits role.

I owe my publisher, John Wiley & Sons, thanks on two fronts. I am grateful to them for believing in me as well as the story I wanted to tell. In addition, I owe them a debt of gratitude for placing me in the care of their dedicated and infinitely able staff. Stephen Power provided concise and revealing comments during the entire process. He helped untangle a narrative that teetered on the verge of chaos and allowed me the freedom to discover the story as it developed. His input was invaluable. I would also like to thank Laura Cusack, senior marketing manager, and Yamil Anglada, my publicist at Wiley, for their hard work and expertise. Finally, I would like to extend my gratitude to Kimberly Monroe-Hill, Mary Dorian, and Devra K. Nelson for their diligent editing efforts.

To say that I am grateful to Jeff Kleinman, my literary agent, would understate the magnitude of his involvement. The influence of his insight and vision can be seen from the first sentence to the final period. The manuscript reads smoother and quicker because of his skill and his pen.

Two years ago, the 29th Bomb Group Association and their members welcomed me into their ranks and allowed me to share their experiences during a biannual reunion. Fred Pawlikowski opened the 29th BG world to me, and the Bomb Group historian, Joe Chovelak, pointed me in the right direction. In addition, members of the association—Robert Karther, Robert Michelson, and Eleanor Cobb—put aside time to share their thoughts.

Under normal circumstances time has a way of dulling and erasing memories, particularly painful ones. It would be easiest to leave them alone. However, the families of the Watkins crew displayed the courage worthy of their lost loved ones. I am indebted to each and every family member who trusted me with their memories and feelings: William Halliday, John Colehower, Jessie Sumers, and Deirdre McMaster. It was an honor speaking with them.

I am indebted to the Watkins family—Glendon Watkins, Louise Watkins, Nancy Eure, Susan Watkins, Michael Watkins, and the late Beatrice Watkins—for their patient cooperation. In particular, I am forever grateful to Samuel Watkins for his untiring efforts and enthusiasm. For two years, he continued to give more of his time while I reaped the benefits of his generosity. Without his help, the story of Marvin Watkins would be nothing more than a transcript.

A number of people helped ensure the factual authenticity of the manuscript. Retired Major Charles Eger spent countless hours explaining the life of a B-29 pilot, the realities of aerial combat, and the dynamics of Superfortress flight. Daniel Resendes shared his recollections of what it was like being an investigator in occupied Japan. Sanjay Patel provided on-the-spot answers for numerous medical questions. Finally, I am infinitely indebted to Dr. Delfin Santos for allowing me to tap his surgical expertise. His involvement and ability to simplify technical terms allowed me to better analyze the story's facts.

During the course of writing *The Fallen*, I found myself confronted with the problem facing anyone working on a manuscript for too long: blurry editorial vision. Thankfully, I had friends willing to act as surrogate eyes for me. Christina Bousquet provided insightful comments, particularly on how the early drafts read. I am especially indebted to Irene Cheung for her meticulous line edits, sharp editorial comments, and late-night venting sessions.

Finding any sort of seclusion in the middle of New York City can be a daunting task. Because of this reality, I would like to thank Wayne Furman and the staff at the New York Public Library for making the Allen Room and all of its resources available to me. In addition, I am particularly grateful to Melissa Roach and the entire staff at the Japan Society in New York for their patience and hospitality while using their private library. Finally, the staff at the National Archives at College Park provided an atmosphere conducive to the detective work necessary to piece together an originally disjointed story.

A number of people played integral roles in assisting me during the seemingly endless phases of research, data compilation, and other necessary tasks. For that I would like to thank Gregory Cassagnol, Alison Schuermann, Lorenzo Pescerelli, Jacqui Edwards, Grellan "Keanoo" Harty, Stu Hackel, David Zerenga, Adina Muncan, Marcela Alvarez, and Jessica Campbell. I also owe Christopher Carvey and Generation X Technologies | New York for their Web design talents and know-how. During the final, hectic stages of writing the manuscript, I was in need of a computer to use. Fortunately, my assistant, Katie Gnagy, entrusted me with her laptop for months—saving my peace of mind in the process—and for this I extend my most heartfelt gratitude.

Because much of my time was spent doing research in the Washington, D.C., Virginia, and Maryland area, I was constantly in need of a place to stay. I am grateful to the Amado family—Zeny, Jennifer, and Jevi; the Cabrera family—in particular, Annie; and Wilfredo and Lorenzo Martinez for allowing me into their homes. Their hospitality made being away from home for extended periods bearable.

As far as mentors go, Robert Dannin has taught me the value of generating a healthy discourse, asking questions that need to be asked, and the responsibility of a writer to ask those questions. From professor to friend, I have only benefited from his constant guidance and encouragement.

Finally, I owe everything to my parents, Nora and Magno. Everything that I am, I learned from them. Without their dedication, support, encouragement, and love, finishing the manuscript would have been impossible. The book is more theirs than mine.

Prologue

The last thing Lieutenant Marvin S. Watkins wanted was a war hero's welcome. He did not want to be tugged or pulled or hugged because human contact still felt strange. Large crowds and loud noises made him uneasy even if they just involved family. The cottage-size railroad station where Marvin's sister waited for him suited his mood perfectly: it was quiet.

Marvin hated secrets but still insisted that Lizzie Belle Watkins come alone and not tell their parents of his arrival in Virginia.[1] Yes, he missed his family. No, a few minutes with them wouldn't hurt him. But his final decision, which he toiled with throughout his brief stay at a convalescent hospital in Florida, still stood. Marvin did not want them to see him in this condition.

The man who greeted Lizzie Belle resembled those Jewish concentration camp victims in the news. Weight loss all but erased Marvin's recognizable features, stretching his face like a reflection in a trick mirror. His blotchy skin—a mixture of flea-bitten lesions, torn blisters, and bruises at different stages of healing—hung from his cheeks like a shroud. Black, bristle-like stubble outlined the curves of his jaw. There was nothing kind or gentle or giving about the face leaning forward to kiss Lizzie Belle that day in September 1945.

Marvin's army uniform sagged where it should have stretched, shifted where it should have held steady. If he stood completely still with his arms dangling at his sides, it would have been difficult to tell that a body supported his clothes. Even when Marvin moved—slow, labored, and timid—there seemed to be an infinite amount of space within his narrow sleeves. The ends of his army air force hat swallowed his narrow head, making him resemble a little boy with a grotesquely mismatched middle-age face.

Lizzie Belle remembered a different Marvin. She knew a man whose slender five-ten frame projected a self-assuredness and grace that came with age and experience; whose dark hair, comfortable eyes, and steady smile put strangers and friends at ease; whose serious expressions, which proved reassuring to those dependent on him, never completely disappeared, even when he told a joke.

But some things hadn't changed. Marvin still spoke with a soft Southern drawl. His deep and confident voice still recalled a well-kept appearance and dignity that he commanded before the war. Though

First Lieutenant Marvin S. Watkins (USAAF)

far from being shy, Marvin was always a quiet man who never startled anyone with sudden exclamations. He was all about steadiness.

Marvin had two brothers—Berkeley Jr. and Glendon—and another sister—Nancy—but he was closest to Lizzie Belle. She was only two years older than Marvin, and they had a lot in common. When Marvin left for the army, he wrote her every week, keeping her updated—at least as much as military postal censors allowed—with his progress in aviation school, then from Guam. Through his letters, Lizzie Belle kept the entire Watkins family apprised of Marvin's military career.

When he first arrived stateside from the Philippines in the middle of August, Marvin contacted his other sister in Newport News, since Nancy was the only member of the Watkins clan who owned a phone. But it was not Nancy whom Marvin needed to contact—it was Lizzie Belle. He asked Nancy to act as a go-between and pass messages to Lizzie Belle until he reached the hospital in Florida. After he was stationary, Marvin and Lizzie Belle would communicate directly.

Marvin's journey home spanned half the world and left an already weakened soldier exhausted: it started in Tokyo, took him through the Philippines, California, and Florida, and finally ended in Virginia. As a result, he found himself drifting through a country similar to the one he defended but at the same time eerily, perhaps dishearteningly, different.

While overseas, Marvin heard about the restrictions placed on American citizens during the war. He now saw the backlash: years of food, clothing, rubber, and metal rationing gave way to the need to own. Boys played with metal toy cars again; girls coddled plastic dress-up dolls; women wore nylon stockings; all types of food could be purchased freely without worrying about a point system that limited what was available; meals no longer revolved around cans of Spam or Treet, Dole Canned Pineapples, Del Monte Peas, Heinz Baked Beans, or Franco American Spaghetti.

The world Marvin understood, enjoyed, and loved before shipping out in 1942 had disappeared. Posters peeled from walls bearing signs that had urged Americans to "Back the Attack" because "The Enemy Is Listening." Blue stars on white and red backgrounds hung in windows of households with sons in active service. A gold star—something nobody wanted to see—meant that a serviceman lost his life in battle. Little boys ran around dressed like G.I. Joe—helmet and dog tag included—shooting rapid-fire friction machine guns at make-believe Japs. Women's stores carried quarter-ounce miniature bomb-shaped bottles of "Atomic Bomb" perfume. America had become a repository of safe war images and soft civilian attitudes because it had not suffered the ravages of war the way the rest of the world had. It was as foreign a land as any far-off country and needed to be rediscovered.

Ironically, Marvin's misfortune during the war sheltered him from the reality of postwar America. Because of his POW status, Marvin's trip home, admittedly arduous and circular, went smoothly without unnecessary delays in middle-of-nowhere barely mapped areas of America. The veterans riding next to him weren't so lucky. The majority of them had been forced to find their own way home and discovered that it would not be easy. Automobiles and buses teetered on a state of disrepair and obsolescence because the last civilian vehicle had been cranked off the assembly line in 1942. Railroads scurried to service the sudden deluge of demobilized veterans seeking passage to all parts of the country. Soldiers jockeyed for seats on Pullman trains, and, in many cases, drifting veterans lost their seats to entire families eager to take the vacation that wartime America had denied them. The spirit of giving disintegrated into unabashed self-centeredness. Most of the nation had already numbed to the needs of returning soldiers.

Marvin's exhaustion entailed more than a simple physical tiredness—he was mentally beaten. Something terrible had happened to him during his captivity, and Lizzie Belle saw it in his eyes: they drooped at the corners and sagged beneath his lids, and a vacant stare—so still he seemed dead—fell over Marvin's face when he thought no one was looking. But someone was, and it tortured Lizzie Belle to know that she could not ask him what had happened. Forcing him to talk about it would only hurt him more.

Lizzie Belle drove Marvin directly to Camp Pickett, about twelve miles from his home in Church Road. Before leaving the convalescent hospital in Florida, Marvin received orders to report to the military installation nearest to the location of his enlistment.

Over the course of a month, the Camp Pickett staff nursed Marvin back to his normal weight, finishing the job that was started in Florida. They fed him a balanced diet with enough fat, carbohydrates, and proteins to bury the ill effects of meager Japanese prison food. They supplemented the meals with a regimen of vitamins and exercise. The staff monitored his progress carefully.

Yet for all of the staff's good intentions, they neglected a crucial aspect of Marvin's recovery. If they had looked past the good soldier act—the charade where the shell-shocked soldier impersonates the valiant, fearless, and emotionless warrior—they would have seen Marvin Watkins, the local boy, struggling to make sense of what he had suffered through. Had they addressed it—the way they would with other soldiers after later wars—the anguish of countless guilt-filled nights might have been lessened.

Marvin's stay at Camp Pickett had an unplanned advantage. While his convalescence delayed his homecoming that much longer, it sheltered him from a populace that had grown increasingly hostile to veterans. In many cases, American society saw the soldier as a monster who would fall into a life of crime and debauchery. Newspapers and experts argued that it was impossible for a soldier to turn off the killer instincts rewarded during times of war. Rumors circulated through the papers that an island in the Pacific had been set aside by the American government where the most brutal Marine Corps units would be quarantined for the remainder of their lives. Another rumor told of how a shipload of American soldiers had been torpedoed at sea by the government because of the danger they represented to American society. In addition, any time a veteran reacted violently to a situation, regardless of how isolated the incident, newspaper headlines barked about psychotic soldiers. Fortunately, Marvin was not thrust into that world.

Marvin left Camp Pickett Convalescent Hospital in late September. Again, Lizzie Belle picked him up. This time, however, the man who greeted her looked like her brother. Marvin had regained all the weight that captivity had stripped from him. His sunken cheeks sprang back to life, his skin rebounded with its former elasticity, and muscles that had softened from inactivity rediscovered their definition. Marvin moved quickly, confidently, and decisively.

After four years, Marvin would see his family. He'd worried that his appearance might distress his parents; now it was out of his hands. The staff at Pickett said he was healthy enough to leave, but did he look healthy? Marvin never wanted the people close to him to worry. How would they react to him now? He did not want special treatment, either. Actually, like most veterans who saw action, all he wanted was to be left alone. He dreaded being greeted as a war hero and had even made his family promise not to have anyone else over to celebrate his return. All he wanted was to be home.

Marvin's family had reservations of their own. Besides the vague responses Lizzie Belle supplied, they knew little about his condition. What they did know was that Marvin had been in a Japanese prison and that it must have been brutal. While they hadn't seen or heard much about Japanese prisoner-of-war camps, they could base their opinions on available information. Recent newspapers overflowed with horror stories about murder and torture in Nazi concentration camps. Marvin survived, but had they hurt him?

The leaves in Church Road had already changed colors. A solid wall of lemon-, orange-, and lime-colored trees outlined the Watkins's five-hundred-acre property and separated them from their neighbors. From the farm's entrance—nothing more than a break in the wall of trees—a dirt road ran through the entire length of the farm, from the first rows of tobacco to the two-story whitewashed house at the far end of the property. Compared with the massive oceans of cropland owned by private companies, the Watkins farm was not very significant, but for generations of Watkinses it provided everything a family could need: food, income, and a reason to rise in the morning.

Rows of tobacco plants dominated the farm. If the soil was tillable, a tobacco plant sprouted from the ground. As far as the eye could see in every direction, knee-high, broad-leafed tobacco plants lined the landscape. Tobacco put clothes on their backs and pulled the entire family through the Great Depression.

The Watkins home sat at the far end of the property, where the road disappeared and a narrow, half-grass, half-dirt footpath faded into the adjacent woodland. A horse wagon–wide driveway intersected the road and led straight to the side of the modest six-room clapboard house. Except for the black tiled roof and gray wood porch, the entire house was painted white: the paneled windows, the front and back doors, the metal doorknobs.

When Marvin saw his mother's garden in the backyard, the final leg of his journey home ended. With Lizzie Belle by his side, Marvin walked through the front door. Because his parents had only learned of their son's return in the morning—it was that much of a secret—they were unable to contact Berkeley Jr. and Nancy, who both lived away from home. It didn't matter, though. Florence, Berkeley, and Glendon rushed toward Marvin, greeting him with the hugs and kisses they had stored since hearing that he had been freed. It startled him, and for a moment he backed away. But it did not take long for Marvin's feelings to conquer his misgivings, and he hugged and kissed everyone as if he would never be allowed to do it again. Marvin had come home.

For the entire time he was back—three months total—Marvin did not work on the farm. Instead, he listened to his family tell him about the changes in Church Road and around the house. They told him about how Lizzie Belle had sensed that something had happened to Marvin when she didn't receive a letter from him for three weeks; about the way the Western Union truck delivered the MIA telegram to his father while he and Glendon worked in the field on a sunny morning in May; and about the way Aubrey Allen, their neighbor, came running to the Watkins's door, on a sunnier morning in August, holding a *Richmond Dispatch* announcing that Marvin had been identified and freed. With all the conversation that went on, nobody ever asked Marvin about his experiences. If he wanted to share them, they reasoned, he would. In that sense, they left him alone.

As weeks passed and the novelty of being home wore off, Marvin grew quieter and more introverted. He lost himself staring at walls and ceilings and listening to the radio. He took long walks through the fields. Memories swirled around the farm like dust caught in a gust of wind: spring days planting crops with his father; summer evenings drying tobacco leaves with Berkeley Jr. and Glendon; long, thoughtful fall walks with Lizzie Belle and Nancy. There was nothing wrong with wanting those days back; every now and again, amid tumbling leaves and swaying blades of grass, Marvin found his childhood, even if only for a moment.

If the farm preserved his past, the future lay just outside its boundaries. When Marvin returned from the war, he discovered one of the world's cruel realities: life goes on. Women had gone to work during the war; kids who had started high school when he enlisted were ready to enter college. Even Church Road—the lazy farm town of Marvin's youth—had moved on without him. Many of Marvin's friends who had not gone into the service were married; some even had children. Others worked jobs that commanded pay commensurate with responsibility.

Before the war, Marvin had lived with his aunt in Richmond. He had gotten a taste of life outside of Church Road and in a major city. He had attended a vocational business school for a while and even worked in a local office. Marvin took advantage of Richmond's social scene and spent his evenings in dance halls with friends. Perhaps he would move to Richmond. Nothing was out of the question, and everything must have seemed wonderfully appealing to a young man who had spent the past three years with his life on hold. It was now Marvin's turn to enjoy what others took for granted.

Marvin was very careful when he came back and did his best to seem the same, to blend in. His naturally quiet demeanor camouflaged whatever remnants of prison he brought home. He acted normal, but what festered in his head was a different story. He told his family that everything was okay—the war, after all, ended months earlier. Only he knew the truth. At this point in Marvin's life, three months may as well have been a day, and the Tokyo Kempei Tai cell in which he suffered may as well have been down the road.

The fate of Marvin's crew needled his conscience. In a purely selfish sense, he missed them. The ten men grew to be brothers—they were his family. Mornings and evenings; weekdays and weekends;

breakfast, lunch, and dinner—they spent it together. They knew one another's families. They relied on one another on the ground, and when they took to the air over hostile territory, they needed one another. When flak exploded nearby and its searing shrapnel bombarded the plane, often cutting straight through the bomber's walls, they checked on one another. They even feared together. If anyone would have understood what Marvin felt after the war, it was his crew.

But where were they? Gone. As lead pilot, Marvin was a father figure to them. They were his responsibility, especially when they were up in the air. Once those Zeroes honed in on a bomber, they attacked like vultures—but maybe Marvin could have avoided them. He did his best to weather their assault—but could he have done more? When one of his engines went up in flames, things looked hopeless—but did he give up too soon? The Zero that smashed into the nose of his plane was out of his control—but could he have maneuvered past it? He had no choice but to order his crew to bail out—but did he issue his orders too soon? Possibilities always existed; and so long as they did, there was no such thing as a good night. His crew was lost because he lost them—and if any survived, he wanted to find them.

The last time Marvin saw his entire crew together, they were flying over Kyushu; the last time he saw any crew members, they were suffering in a Japanese prison cell. Since then, he had not heard from any of them. By October, Japanese POW camps had been liberated all across Asia—the ones in Japan now held war criminals awaiting trial—and he knew that if any of the crew had survived, someone would have contacted their families.

During his four-month captivity, Marvin's life belonged to the infamous Kempei Tai—the Japanese Gestapo. After his plane was shot down over southern Japan, he fell into the custody of the local military police. They questioned him and the other members of his crew about their mission, past missions, and future orders. When Marvin's interrogators learned that he was the plane's lead pilot, they immediately sent him to Tokyo. Pilots, especially lead pilots, meant more than other prisoners. The Japanese hoped they might divulge top-secret intelligence information regarding America's current bombardment strategy. Within days of apprehending Marvin, they transported him to the Tokyo headquarters of the Kempei Tai for further questioning. There, the Japanese tribunals would decide his execution date.

The Kempei Tai prison consisted of six 8-by-10-foot cells, holding 108 prisoners, total. Three adjacent cells lined each side of a narrow hallway. Prior to the war, the holding cells served as the emperor's horse stables and were only converted because the Kempei Tai headquarters lay a few hundred feet away.[2]

Large wooden planks lined the floors and ceilings of each cell. Six-inch bars separated prisoners from the Japanese guards pacing through the hall. Toward the rear of each cell, a hole with a wooden box served as the toilet. Just outside the cells, a long, white sheet suspended by a cord prevented prisoners in facing cells from making eye contact.

Marvin and seventeen other men waited and wasted away, drowning in perpetual uncertainty. You never knew when a Kempei Tai officer dressed in an ill-fitting beige uniform, would stand in front of your cell and peer between the bars. The officer always seemed to stand there, left hand resting on the handle of his sword, taking forever to decide who would suffer that day. Then he'd lift his arm and extend his index finger in your direction and you would hang your head, cursing your luck. A week could pass without the cell door sliding open except when you would empty out the toilet box—heavy, swooshing, and overflowing with dysentery-loosened fecal matter—or they could pull out three or four of your cell buddies at a time. There was no system; nothing to count on; nothing to place your hopes on: only chance. And if the finger fell on you, you froze for a breath, then said good-bye to your buddies with an eye-shake—a second's worth of eye contact—and stepped out of the emperor's dank, dung-riddled horse stable with the dignity of a proud American soldier.

Putting on a brave front meant ignoring the realities of what the Kempei Tai were: state-sanctioned military policemen with the power to detain, interrogate, and execute. They ruled through intimidation. Their reputations preceded them: surrounding nations like China, Korea, the Philippines, French-Indo China, and the Dutch East Indies trembled at the mere mention of their name. According to an Allied soldier, "The Kempei Tai were without a doubt the elite of the Japanese military forces. In Japan, army personnel saluted any member of the Kempei Tai with meticulous correctness. When a member of the Kempei Tai was within sight of civilians, no matter how far away, the civilians went down on their knees and then bowed with their faces only an inch or two from the ground. And they stayed in that position until the Kempei Tai was completely out of sight."[3]

In one infamous incident in Java, the Kempei Tai captured Dutch soldiers and decapitated them. When all the soldiers had been executed, the Kempei Tai loaded their bodies into bamboo boxes normally used for transporting pigs. They dumped their remains into the Java Sea so that the sharks roaming the waters could devour the evidence. After the war, the brutal slayings became known as the Pig Basket Atrocities.[4]

The Kempei Tai tortured their way to confessions, refusing to stop until they heard a story to their liking. They created novel ways of forcing people to implicate themselves. They often tied cords around suspects' middle fingers and hoisted them off the ground, leaving them suspended and swinging in the air by two fingers. It did not take much weight to tear bone from cartilage.

Another Kempei Tai torture entailed binding a prisoner's hands behind his back tight enough to impede the flow of blood. Keeping the restraints secure was key because his hands could not be allowed to slip free. A separate rope ran from a Kempei Tai officer a few feet away, then over a high beam, usually in the ceiling, and finally ending at the prisoner's hands. The Kempei Tai fastened the hanging rope to the prisoner's bound hands, then hoisted him off the ground. With his arms pulled back so far and supporting so much weight, the prisoner's shoulders often snapped into dislocation.

A Kempei Tai favorite entailed laying a prisoner in a tight coffin-like box and pouring water on his face. Gallons of water were added, a bucket at a time. The combination of accumulated and newly added liquid acted like a plastic mask, smothering the prisoner until he began to suffocate. Confessions followed soon after.[5]

Marvin's cell was his sanctuary. Sitting with other American POWs meant that he was safe from his captors for the time being. He could close his eyes and not brace himself for a blow to the head; he could speak without thinking twice about his words; he could breathe without worrying about a karate chop to the windpipe. It did not matter that he suffered in a dark, steamy, and flea-infested box. What mattered was that he could open his eyes and see the dark; smack at the mites sucking on his skin and feel their crushed bodies roll into a ball. The pleasures in life came down to one thing: being alive.

Marvin eventually saw his captivity for what it was: another form of violence. All he needed to do was look around him at the gaunt, beastly men pooled together in the humid cell, or close his eyes and smell the putrid stench of thick, bacteria-infested pus seeping from untreated wounds. There was nothing safe about his cell.

Every aspect of Marvin's captivity represented a concerted effort to humiliate and dehumanize. The Kempei Tai created rules that served no purpose, unless from the point of view of systematically peeling away every layer of humanity the prisoners possessed. The ultimate goal was to reduce soldiers into animals.

Unlike detainees in most other camps, Marvin and his prison mates were refused the right to exercise or engage in any activity. They never left the cells unless they were taken for questioning or were responsible for emptying out the toilet. Stripped of sunlight, skin lost its life, fading from tan to gray. Weeks without sun tormented the body—a punishment straight from Dante or De Sade—and soon enough the epidermal melancholy seeped into the soul and depression followed.

Marvin and the other prisoners sat in silence for the duration of their internment—yet another torture imposed by their oppressors. The sounds of captivity were faint and few: the sandy click of a guard's heels against the dirt, the occasional moan of a cell mate nearing death, the scratch of the wind against the side of the prison, the chirp of a nearby bird ready to take to the sky. The only voices belonged to the Japanese; the only laughter came from Kempei Tai officers. It reinforced the captive's isolation.

The prisoners, however, were not only separated from the outside world; they were cut off from one another and from humanity. They huddled together so tightly that they could hear one another breathing, yet prison rules forbade them from talking with one another. Human contact, they learned, entailed much more than physical proximity with other people. It necessitated speech—something inherently human. But to speak meant risking physical harm and even death. In an environment of almost complete silence, a whisper was amplified to a scream. With guards pacing back and forth, ready to pummel prisoners through the bars or up close, the risk was too great. If the prisoners communicated—and at times they did—they grunted and waved and jabbed their fingers. The millions of years of evolution preceding the development of vocal cords disappeared in a matter of months; the cornerstone of civilization—the spoken word—was stripped away.

The symbolic assault went further. The Kempei Tai prohibited captured soldiers from standing up in their cells under any circumstance. They would spend every hour of their captivity seated on the hardwood floors. As a result of their inactivity, many prisoners lost the use of their legs; others were unable to walk on their own. Yet another facet of humanity that separated them from the animal kingdom—the ability to walk upright—died of atrophy. If the prisoners needed to move about the cell, they crawled on all fours: hands and knees shuffling across the floor, head pointing anywhere but up.

Since the prisoners never left their cells and were not allowed to stand, bathing was forbidden. All forms of hygiene, from shaving to washing hands, became a remnant of the past. Beards extended down to their chests; teeth turned brown with decay; pants bore amorphous stains that were testament to dysentery's ravaging effect. The hair on their heads knotted together and lay matted to their scalps, held in place by layers of body oil, dirt, and flaking skin. A horrid odor hung around them: sweat mixed with feces and pus. For newcomers or outsiders, the stench was stifling; the prisoners, however, smelled nothing. They had lost civilization's sense of smell and no longer cared about their appearance or society's rituals of cleanliness. It simply did not matter. If appearances were reflections of pride, the Kempei Tai succeeded in destroying yet another vestige of civilized man.

Marvin survived on the most meager of meals. The prisoners ate like animals in a zoo. Their single meal consisted of a tightly packed ball of rice a little smaller than a baseball that the guards rolled into the cells. Marvin ate off the floor or out of his hands, shoveling the rice into his mouth with his fingers. If he looked around him, he saw his cell mates crouching, cowering, and feeding much the same way. The Japanese denied them something as basic as a container to hold their food because they knew that all societies valued and held the rituals of eating in high esteem. Anything would have sufficed—a piece of wood, a patch of cloth, a leaf from a tree—but they gave nothing. To deny the Americans a dignified meal meant denying them civilization. Eating degenerated to the point where prisoners, on hands and knees with their faces only inches from the floor, pinched at individual grains of rice that had broken free while the balls were rolled into the cell. Sometimes enough grains could be retrieved to cover your tongue. Dirty or not, it was food.

The everyday humiliations, while vicious, by no means broke Marvin. He held strong. Things could not continue this way forever, and when America won the war, he would return to his friends and family and to the things he enjoyed before he left. Thinking about the future kept him from giving up on the present. You never gave up. It was a matter of pride. The Japanese, however, would challenge that.

One day's interrogation proved worse than the others. A room of Japanese officers—Marvin's peers on a purely military level—pressed him for a confession as he knelt before his interrogator's desk. Admit to the indiscriminate bombing of Japan, a crime punishable by death, and die painlessly, they said. His interrogator—always the same sadistic man the POWs nicknamed "Whiskers"—insisted that Marvin's last name was Watson, an American bomber the Kempei Tai had sought for some time. He told them that he was First Lieutenant Marvin S. Watkins, Army Air Force, 6th Bomb Squadron, 29th Bomb Group, 314th Wing. Each time Marvin refused to admit he was Watson, he was beaten—kneeling on the floor, lying on his back, or standing on his feet—with cane-length bamboo sticks, or, if he was lucky, Japanese government–issued fists and steel-toed boots. Still, he never gave in to them.[6]

That day, unable to break him into a false confession, Whiskers told Marvin that he would be executed on the spot. You're guilty, they told him. We know who you are. Marvin was not allowed to raise his head, but the soft metal hiss of a bayonet sliding from its scabbard told him that he was about to be beheaded—the most common means of execution among the Kempei Tai. He would never make it home. It was over.

Whiskers forced him to expose his neck and hang his head while still kneeling. Then Whiskers stood over him, weapon suspended in the air and over his head.

Marvin inhaled—his head swirled—his eyes shut—his hands trembled—then exhaled.

In one swoop, hand and blade descended. Whiskers did not decapitate with his blow; instead, he simply tapped Marvin's neck with the side of the blade.

Marvin was not dead. It was worse. Whiskers had obliterated Marvin's faith that his own life was under his control. From that moment on, Marvin understood that his captors could take his life at a whim. It was the ultimate feeling of impotence. His survival was almost a privilege bestowed on him by someone who had power. Marvin's every breath thereafter, for the rest of his life, was a gift from Whiskers, and, in a sense, Marvin would always be that man's inferior.

When the sword touched his neck, Marvin gave up. He had been broken and would have to live with the shame. No matter what he did or where he ran, it would never go away. It would curse him in his sleep, but that was war.

Less than six months after being liberated from a Tokyo prison and brought home, Marvin S. Watkins said good-bye to his family for the second time. They did not know what he had been through; nor could they understand why he had to leave, or why he could not just put the past where it belonged. But they did not stop him. Nothing could. Marvin knew what he needed to do. He gripped the steering wheel of the car and pushed past everything—his fears, memories, and guilt.

A few days earlier, Marvin had spoken to his crew's families and told them that he was coming to visit. He was the lone survivor. They had questions that he might be able to answer. He owed it to his crew. Each family needed to see him and speak to him and drag the past into the present because it would help them. Perhaps it would free him, as well.

On a crisp winter day, First Lieutenant Marvin S. Watkins eased his father's green 1941 Chevrolet out of the driveway and down the dirt road much the same way he coaxed giant B-29 bombers into the sky during the war. This time, however, he would make the journey alone.

1

October 1945: CIC Headquarters

When rumors of atrocities against American fliers in Kurume first crossed Special Agent Philip Cheles's desk in November 1945, there was no way to imagine the horror he would discover. They were, after all, rumors. And those kinds of things usually proved unfounded. False leads sprouted out of the fertile Japanese countryside—a landscape littered with tiny towns and teeming with superstition—like narrow blades of grass. In retrospect, the pieces of the puzzle that would explode into the most sensational war crimes trial to come out of Japan had not even been discovered, much less assembled. As Cheles would later recount to a military tribunal in Yokohama, he did not know the true details until much later.[1] The puzzle Cheles envisioned appeared much more benign. But behind the opaque truths he unearthed, a tunnel into the recesses of man's inhumanity lay hidden.

The pieces of the Kyushu University puzzle still lay buried. Cheles reported for duty unaware that he had been touched and drawn into Case 420's twisted world. But it was only a matter of time. There were clues hiding and lurking and not fitting in, like a stray piece from a nearby puzzle mixed into the confusion of another puzzle.

Cheles belonged to the Counter Intelligence Corps (CIC), an

organization that fell under the government umbrella of Military Intelligence, commonly referred to as G-2. Before World War II, the CIC was known as the Corps of Intelligence Police and was infamous for being one of Washington, D.C.'s most underfunded wings. CIC Headquarters bounced around the capital like a pinball. Nobody seemed to want them. Headquarters eventually found residence in a house on a sleepy, inconspicuous, tree-and-lawn–lined street in Baltimore—chosen because the CIC budget allotted to them by the War Department was as fleeting as their past headquarters. It would take some time for the military brain trust to figure out that espionage and sabotage—later the CIC's prime objectives—tipped wars toward victory.

The wartime role of the CIC special agent involved many of the duplicitous dealings that have become ingrained in the pop-culture perception of the spy. Each agent was expected to perform certain core duties. If he was behind enemy lines, the urgency of his duties skyrocketed. His job required perfection. He surveyed public utilities, buildings, and supply dumps, then reported on them. He seized telephone and radio stations for their records. Civil communications—mail, radio, telegraph, and telephone—were to be ended; all mail in local drop boxes was to be impounded and turned over to the field censorship bureaus in the given area. Publications of all kinds—particularly newspapers and periodicals—were to be halted. In order to execute their directives, CIC agents familiarized themselves with local political, social, and economic affairs. This also kept them alive.[2]

During the war, the CIC's branch in the Far East theater went by the name CIC Forces Far East. In addition to their covert duties, CIC agents participated in a number of more traditional military operations. They were particularly active during the final year of the war. Many agents found themselves among invading Allied troops as Japan's deteriorating forces retreated. Thirty CIC detachments took part in the invasion of Luzon in the Philippines on January 9, 1945; members of the CIC were among combat troops when Manila was liberated from the Japanese on February 3, 1945; three CIC special agents died during the Allied landing on Okinawa on April 1,

1945.[3] The CIC were as much a part of the war's everyday struggle as anyone else.

The Pacific War officially drew to a close on September 2, 1948. Amidst the triumphant Allied sneers and a beaming General Douglas MacArthur, General Umezu Yoshijiro signed the instrument of surrender onboard the USS *Missouri* in the name of Emperor Hirohito. While most branches of the U.S. military embarked on the painfully random process of demobilizing their troops, the CIC witnessed an increase in the demand for agents. The CIC Pacific radioed the War Department on August 20, 1945, that because of the occupation of Japan, CIC personnel were urgently needed. Three days later, the War Department informed the CIC Pacific that "since the Japs' surrender, requirements for CIC personnel have increased and recruiting should be continued." The last week of August and the first week of September witnessed the arrival of a number of CIC units in Japan from around the world. The strength of the CIC in Japan increased significantly.[4]

Postwar, occupied Japan demanded a shift in the special agent's responsibilities. While he still functioned in his traditional role, he also acted as an investigator. CIC detachments across Japan sent agents out into the field. The responsibility of investigating hundreds of low-level war crimes—future B and C war crimes—fell on the CIC. They checked the validity of each incident where a war crime—anything from murder to bribery—might have been committed. Sometimes, they acted on tips from anonymous informants; other times, people spoon-fed them leads. Regardless of how implausible the claim, their job required them to either uncover the truth or reveal the misinformation. If war crimes had been committed, the case would then be turned over to the proper legal departments.

On November 15, 1945, an informant known only as 106-K marched into the 496th Counter Intelligence Corps Detachment in Kurume with information that in July 1945 an American B-29 plane crashed somewhere in a local mountain range.[5] One or more of the survivors died at the hands of local villagers—a frequent occurrence. While murder between soldiers was acceptable, the murder of a soldier by a civilian went against the rules of war. It was considered a war crime, an atrocity. As a result, the Supreme Commander Allied Power (SCAP) made it a priority to investigate all incidences involving downed American planes.[6]

On November 17, 1945, Cheles proceeded to Japanese Division Headquarters, also located in Kurume, accompanied by an interpreter, Okino Shuichi.[7] It was the most logical place to start. The Japanese military kept records of all downed planes and conducted investigations into the fates of the crew. They would know if an American airman had been killed—and by whom.

Cheles first questioned the commanding officer, Lieutenant General Sonobe Waiichuro.[8] As the officer in charge, it made sense to go to him first; theoretically, Sonobe's responsibilities included being aware of anything that went on under his command, particularly if American prisoners had been brought to the headquarters.

Initially, Sonobe denied any knowledge of the crash: an understandable and probably expected response. Cheles refused to quit, continued pressing like a one-man good cop/bad cop, and forced the general to recall the event in detail. Sonobe submitted a written statement outlining the part the division played in retrieving the downed crew members.

Interrogation of other Japanese Division Headquarters staff members, from the chief of staff down to the common jeep driver, yielded more information. Naturally, some people knew more than others; some were more open than others; some simply liked to talk. Whatever the case, the pieces of the puzzle that Agent Cheles struggled with started revealing themselves. It was only a matter of time until they started making sense and patterns started forming. The picture would start to congeal.

First Lieutenant Yamaguchi Tetsuo revealed that in July 1945 a plane crashed near Yokoyama-mura, Kyushu. Three crew members, presumably American, died in the crash. Nine survived. Japanese authorities captured the fliers within ten days of their descent into enemy territory, brought them to the Kurume Division Headquarters, and placed them in the custody of the Kurume Kempei Tai—the local branch of the notorious and much-feared Japanese military police.[9]

Three of the captured Americans suffered injuries bailing out of the plane. Jumping from a moving B-29 Superfortress was a brutal affair: pulling the rip cord caused a jolt that could crack bones to the marrow; drifting down in turbulent skies entailed bone-shifting herky-jerky motions and sudden tugs to and fro; landing often involved tumbles even a gymnast would struggle to control.

The Yokoyama-mura chief of police revealed that a crew member was murdered by local farmers. The farmers signaled for the soldier to drop the .45-caliber pistol he was wielding like a shield. He refused, as any fearful man in a hostile land would do. Perhaps he thought he had a chance to survive, to find some more Americans, a chance to fly back home, to see his family again. Whatever the case, he fired each of his twelve bullets, spraying them without aiming. A chase ensued and the downed airman managed to shoot one of the farmers, wounding him in the shoulder. Rather than fleeing, the remaining farmers attacked. He had no chance.[10]

A civilian named Ushijima Nagaki had acted as an interpreter during a Kempei Tai interrogation of one of the captured crew.[11] For the first time, Cheles actually spoke to someone with firsthand knowledge of the fliers and a portion of their fates. Ushijima, a U.S. native—born and raised in California—had moved to Japan nine years earlier. Because of his familiarity with Western names, he turned out to be a much more useful witness than most Japanese nationals who had difficulty recalling any American names, even when read from a list.[12]

According to Ushijuma, the Kempei Tai brought him to a little village, Kyura, on top of a mountain in the vicinity of the crash scene, where one of the American crewmen was being held. The Kempei Tai ordered Ushijima to act as a translator, forbidding him from asking any questions of his own. Everything came from the Kempei Tai officer in charge of the interrogation.

Ushijima: What base did you come from?
Prisoner: Guam.
Ushijima: How many were on the plane?
Prisoner: Twelve.
Ushijima: That is incorrect. When your fellow crew members

were captured and questioned earlier, they stated another number. They said eleven. Are you telling the truth? Explain the discrepancy.

Prisoner: There were twelve men on the plane, including myself. There was an extra person on the plane, a special passenger. The other crewmen were unaware of his presence.

Ushijima: What are the names, ranks, and ages of the crewmen?

Prisoner: (The prisoner then gave requested information in full. Ushijima, however, was unable to recall the plane's roster in full.)

Ushijima: What is your name, rank, and age?

Prisoner: Captain Hewitt. Age twenty-seven.

Ushijima: How did the other crewmen escape?

Prisoner: I do not know.

Ushijima: What part of the plane exploded?

Prisoner: I'm not certain, but I believe that the left engine exploded.[13]

There were more questions relating to the plane crash, though Ushijima could not remember them. He did, however, recall a brief exchange.

Prisoner: May I have some cigarettes?

Ushijima (with the Kempei Tai's approval): Certainly.

Prisoner: And may I have some water? I'm very thirsty.

Ushijima (again with the Kempei Tai's approval): Yes.

(Captain Hewitt is given cigarettes and water.)

Prisoner: Thank you so much. (Pause) May I inquire about the status of my crew?

Ushijima turned to the Kempei Tai officer who shook his head. It was not permitted.[14]

The Kempei Tai got the information they desired, and after collecting the data, they shipped the entire crew and all their effects to Western Army Headquarters in Fukuoka. They ordered Ushijima to return home.[15]

Ushijima's cooperation struck a chord with the investigator. As a result of what Cheles called Ushujima's "untiring efforts and his willingness to aid the American cause," the former California native found himself appointed as a "special aide" in locating the farmers responsible for the death of the B-29 crew member. Undoubtedly, the fact that Ushijima spoke fluent American English influenced the CIC officer's decision-making process.

On November 17, 1945, Cheles stood in front of three graves constructed at the edge of a forest.[16] The familiar smell of grass, a sweetness that differed little whether you were in Kansas or Kurume, floated through the countryside. Some things held true, regardless of context; most played according to different rules—for example, the investigation—and Cheles had proof. Sometimes, rumors turned into hard facts. If you were lucky, those facts were tangible, like the three makeshift wooden markers standing stationary before him.

The war had ended for these three men; the war had long since delivered them from boyhood. There would be no more violence. No more orders. No more guns. No more bombs. No more shaky takeoffs to fray their nerves. No more explosions with scalpel shards glowing like branding irons.

They died for their country. They sacrificed their lives for their families at home, for the warm-crusted apple pies sitting atop wooden tables, for the waving wheat fields drenched in sunset, for the homecoming queen and the captain of the football team. Freedom and justice and God were on their side. Or so they were told.

To Cheles, it seemed that a major portion of the Kurume puzzle had come together: corners set in place, the frame sturdy, and the center of the picture assembled. All that remained was to fill in the incomplete patches—a task that in all likelihood would not prove impossible. The perpetrators were rural villagers. People would talk.

Two days later, November 19, 1945, Cheles returned to Yokoyama-mura. Ushijima managed to track down the four farmers and did the grunt work of collecting the facts surrounding the cremation and burial of the victim. Each man confessed his guilt.

Mizota Masaru, for example, confessed: "When I was at home on the morning of July 28, 1945, I heard somebody crying, 'An American soldier is there.'

"I hurried to the scene, and immediately afterward the sound of guns was heard. I saw Mizota Mitsuo cutting at the American. When Kawaguchi cried, 'Wounded,' I got exasperated and knocked the American on his head with a club. I dimly remember that some others knocked him after I did."[17]

Cheles's hunch about appointing Ushijima a special aide ended up rewarding him with a closed case. Voluntary confessions and signed statements from the accused and witnesses piled into the CIC office. Philip Cheles filed his report on November 24, 1945, with the approval of Robert Tait. Yet, nobody—Japanese or American—ever mentioned or acknowledged for the record that a man tumbled from the clouds and found himself lost in a strange, dangerous land and that he was scared and confused and young. He was alone. He died that way.

The puzzle, however, was solved. The pieces fit nicely. The picture was complete. All that remained were red-tape formalities. But that was on the surface. Nothing was ever that simple in occupied Japan.

With his interpreter sitting beside him, Philip Cheles questioned yet another confidential informer on November 20, 1945—the day after Ushijima handed him the four farmers responsible for the murder of the American crewman. He was about to discover a stray piece from a different puzzle.[18]

"I have more information to report about the American crewmen who were captured by the Kempei Tai," the informant said.[19]

"Tell me."

"I believe some of them weren't treated according to proper fashion."

"How so?"

"Two of the captured crewmen were beaten by the Kempei Tai."

"Are you sure of this?" Cheles asked.

"Yes."

"How do you know they were beaten?"

"Their faces were severely swollen when they were delivered to the Kurume Japanese Division Headquarters."

"And you saw this?"

"Yes."

Cheles made note of his informant's revelation. The case was essentially closed, however.

"I have more to say," the informant added before Cheles could dismiss him.

"More about the airmen in Kurume?"

"No. Something different. It is very bad."

Cheles's neat Kurume puzzle might have been assembled and ready to frame, but now the extra pieces—the stray tangents that never led to anything positive—began revealing themselves.

The informant continued: "I have heard rumors of horrible things that happened toward the end of the war. I believe that executions took place and that some of the Americans involved were from Kurume."

"Executions?"

"Yes."

"Where?"

"I believe they took place in Fukuoka. Nine captured Americans were executed, and some of those nine had been sent from the Kurume Division Headquarters."

"How were they executed?"

"The men were beheaded."

"How did it happen? Who ordered the executions? Who performed the executions?"

"I'm sorry. I do not know the specific facts surrounding the executions. But I do know something else that is related to the executions. It might help. There is a Colonel Sato Yoshinao at Western Army Headquarters. He is a staff officer. Shortly after the war ended, he visited the Kurume Division Headquarters. He spoke to all of the officers there. He warned them that the Americans would be conducting investigations into the fates of lost soldiers. He told them to conceal all facts pertaining to the executions. He told them that in the event the Americans inquired about the whereabouts of the surviving prisoners, they were to mislead them. Sato's explanation was that three of the prisoners had been killed in Hiroshima when the Americans dropped the atomic bomb. If you speak to Sato, I'm sure you will learn the truth."

2

October 1945: Western Army Headquarters

If the world ever discovered the truth, Colonel Sato Yoshinao would hang. That much was obvious. Still, as Sato stood before Lieutenant General Inada Masazumi, his state of confusion could only have been superseded by his raging sense of indignation because no man wants to die.

"I was granted permission to carry out the executions," Sato insisted, barely managing to maintain his composure and keep his volume to a respectful level.[1]

"Permission by whom?" Inada shot back.

"Lieutenant General Yokoyama."

"How is that? I would have known about it since everything intended for him must go through me first. If you had a request for Yokoyama, wouldn't you speak to me first?"

"Yes, but . . ."

"I do not know how you can say that you were granted permission. The commanding officer of the Western Army does not issue orders to lower officers without going through me first."

In the months since the war's end, Sato's struggle for survival never ended: it intensified. American investigators searching for proof of wrongdoing—so-called atrocities—hounded him; eager to appease occupying forces, Japanese investigators and now his own comrades at what was once the Western Army Headquarters in Fukuoka, harassed him.

Inada had good reason to doubt Sato's claims. He was correct to assert that nothing came in or out of Western Army Commanding Officer Lieutenant General Yokoyama Isamu's office without his clearance. It was his job, after all. Under normal circumstances, Inada had to be contacted first. In the case of an execution, there was no way that he should have been left out of the loop, or so he believed.[2]

Of course, toward the end of the war, Inada shouldn't have been surprised. Everyday life on Kyushu, like most of Japan, had steadily crumbled into a constant state of alert, apprehension, and fear. It was no secret that an Allied invasion of Japan would focus on its southernmost island. Everyone—soldiers and citizens—knew the Allied intentions. The storm of bombs pounding the island every day ensured them.

Kyushu lay roughly a thousand miles north of the Philippines. At the war's onset, when Japanese forces pierced through Pacific waters and countries like a spear through flesh, its proximity to South Pacific islands meant that they would fall quickly and without much struggle. Even the Philippines, long hailed as a key American stronghold in Asia, keeled over within weeks of Japan's initial assault, forcing a not-so-defiant General MacArthur to seek refuge in Australia.

Japanese ambitions ran high at that point, and under the guise of building a new order—the Greater East Asia Coprosperity Sphere—they promised Eastern liberation from Western imperialists. For Eastern nations, however, the distinction between an Eastern colonizer and a Western colonizer amounted to the same thing: colonization. Oblivious to the concerns of the countries they invaded, the Japanese pressed forward, toppling, plundering, and pillaging their way to Asian supremacy. It was their right, after all. Everything from their twentieth-century status as the Far East's only member of the League of Nations to their glorious tradition pointed toward their position in the Asian vanguard. If their prominence meant destroying everything in their path, so be it. It was, after all, their way. That all ended, however, and did so very abruptly.

Sato and Inada plunged into a verbal tug-of-war that could not be resolved by the two alone. It was one man's word against the other—a colonel's against a general's—and ultimately Inada's word mattered most. Sato had everything—including his life—to lose.

Sato, a sizable five-six compared to the average Japanese man, wore a chiseled smirk and wielded a sharp stare that shot out from his slightly inset marble eyes. He lacked facial hair, making him look younger than his forty-seven years—something that could have been misleading.

During the war, Sato was stationed at Western Army Headquarters in Fukuoka on the island of Kyushu. The headquarters fulfilled two purposes: From a purely military perspective, it oversaw the defensive forces on Japan's southernmost island. The Fukuoka office also supervised the relationship between the military and civilian sectors on Kyushu. It organized and mobilized the farmers and villagers, coordinating their efforts in a way that would best complement the army's. It also pumped wartime propaganda into the scattered agrarian communities throughout the mountainous island's countryside.[3]

Members of Western Army Headquarters fell under the designation of either First Staff or Second Staff. First Staff officers dealt solely with the military aspects of the command while Second Staffers functioned within the civilian sector.

Lieutenant General Yokoyama Isamu stood at the top of the Western Army hierarchy. As commander in chief, he oversaw all aspects of Western Army affairs and everyone answered to him. The headquarters' second in command was Lieutenant General Inada. As the chief of staff, Inada served a more hands-on role in the day-to-day functioning of Western Army Headquarters. His approval was necessary before any requests were filtered to Lieutenant General Yokoyama. He represented the lower-ranking officer's bridge to the commander in chief's attention.[4]

As director of Air Defense and Tactics, Colonel Sato belonged to the Western Army Second Staff. At times, however, he functioned

Western Army Headquarters

under the First Staff's military umbrella. Since all of the prisoners brought to Western Army Headquarters consisted of downed Allied airmen, who fell under Sato's supervision by default, he found himself under constant pressure to deal with them appropriately. This entailed intense interrogations in an attempt to discover any hints pertaining to the American bombing strategy. Any airmen who appeared to have information, particularly crew chiefs, lead pilots, and squadron leaders, were sent to Tokyo for further questioning.[5]

"Colonel Akita knew about the executions," Sato persisted, referring to Inada's assistant.

"Oh did he?"

"Yes."

"Akita is just outside the office, Sato. If what you say is the truth, then you wouldn't mind if I called him into the office?"

"No." Akita knew the truth.

"Then I will ask him." Inada rose from behind his desk and marched toward his office door. He called Akita into the room.

Colonel Akita Hiroshi served as the Western Army Headquarters' senior staff officer of the First Staff Section. He functioned as a liaison between Inada and other officers. Anything that pertained to the First Staff Section, particularly paperwork, ultimately passed through his desk.[6]

"Colonel Akita, Colonel Sato tells me that you knew about a series of executions that took place during the final months of the war—executions of which I was not aware. Please tell me everything you know about those executions."

"Sir, I regret to say that I know nothing about any executions."

Sato listened in disbelief. Akita lied and showed neither remorse nor shame in betraying him.

"So you knew nothing?"

"No sir."

"Are you certain? Are you saying that Colonel Sato is lying?"

"Sir, I know nothing about the executions. At least, I didn't know about them when they were taking place. I wasn't even here. I only heard of them after they happened."

Sato stepped toward the desk.

"That is not true."

The room's attention shifted back to Sato. He had more than one enemy in the room.

"Akita does not tell the truth."

"Explain." Inada's leanings were obvious. He believed Akita.

"Before carrying out the executions, I visited the staff office and asked for permission to see you."

"Is that so?"

"Yes," Sato insisted. "I spoke to Akita instead. He said that you were not in the office."

Inada turned to Akita, who immediately defended himself.

"That is a lie. I was not even in Fukuoka at the time. How could we speak?"

"Didn't you go into Yokoyama's office yourself and ask him about the prisoners for me?" Sato seethed. It was useless, however. Akita refused to alter his story. Yet someone, besides Sato, knew differently.

Major General Fukushima Kyusaku, one of several vice chiefs of staff at Western Army Headquarters, sat to the side, doing everything he could to stay out of the exchange. It wasn't in his best interest to get involved even though he knew Sato told what from his eyes was the truth and that Akita lied. Fukushima was no fool and refused to put himself in a position where he would have to lie to Inada. The wise thing to do was to sit back and watch.

The Japanese warrior had fallen so far in so short a time. The bickering soldiers in front of Fukushima belonged to a proud tradition at least a millennium old. It stretched back to the dawn of recorded history in Japan during a time of warring clans. Buddhist thought had not yet been introduced to Japanese society. Their lineage included Minamoto Yoshitsune, Kusunoki Masashige, Hosokawa Sumimoto, Yamamoto Kansuke, and Kato Kiyomasa. Yet, they were conquered and acting like scared children.

Fukushima stood up, excused himself, and escaped the room without having to join the conversation. He was safe temporarily. For Sato, however, the trouble was just beginning.

3

October–November 1945

From Yamae, Yokoyama laid out the plans for the defense of Kyushu. Every day, he pondered how, when, and where the American landing would occur. He monitored the frequency and intensity of the Allied air raids. It was where he could have achieved greatness but where he ended up receiving notice from the War Department that he was relieved of his command and ordered to retire from the military, effective November 1945.[1] Now, with his separation from the Japanese military permanent, Yokoyama spent most of his time on his farm in Fuksukaichi.[2] That was where Colonel Sato found him later in November. They spoke frankly.[3]

"The decision to reveal the truth came from Tokyo. It was not ours," Sato said.[4]

"Tokyo's?" Yokoyama could not believe what he was being told. He was practically being handed over. In occupied Japan, every man fended for himself, and even a retired general could only hide for so long.

"The War Department."

"And what information is to be surrendered to the occupation forces?"

"According to them, the truth."

"The truth," Yokoyama grunted. "And what is that?"

"Everything concerning the atrocities."

Yokoyama shook his head and contemplated the situation. The tranquility he fostered on the farm spiraled to oblivion like water being sucked down a drain. If an investigation ever established that POWs had been executed under his command, he would be held accountable and definitely hang, regardless of whether he knew about them. In the past, when the old order still stood, that never happened; generals were never held accountable for the actions of their subordinates. But that was before General Yamashita swung from the gallows for the misdeeds of his soldiers.

"Is it an order?"

"A request." It was as good as an order.

Yokoyama nodded.

"But that is Tokyo." Sato's tone was oddly calm. "Western Army has decided otherwise."

"What do you mean?"

"We are still going to try to conceal the atrocities. Tokyo can only know as much as they are told, and the occupation forces will only know what Tokyo tells them. We will continue to hide the facts."

"Who is 'we'?"

"Myself and Fukushima."

"How do you plan on covering up the events?"

"That has not been settled yet, but we have ideas."

Yokoyama's silence indicated that he wanted more information.

Sato continued. "One option we have to account for a portion of the prisoners is to say that the POWs were killed when the atomic bomb destroyed Hiroshima. There is no way for the bodies to be traced. The city was incinerated. You saw Nagasaki in person. The devastation was enormous. Let the American bomb be used to our advantage."

"The situation is no good. Things are out of control." Yokoyama would never be able to leave his military life behind, no matter how many crops he planted.

"Do not worry. Nothing will be revealed that does not need to be. We will only admit to what is necessary and when it is our only option."

"The record shows that I knew nothing about the executions. There were no reports filed. I issued no orders. Yet, I will be hung on account of your decisions." Yokoyama paused. "All I can suggest is that you take the best possible course."

"Your intervention might be necessary. I fear the situation has grown increasingly complicated," Sato said.

"What do you mean?"

"The higher-ranking officers—Tomomori, Ito, Wako—they are all trying to escape their responsibilities, though they played roles in the executions. Someone of considerable rank needs to bear the brunt of the responsibility. The situation does not make sense otherwise. They were there. They issued orders. One of them must be held accountable. It will be difficult to hide anything from the occupation forces unless someone of rank—at least the assistant chief of staff—is brave enough to accept some of the responsibilities."

"I would be willing to accept complete responsibility. It was my command."

Sato listened intently.

Yokoyama continued. "It is impossible, however. I cannot have my name and my position in the Imperial Army tainted by the executions. As a commanding general, I am directly responsible to the emperor. The power and authority I wield originates in him. It is an extension of the emperor, and, as a consequence, any wrongdoing on my part represents a direct reflection on him. That cannot happen."[5]

Lieutenant General Yokoyama Isamu spent the majority of his tenure as the supreme commander of the Western Army in Yamae, away from Western Army Headquarters, away from the scruffy American prisoners, and away from Colonel Sato. When the Allied bombing of Kyushu reached its peak, Tokyo decided to split the 16th Army command between the Fukuoka headquarters and another in Yamae. A portion of the staff would stay in Fukuoka while Yokoyama, Inada, and the 16th Army relocated. Sato was one of the officers who remained in Fukuoka. Fukushima was another.

Lieutenant General Yokoyama's military career fell one battle short of historical significance. Ever since Tokyo placed him in charge of the 16th Army and the Western Army, the defense of Japan's southern and most vulnerable island rested in his hands.[6] His homeland's destiny depended on the plans he drew up at his desk. During the waning months of the war, when Allied bombers sliced through Kyushu skies, Yokoyama focused all of his attention on devising a solid defense of the island. The Allied invasion would concentrate on the shores of Kyushu. Somehow, all invaders saw the island's shores as the doorstep to conquering Japan. Genghis Khan did in the twelfth century and now General MacArthur did in the twentieth. Yokoyama dedicated all of his time to making sure the "invincible" Americans would meet their demise the way the equally "invincible" Mongols had long ago.

The rigidity and discipline of military life surrounded Yokoyama from a young age. His father, a Japanese army colonel, made sure that his son followed in his footsteps.[7] Great things awaited young Isamu; he would certainly excel and eventually exceed his father's own accomplishments. He only needed the chance. So by thirteen years of age, Yokoyama was already studying the Bushido Code and its military tactics in cadet school. From that point, Yokoyama dedicated his life to becoming a member of the emperor's army.

Yokoyama scaled the army ranks like a cat up a tree. In May 1909, he graduated from the military academy in Tokyo at the age of twenty. Seven months later, he belonged to the 3rd Infantry Regiment and held the rank of second lieutenant in the Imperial Army. By 1924, Yokoyama had ascended to the rank of major.[8] After attending military staff school, Yokoyama did a brief stint at the War Ministry before being sent to Germany in 1925. During his two years in Europe, he studied Western warfare and culture. It was an honor to be sent abroad. You represented your country, the land, its people, and, most importantly, the emperor. Only the best army men went to Europe, and Yokoyama was one of them. In April 1932, Yokoyama—now a full colonel—served in the Kwantung Army in Manchukuo (Manchuria). A year earlier, the Japanese Kwantung Army marched into Chinese Manchuria and never left. It was his first taste of a historical moment. It would not be his last.

To be in Manchukuo during the Japanese occupation meant being part of a situation so unique and compelling that any history of World War II would be incomplete with its omission. Without it, perhaps the Pacific War could have been avoided. If it was not the hinge that swung Japan toward conflict with Western powers, it was definitely one of the screws holding the door in place.

Chinese Manchuria sits atop the arch of Korea's northern border. Most of the region's landscape consists of sweeping plains, though forests to the north, east, and west cup the land like a football helmet. Local farmers, following traditions handed down to them through generations, till tobacco, grains, and cotton. Coal and iron deposits—essentials for the production of steel—dot the terrain; columns of soot and smoke billow from the matrix of factories that convert raw materials into exportable products.[9]

Since the turn of the twentieth century, Japan wanted Manchuria for its resources. On the evening of September 18, 1931, an explosion on the Japanese-owned and -run South Manchurian Railway destroyed thirty-one inches of track and lots of dirt. Though definitive proof of who was responsible failed to surface, the Japanese blamed the incident on Chinese terrorists and the rest of the world blamed Japan. Chinese officials responded by sending enough troops to quell the disturbance; Japanese officials responded by sending enough troops to take the entire territory by force, which they did. The fiasco became known as the Manchurian Incident. Under Japan's thumb, Manchuria declared its independence from China in February 1932, renaming itself Manchukuo and installing China's last emperor, Henry Aisin Gyoro Pu'yi, as its ruler. The West, by way of the League of Nations, refused to acknowledge the newly formed country's sovereignty as well as Japan's interests in the area. They denounced the outward use of military aggression in order to obtain a colony and demanded that Japan withdraw immediately. The league's opposition prompted Japanese delegates to storm out of the organization. It represented yet another slap in the face by Western imperialist hypocrites.

In the end, however, it mattered little. Japan now controlled Manchuria and everything inside it. They could do whatever they wanted to the land and its inhabitants. It was their new playground.

On November 30, a few days after Sato's meeting with Yokoyama, the colonel spoke to Fukushima, who had just returned from the War Department meetings in Tokyo. He, along with General Nishihara Kanji, who now commanded the former Western Army, had remained in Tokyo an extra day.[10]

Sato and Fukushima discussed Tokyo's decision and both agreed that the powers in the War Department were mistaken. Whether they wanted to genuinely cooperate with the Americans or were simply trying to protect themselves didn't matter. Either way, the outcome remained the same for the two Western Army officers: they would be handed over to the occupation forces to stand trial for war crimes.

Fortunately, the War Department meeting had been a gathering of every Japanese command. That meant there was no way for any information to be gathered. Tokyo established the policy that all atrocities be reported, but that did not mean that Sato, Fukushima, or any other Western Army officer would reveal anything. Only if they found themselves in a compromised position would they allow the truth to come out. Even then, it would only be at a trickle. During the war, horrible things occurred in Fukuoka that had to be suppressed.

Maintaining any degree of secrecy in Fukuoka did not come easily. The situation tumbled out of control at Western Army Headquarters since the surrender. Some of the responsibility fell on the command's carelessness, and even under perfect conditions concealing the facts behind the executions would have been difficult. Unfortunately, postwar existence drifted further from perfection with each passing day. The situation continued to deteriorate in November when a special investigator from Tokyo, Lieutenant General Oki Genzaburo, arrived and began interrogating every officer and soldier associated with Western Army Headquarters.[11] In an attempt to play both sides of the fence, the War Department launched their own investigations into suspected atrocities, independent of both the subordinate commands and the occupation forces.

In early December, an agent from the American Counter Intelligence Corps contacted Sato. He was to report to the Kurume CIC Headquarters for questioning. His interrogator's name was Special Agent O. Vincent Esposito.[12]

Once the complete truth surfaced, his fate would no longer be under his control, much the same way his country laid helplessly stripped of its autonomy. Years of faithful service to an emperor-god left him with nothing; his fate no longer belonged to a divine ruler but to a Western imperialist. The manhunt of the victors threatened to wipe out hundreds if not thousands of Japanese soldiers, including Sato, for serving their country. Times had changed in Japan, and Colonel Sato Yoshinao was a marked man. A white barbarian would stand as his final judge.

For Colonel Sato, being subjected to interrogations by the CIC must have felt like another in a long line of gaijin insults that went back to the Harris Treaty. Esposito, Sato's interrogator, must have seemed like just another weak-skinned, big-nosed, featureless white-face brute. They all looked the same, after all. Yet, Sato sat before him, powerless to maintain his silence, much less leave.

"Tell me about the nine American fliers sent to Western Army Headquarters from Kurume," Esposito asked through an interpreter.[13]

"American fliers were never sent to us from Kurume," Sato said.

"Are you telling me that you have no knowledge of any American POWs from that area?"

"Yes," Sato insisted.

Esposito remained skeptical. He had information to the contrary. One of his sources at the Kurume Division Headquarters divulged that Sato had visited the office shortly after the war and had asked the officers at Kurume to conceal all evidence of the Western Army Headquarters beheadings. Sato clearly realized that his actions during the war placed him in jeopardy and that the repercussions could cost him his life. He warned Kurume Division Headquarters that if the Americans conducted an investigation into the fates of the prisoners, they should say that three Americans had died during the atomic bombing of Hiroshima.

So now Esposito prodded Sato for more information. Someone was lying—either Sato or Esposito's informer. Either way, it was Esposito's job to discover the truth.

"Sato, the information coming out of Kurume indicates otherwise. According to them, nine captured B-29 fliers were sent to Western Army Headquarters. It would be your responsibility to deal with them if they had been, is it not?"

"Yes," Sato agreed. "That is true."

"And you have no knowledge of nine prisoners from Kurume?"

"No."

"So are you saying that the command at Kurume Kempei Tai are lying?"

Sato paused. There was no way to circumvent the fact that the staff at Kurume had contradicted his claims. Finally, he admitted, "There might have been fliers from Kurume."

"Were there or weren't there?"

"There were."

"How many Americans?"

"Nine."

Kurume hadn't been lying—Sato had. Esposito pushed further.

"Are you sure only nine?"

"Yes."

"Sato, tell me what happened to those nine prisoners."

"They arrived at Western Army . . ."

"After their arrival, Sato."

"Three of them were sent to Hiroshima."

"Around when?"

"I would guess around 31 July."

"And what happened to these Americans?"

"They died when the atomic bomb destroyed the city on 6 August."

"And what happened to the other prisoners?"

"I believe they were sent to Tokyo by airplane sometime between 16 and 18 August."

"Sato, were the nine Americans beheaded?"

"No." Sato shook his head.

"Are you certain?"

"Yes, I'm sure. That could not happen. I'm sure of it. They were not beheaded."

Sato continued. "Personally, I had no responsibility for them. I took no part in handling them. There are others who can support what I say."

"Who are these 'others'?"

"One is a Colonel Kusumoto and the other is a Major General Fukushima. Both were officers at Western Army Headquarters."

Satisfied with what had been discovered thus far, Esposito stopped questioning and ordered Sato to produce proof verifying his claims that the fliers had been sent to Tokyo and Hiroshima. In the meantime, Esposito sent for Kusumoto and Fukushima. He held Sato there until they arrived. On his departure, Sato was ordered to report to the Kurume CIC with the requested information.[14]

Up until this point, Sato's words and actions made sense for an increasingly desperate man. After the war, Sato agonized over his fate. He understood the precariousness of his situation and what his fate held if the truth were uncovered: death. Sato's health deteriorated as a result. His worries became so pronounced that other officers noticed his haggard appearance. Matters had regressed to the point where Sato even told Major General Fukushima that he suffered from a bad heart.[15]

Whatever fable Sato and Fukushima concocted was doomed from the start. Sato, while probably a man of reasonable intelligence, lacked vision. His shortsightedness cost him and the Western Army Headquarters command dearly. Had Sato been able to see the big picture, he would have realized at the time of the executions that the records of other headquarters who had sent their prisoners to Sato would not add up—that thirty-nine fliers would be recorded as being imprisoned while none would be on the record as being released. If anything, that was when the cover-up should have started, not in American-occupied Japan. Worse yet, Sato, in his postwar panic, destroyed all of his records pertaining to the prisoners and their executions. When the time came to implement a cover-up, Sato could not even recall the exact number of executions that needed to be concealed. As a result, the duo created elaborate and unbelievable explanations with no chance of succeeding.[16]

In the time between Sato's initial interrogation and the subsequent one, he went through the motions and conducted a fake investigation, knowing that there was no proof to be found. He flew to the main headquarters in Tokyo and demanded proof that six American POWs were sent there from Fukuoka. Sato questioned Lieutenant General Yoshizumi, head of the Military Affairs Bureau of the War Department, regarding the fate of the fliers. Yoshizumi checked whether any flights had been dispatched around the time in question with the purpose of bringing prisoners from Fukuoka; he discovered that none had been sent. The facts were reported to Sato, and he returned to Fukuoka ready to continue his imaginary investigation.[17]

During this time, Sato chose to employ the story that he and Fukushima fabricated in September detailing the fates of the prisoners sent to Tokyo. According to their tale, the American prisoners were kidnapped by a band of renegade Japanese soldiers at the end of the war. The kidnappers were diehards who refused to surrender to the Allied forces. In a swirl of confusion, the soldiers loaded the American POWs onto the plane and flew off, never to be heard from or seen again. Sato, however, did speculate that the flight crashed somewhere in the middle of the ocean.[18]

Sato reported back to Esposito on December 7, 1945, carrying the "proof" that he hoped would put an end to the investigation.[19] He handed over a telegram from the vice war secretary that ordered all division commanders to submit "complete data concerning those enemies who died in their districts."[20] Sato informed Esposito that the reports were sent to General Douglas MacArthur's headquarters in Tokyo. He also produced forged statements from the Prisoner-of-War Information Bureau, Gendarmerie Headquarters, and from the chief of the Imperial Headquarters Flying Department, corroborating Sato's earlier claim that no prisoners had been transported from Kyushu.[21]

Esposito pushed the documents and Sato's fairy tales to the side and proceeded to subject him to yet another intense round of questioning. They went over Sato's initial story, and, when they finished, went over it again. With each rehashing, Sato contradicted himself more, becoming confused by his own inconsistencies. When pressed for exact numbers—something that even Fukushima identified as Sato's weakness—and presented with documents from Kurume that completely contradicted his claims, Sato crumbled.

"Americans were beheaded," he admitted. "But I cannot speak about it now. I will return in five days with all the data pertaining to the executions."[22]

Esposito's first instincts must have been to detain Sato and force more information from him. He consented, however, and granted Sato the time necessary to procure the data and put together a written report. Esposito's gamble paid off.

Sato returned to the Kurume CIC, as promised, on December 12. He brought documents verifying that American POWs had been executed, all without trial. In addition, he handed over information indicating that more executions took place, separate from the original ones Esposito investigated. This time, Sato, when questioned, volunteered information freely.[23]

"I think I will disclose the real state of things," Sato told him. "Feeling righteous indignation for those who had nothing to do with the matters but are receiving pain at the sacrifice of concealing the truth of the case on the part of the superiors. The inferiors of those days are being destined to take the guilt of their superiors."

"Continue," Esposito said.

"I have been charged with the duty to make every arrangement for concealing the truth of the case and have had hard work for four months up to this day, since the close of the war. But the truth of the case will come to light sooner or later and cannot be kept secret forever.

"Though I have often presented my opinions to disclose the case to light, my advice has not been taken. Such being the situation, I have made up my mind to tell the real state arbitrarily.

"In the meantime, the superiors are still resorting to petty tricks, bringing disgrace upon the Japanese Army. On the contrary, it is a pity that those young officers who were directly concerned with the case be condemned to heavy penalties because they did it in accordance with the situations, their superiors' guidance, etc. I heartily wish you would take these points into consideration and sympathize with them."

"Sato," Esposito said, "tell me about the executions. When did the first one take place?"

"It happened on 20 June, just after the Fukuoka air raid."

"And who was in charge of the executions?"

"Judicial Lieutenant Murata Sadayoshi oversaw the incident."

"How many executioners were there?"

"Only one," Sato answered. "Lieutenant Toji Kentaro."

"And he killed the nine Americans?"

Sato's answer startled Esposito. "No, more."

"More?"

"Yes," Sato said. "There were in fact more than ten Americans beheaded. Their bodies were immediately buried within the Western Army compound behind a hut. When the war ended, their remains were dug out and cremated.

"It was not by his own judgment that the commander committed the crime.

"Yokoyama Isamu, commander in chief of the Western Army, had been telling his inferiors that he would not spare any captives in Kyushu.

"Lieutenant Murata fulfilled his duty, thinking, of course, that it had been decided by the commander in chief."

Esposito could not believe what he heard. Had the deaths of at least ten American soldiers been the result of a misunderstanding?

Sato and Esposito moved on to the second incident.

"Tell me what you know about the following set of executions," Esposito said, guiding Sato through his testimony. Again, the colonel spoke freely.

"Staff Colonel Akita Hiroshi is pleading that the commander in chief did not directly give the order to kill them, and especially denied it on the grounds that he was absent on the 20th. It will come to light, however, that he is telling a lie, if you interrogate Captain Kazumitsu."

"The executions," Esposito interrupted. "Tell me when they took place."

"I am not sure of the exact date," Sato replied. "It was in August, though."

"Who ordered them?"

"Major General Fukushima Kyusaka gave consent to the beheadings."

"How many Americans were killed and who killed them?"

"Lieutenant Hashiyama Noboru carried out the beheadings at two different times."

"Where did they occur?"

"The soldiers were executed at Aburayama in the suburbs of Fukuoka City," Sato said.

"What happened to their remains?"

"Major Idezono and Lieutenant Murata saw to it that the bodies were cremated in Aburayama with the bodies of the first executions. I don't know about the disposal of their belongings. As for their ashes, Lieutenant Murata disposed of them. Though I am not sure, I hear that their ashes were buried at sea, for Murata was too sorry for those brave air warriors to bury their ashes in the ground."

"You never mentioned how many were executed."

Sato thought, then answered. "Nine. They were the prisoners from Kurume."

That was how Sato's interrogation with the gaijin investigator began in earnest. As it stood, the CIC knew about at least nineteen executions. At least they didn't know about the other fliers and how they died.

4

December 1945–February 1946

Special Agent Esposito sat across from Fukushima. His eyes burrowed a hole through the suspect. Earlier in the day, during his initial interrogation of Colonel Sato, Esposito failed to draw out information corroborating the informant's story. His admission would come during subsequent meetings. Clearly, however, Sato hid something. If the colonel would not volunteer the facts, perhaps he could be coerced into divulging the information. And if Sato, Fukushima, and Kusumoto failed to cooperate, Esposito had more tricks. That was why he made sure that they saw one another at the CIC headquarters. Self-preservation was a powerful motivator. He would play on their doubts and fears and insecurities. They would crack—it was only a matter of time. The question was: who would crack first?

Major General Fukushima Kyusaku's position with the Western Army sounded innocent enough: he was one of the many vice chiefs of staff. In that capacity, he served a primarily administrative role: something like a glorified assistant to Lieutenant General Inada, the chief of staff. In certain ways, the war might have seemed a little distant. But Fukushima's duties extended beyond his title—he served as the main link between the Western Army command and Kyushu's civilian population.

Under the stifling duress of waiting for an imminent Allied invasion, establishing a healthy and open line of communication between the military and civilian population became a priority. Fear-driven rumors, fabrications, and falsehoods threatened to send the island into anarchy if they were not dispelled immediately. Order had to be maintained because the defense of Kyushu demanded cooperation from all sectors of society. It fell on Fukushima to ensure that these things occurred. He kept in constant contact with prefectural governments, ensuring that their governing efforts complemented those of the Western Army.[1] Contradictions circulating between the two bodies could only hurt their efforts at maintaining the tentative order on the island. Controlling the flow of information to and from the media—radio and print—also contributed to keeping a grip on civil order.[2] Not only could it be used to maintain order, it could be used as a preventive: a well-informed public was less likely to panic than an uninformed one.

Fukushima's most important function, however, lay in his role organizing Kyushu's citizens into the Civilian National Defense Corps.[3] Enlisting the active services of nonmilitary civilians, mostly villagers and farmers, meant adding thousands of hands to a severely depleted force. At a time when able-bodied young men were being drafted in droves to act as human guided missiles with no hope of ever returning, any help—whether from a fourteen-year-old schoolboy or a seventy-five-year-old seamstress—was useful. If Kyushu's men could form an armed defense unit, Japan would benefit. Earlier in his military career, Fukushima served as the company commander of the 2nd Infantry Regiment,[4] so he understood what aid from the civilian sector meant: Japan's survival. Preserving his homeland mattered most.

But on August 15, 1945, when the emperor announced Japan's surrender, the Japan cherished by Fukushima ceased to exist. The entire nation flipped a switch on their radios and tuned in to hear the end. That night Fukushima retired directly to his home. Sorrow overwhelmed him. He did not emerge from his room for the rest of the night.[5]

Fukushima had walked into CIC Headquarters not knowing what to expect but uncomfortable with his conscience. Had it not been for the plan that he and Sato had drawn up, he might have felt more nervous. It helped to know what you were going to say ahead of time. If you delivered your lines well enough, you avoided hesitation; uncertainty was as good as an admission of guilt. There would be none of that, however. The general knew his lines.

Then Fukushima saw Sato and Major Kusumoto at the CIC.[6] Their presence changed everything. The stakes were much higher than he initially suspected. There was only one reason why three officers from the Western Army Headquarters would be in the same American intelligence center at the same time: the Americans had something tangible, something serious enough to warrant questioning a Major General. What did they know? Even worse, what did Sato tell them?

Say Sato divulged the true facts and Fukushima lied. It would taint him in the eyes of the American investigators. Hiding the truth amounted to an admission of guilt. The horrible deaths would be placed on Fukushima's head. He would hang. His hands and arms and legs and ankles would be tied as he swung from the gallows. The irony of surviving war only to die in peace had no appeal.

But what if Sato stuck to the story and Fukushima did not? A cowardly act, for sure. Imagine the disgrace, the shame he'd bestow on his family. Sato's life depended on Fukushima's courage.

But did he trust Sato? Yes.

Did he really trust Sato? No.

Did Sato trust him? Fukushima had no way of knowing. If Sato held any doubts, surely he would tell the truth in order to save himself. Yet if Sato trusted him, their stories would match perfectly.

It was all too complicated. He needed time to think things through carefully. But as he entered the interrogation room, Fukushima's moment had arrived.[7]

"What role did you play in the handling of POWs?" Esposito asked.

"I did not deal with POWs. It was not my responsibility."

"You never came into contact with them?"

"No. They were held in different parts of the headquarters. In order to have any contact with them, I would have to go out of my way to see them. Since they were not my responsibilities, I never went to their barracks."

"Never?"

"I had no reason."

The warm-up session ended and Esposito confronted Fukushima head on.

"If you had nothing to do with POWs, why is Colonel Sato identifying you as one of the people who can corroborate his story about the fates of nine POWs?"

"I don't know."

"You know nothing about them?"

Fukushima flinched. "I did not say that."

"I asked you why Sato ID'd you as someone who knew about the nine POWs and you said, 'I don't know.' "

"I didn't say I didn't know anything about the POWs. I just said that I didn't know why Sato pointed to me."

"Fukushima, are you a liar?"

"No."

"So what do you want to tell me about the POWs?"

Fukushima shuffled in his seat. He hesitated. The lines he had studied and rehearsed melted in his head. Esposito obviously knew something. He came on too strong to not know anything. Had Sato told them a different story? No. Sato had told the story they agreed to tell. That was why he identified Fukushima. Yet, Esposito appeared skeptical. He doesn't believe Sato's story, Fukushima thought. Nonetheless, he began to tell the same story.

"There were a number of POWs who were sent to Hiroshima before the hostilities ended."

"How many?"

"Three, I believe."

"Americans?"

"All of the prisoners at Western Army were American."

"Why is that?"

"We were responsible for all downed airmen and the only planes bombing Kyushu at that time were American B-29s."

"Continue."

"I am not certain about the fates of those Americans sent to Hiroshima, though I believe I heard that they died when America dropped the atomic bomb on the city. Many Allied prisoners perished as a result of the bomb."

So far, Fukushima's story matched Sato's. Esposito pressed for more information. If the story matched too perfectly, it indicated a conspiracy. If there were too many blatant inconsistencies, it pointed to wrongdoing and an ill-conceived conspiracy.

"Is that all?"

"No, there were more," Fukushima replied. The lines came out more confidently now. "During the end of the war, a number of prisoners—I am uncertain as to the exact numbers—were sent to Tokyo by plane."

"And what happened to those prisoners?"

"I do not know. They never arrived in Tokyo. The plane seemed to have disappeared. At first we didn't know anything about them, but we soon discovered that they never reached their destination."

"Is that the truth?"

"Yes," Fukushima insisted.

"I don't believe you." Esposito's voice trembled. "What are you hiding?"

"I hide nothing."

"What happened to those prisoners? Were those boys executed?"

"I don't know."

"Sato knows, doesn't he?"

"I don't know."

"And you do, too."

"I don't."

"You're trying to hide something bad. Did something bad happen to those boys?"

"I don't think so."

"But something could have happened? How do you explain them disappearing?"

At that moment, Fukushima could have repeated his story. He didn't. He weakened. He made a mistake. He tried to appease his inquisitor. He wanted the ordeal to end.

"I believe something must have happened to the American prisoners. You are right. I just do not know exactly what right now. I would like some time to conduct an official investigation into their fate."

"What do you think happened?"

"I will find that out. I will investigate."

"How long will this investigation take?"

"Five days," Fukushima replied.

Esposito was skeptical. Why five days, he asked. The general replied that many of the officers he would have to question had gone home already. Contacting them took time. The CIC granted him five days exactly.

The proximity of SCAP general headquarters to the Imperial Palace and the Japanese government exerted immeasurable pressure on Tokyo's officials. The prime minister, members of the Cabinet, Diet members, and various ministers wanted to stay in power and also tried to avoid antagonizing SCAP's attempts at democratization. In an attempt at appeasing their occupiers, they carried out the directives sent to them from SCAP with considerable zeal. One such area was the investigation of atrocities at the various POW camps and holding barracks scattered throughout Japan. They formed the Prisoner-of-War Information Bureau. By conducting a vigorous initial investigation, Tokyo was able to display their cooperation but at the same time filter as much information as they possibly could within limits. Legal officers from Tokyo spread throughout Japan interviewing former Imperial officers and reviewing whatever documents survived the initial day of surrender.

Order at Western Army Demobilization suffered as a result. Perhaps in some subconscious attempt to appease the gods of retribution, an investigation frenzy gripped the office. Whatever the reasoning, a dizzying web of quasi-investigations emerged.

Immediately after hostilities ceased, Sato and Fukushima embarked on an investigation charade, going through the motions of digging for the facts.[8] Anyone not directly involved in the executions needed to see the two officers endeavoring to bring the guilty parties to justice. Their efforts served two purposes, of course: first, these efforts announced their innocence to the world. After all, had they been guilty, why would they be so zealous about spearheading an investigation? Their proactive attitudes would surely dispel any doubt. Second, Sato and Fukushima attempted to sow the seeds of a legal defense, albeit indirectly. They were already working on contingency plans in the event that their guilt emerged. All of the people convinced of their innocence provided a stable of character witnesses.

At about the same time, Lieutenant General Inada started asking around about the fates of the prisoners who had been interned at Western Army Headquarters. Rumors circulated throughout the Western Army about the executions. During a time when the discussion about war crimes gathered momentum, people naturally allowed their mouths to run freely in between you-and-me conversations. No matter that all the facts did not hold up; the trickle of knowledge proved empowering. It was only a matter of time until Inada heard something, true or false. If the rumors proved true, he needed to distance himself from them. For a man in his prominent position, being tied to such atrocities would prove fatal. Inada approached his officers—Sato, Fukushima, and Akita—and spoke to them, first alone, then all together. The rumors had not been rumors after all.[9]

Inada ordered Sato to conduct an investigation and consolidate all of the facts. Inada's logic—genuine, although head-scratchingly sophomoric—was as convoluted as the nation's sense of identity. His explanation for placing a guilty man in charge of his own investigation: "Because Sato was the only one that knew the facts, I felt that the only way to determine the true facts was through Sato." Inada even went so far as to admit that he never entertained the illusion that Sato would conduct an "impartial, unprejudiced investigation."[10] Of course,

Sato's "official" investigation proved to be nothing more than an elaborate cover-up of the concealment plans that he and Fukushima continued to nurture.

In December 1945, Colonel Oki Genzaburo replaced Colonel Ito Shoshin as head of the Western Army Headquarters Legal Section.[11] Because Oki was a newcomer with no strings attached to the wartime command, he took it upon himself to initiate an investigation of his own. His investigation came closer to revealing the actual events surrounding the executions than any of the preceding attempts. Oki's lack of connection to the headquarters command worked against him, however, and numerous facts were ultimately held from him.[12] Sato, Fukushima, and the rest of the officers responsible for the atrocities could at least take solace in the fact that Oki still represented the Western Army, and as a result, had the best interests of the outfit in his mind.

The investigator-as-enemy arrived in Kyushu in the form of Lieutenant General Suzuki Shigeo. He hailed straight from Tokyo, Western Army Headquarters' newfound adversary. He was sent to Fukuoka by command of the higher court of the Demobilization Ministry. His sole purpose lay in teasing out the facts behind one of the executions.[13] He would report back to Tokyo with an affirmation or a negation of the War Department's suspicion that Western Army actively concealed wartime atrocities. Suzuki's prying and poking and probing proved to be Sato and Fukushima's worst nightmare. Then the Counter Intelligence Corps came calling.

Fukushima returned to the Kurume CIC five days later, as promised.[14] The contents of his report hampered any chances of exculpating his guilt. After a CIC translator rendered Japanese into English, it became evident that new ground would not be broken. Fukushima decided to simply regurgitate the same story about the American prisoners being flown to Tokyo. In addition, he documented his daily attempts at questioning the Western Army Headquarters staff responsible for handling captured airmen. In hindsight, it would probably have been better to have skipped the description because it only exhibited how little effort Fukushima put into his investigation. He named nine people:

Colonel Sato	Staff Chief
Lieutenant Ono	Assistant Staff Officer
Captain Aihara	Assistant Staff Officer
Nakao	Interpreter
Lieutenant Colonel Kami	Adjutant
Captain Goiyama	Assistant Adjutant
Major Kusumoto	(Temporary) Deputy Adjutant
Captain Yukino	Assistant Adjutant
Lieutenant Nakamura	Assistant to Captain Yukino

Fukushima admitted speaking to two: Sato and Yukino. Everyone else was either out of town, sick, or simply stood Fukushima up after making appointments. At least that's how he presented it.

Five hundred thirty-six words said absolutely nothing. He noted, "Within the sphere of investigations up to now, there seems no particular data of criminals in the Headquarters." He had no data, so of course his "data" failed to indicate the presence of criminals; they would fail to indicate any innocent parties had there been any. Fukushima's feeble attempt at manufacturing an investigation report accomplished two things: it implicated him as a definite suspect and managed to insult the Counter Intelligence Corps agent conducting the investigation. Interestingly enough, Fukushima showed that he failed to grasp the gravity of the situation: "While the Japanese Demobilization department was determined to investigate the case, it was surprised at the seriousness which the Kurume CIC Detachment gave to the matter."[15]

When Maki Hiroyuki—the CIC's Western Army informant—waded through the halls of the Oita CIC headquarters, he carried a purpose and told a story different from Fukushima's version. Maki's account became the CIC's working story. He was there to enlighten the Americans with information they would not have had access to otherwise. That was what informers did. They informed. As an assistant to Major General Fukushima, which was how he presented himself to the CIC, the depth of knowledge he possessed made him invaluable. The Americans fawned over him, pampered him, complimented him, and exalted him. The head of the Kurume CIC, First

Lieutenant P. Vincent Esposito, praised him and pleaded lenience for Maki in an official report: "His [Maki's] diligence and earnestness, at the risk of his life, deserve full consideration in any trial of the conspirators." From the end of December 1945 until February 1946, Maki spent a considerable amount of time divulging everything he knew about Western Army Headquarters, the command structure, and the executions of thirty-one American soldiers.[16]

Thirty-one beheadings.

The staggering number revealed itself after closer investigation of Colonel Sato's testimonies and the reports submitted by Maki and Fukushima. Maki confirmed the number himself. Thirty-one premeditated murders spanning the course of three days, one in June 1945 and the remainder in August.[17]

Maki systematically implicated the majority of the Western Army Headquarters high command. He supplied a list of each person responsible:

Major General Fukushima Kyusaku
Major General Ito Akinobu
Lieutenant General Yokoyama Isamu
Lieutenant General Inada Masazumi
Colonel Akita Hiroshi
Major Kusumoto Tomonosuka

From the top down, ranking officers advocated the execution of Allied airmen without a trial. They didn't even make believe. All they wanted was American blood. On June 20, Lieutenant General Yokoyama issued the command, and eight U.S. Air Corps men perished directly behind Western Army Headquarters. Maki listed the victims' names to the best of his recollection:

Second Lieutenant Baile, Jack M.
Sergeant Denglar, Jack
Corporal Coaks, Arving Atwood
Second Private Calvin, Muran
Sergeant Major Fresh, Edgar L. Macwell

Sergeant Romance, Ralf S.
Sergeant Balmgarten, Otto W.
Sergeant Major Aspinal, Robert J.

Although many of the names were spelled incorrectly, Maki's list served its purpose. He could not recall all of the executioners involved but recalled one name: First Lieutenant Toji Kentaro. It was enough for the CIC to investigate.

Esposito asked Maki why the executions occurred. The response was simple: revenge for the Allied bombing raid on Fukuoka the morning of the same day.

The second set of executions took place on August 12 at a rifle range at Aburayama, just south of Fukuoka. The orders came from Yokoyama and Fukushima. Eight more airmen died. Maki, however, could only recall two of the victims—Billy Brown and Chas Palmer—and one of the executioners—Major Itezono Tatsuo. Like the first set of executions, the Japanese wanted revenge, this time for the dropping of the atomic bomb.

The final set of executions involved fifteen airmen under orders from either Yokoyama or Fukushima. The murders took place after the emperor's broadcast. They died after the war had ended. The Japanese took advantage of the opportunity to exact one final injury on their enemies.

A conspiracy to conceal the murders emerged in the months following the war. Western Army command decided that neither Japanese nor American forces could ever discover what happened. According to Maki, the conspirators planned to direct Allied attention away from Fukuoka and toward Tokyo. In order to achieve this, false reports were prepared and submitted to the Department of War. They understood the unlikelihood of the Tokyo story going over without a snag. Should the atrocities be discovered, the responsibility fell on Fukushima to state that the airplanes carrying the prisoners crashed at sea and that the bodies of the crewmen disappeared.

The CIC informer's numbers did not add up, however. When questioned about this, he recalled that nine prisoners had been sent to Hiroshima from Fukuoka. He explained that these men perished when the atomic bomb destroyed the city. Their remains would never be found. For Esposito, the matter bore further investigation.[18] Who were the nine?

The investigation rose to another level. On the strength of Maki's efforts, arrest warrants were issued. Japanese policemen, under orders from the CIC, searched Fukuoka for the men responsible for murdering the American prisoners. Once in custody, the occupation forces interned them at Dotemachi Prison—everyone except Colonel Sato. He retained his freedom on account of the aid he supplied to the CIC. It made sense. The man who entered the Kurume CIC as Maki Hiroyuki left the office and returned to Fukuoka with a different name and identity. By serving as an informant for the Americans, Colonel Sato Yoshinao hoped to keep them at arm's length.

5

April 1946

Sato presented himself as the ideal witness, and his story made perfect sense. It chronicled the series of atrocities that occurred at Western Army Headquarters during the final months of the war. Sato implicated the main players involved in the murders—the important high-ranking decision makers who bore the brunt of the responsibility. He stated with certainty that Lieutenant General Yokoyama and Major General Fukushima issued the orders. He indicated that three sets of executions occurred on separate occasions: June 20, August 12, and August 15. The first executions took place in the yard behind Western Army Headquarters; the subsequent executions were at Aburayama Crematory. Sato even supplied Esposito with the concealment plans that had been set in motion and that might have hidden the atrocities had it not been for the colonel's heroism. All that remained was for Esposito to confirm the facts that Sato supplied and to fill in the gaps that resulted from confusion in the colonel's memory. It was all very neat.

During the first week of April 1946, the CIC arrested every high-ranking officer, except Yokoyama, identified by Sato: Major Kusumoto Tomonosuka, Colonel Akita Hiroshi, Lieutenant General

Nishihara Kanji, Lieutenant General Inada Masazumi, and Major General Fukushima Kyusaku.[1] The suspects were held at Dotemachi Prison, a local jail in Fukuoka that had previously housed Allied prisoners of war. Like most of the internment centers scattered throughout Japan and the Pacific Rim countries, Dotemachi Prison housed former Japanese soldiers awaiting judgment by the victorious masses. It was just one more situation that became inverted during the occupation.

The CIC investigation verged on closure. All they needed was for Sato's facts to be supported by a handful of admissions of guilt and the case could be closed and prosecuted. It would save time for the SCAP Legal Section and make the Counter Intelligence Corps look terribly efficient.

Special Agent Esposito interrogated the Western Army Headquarters officers on April 16 and 17. Tension, anger, and outward hostility dominated the sessions. The questioning often fell into pure badgering. Esposito had a story that had taken him months to construct and demanded to hear facts supporting it. His strategy revolved around establishing everything Sato told him. He repeated questions, hoping to catch contradictions; he stated "facts," coercing agreement from the prisoners; he played officer against officer, fostering insecurity and doubt; he yelled and screamed and tried to psychologically intimidate the suspects. He expected them to lie—which they all did—and hoped to weaken their resolve. Emotions ran high. Esposito wanted to see the guilty punished and the officers desperately wanted to avoid being hung. Some sessions simply tumbled into chaos. The most important thing for Esposito—the thing that would make weeks of interrogations worth it—was simply to establish who saw to it that the executions took place. Yokoyama and Fukushima. In the end, however, nobody got what they expected. Once again, the case proved that it made the rules and had a life of its own. Whenever it wanted to change the stakes, it did.

Major Kusumoto Tomonosuka grew up a few miles from Fukuoka in Oita. Prior to enlisting in the Imperial Army, he graduated from farming school and worked for the Oksaka Electric Company. After a year of employment, he joined the army on December 10, 1920, entering as a second-class private. In 1934, Kusumoto graduated from officers school and made second lieutenant a year later. It took nine years for him to reach the rank of major.[2]

Kusumoto served at Western Army Headquarters for a little over three years. He belonged to the Adjutant Section and was in charge of the General Affairs Division that handled the day-to-day affairs such as personnel issues and office supplies. He served as junior adjutant until his discharge.

Unfortunately for Kusumoto, demobilization did not free him from culpability for crimes committed during the war. When Sato identified him as a participant in the executions, the CIC ordered his arrest. Kusumoto was the first to be interrogated. Esposito wasted no time and interrogated aggressively, speaking to Kusumoto through an interpreter.

Kusumoto admitted that atrocities had been committed at the headquarters during the war, though he refused to provide specific dates. Much to Esposito's delight, Kusumoto identified Yokoyama as the Western Army Headquarters commanding officer during the span of time in which the murders had been committed. It corroborated the information Sato supplied, mainly that Yokoyama authorized the murders of the captured airmen. Kusumoto, however, denied being present for any of the executions, though he admitted being at Western Army Headquarters at the time. He also claimed ignorance of how many prisoners died altogether.[3]

Esposito addressed Kusumoto directly. "Did you hear any rumors about how they were going to cover up the deaths of these men?"[4]

"Yes, from Fukushima and Sato," Kusumoto replied. "I heard the story mainly came from Tokyo on or about the 18th of August that thirty-one American fliers left by plane for Tokyo. I do not know the fates of these men, though."

Sato and Fukushima. Not the expected reply.

Esposito asked whether Kusumoto had ever seen a POW and where. He then asked about the yard where the POWs had been executed. Kusumoto indicated seeing a prisoner at Western Army Headquarters but not knowing where the murders occurred.

Kusumoto placed responsibility for the beheadings on Yokoyama and explained that he hadn't heard about the June 20 execution because the air raids made his work multiply. He never saw any written orders pertaining to the incident and speculated that a trial may have taken place, though he knew nothing about it. He identified a number of Western Army Headquarters officials who might be able to supply information—Yokoyama, Inada, Fukushima, Akita, Sato, Akamine, Yukino, and Nakamura—and identified General Inada as the adjutant and Major General Ito as the judge advocate. Kusumoto failed to identify any men who actually attended the executions, however, and added that nobody at the headquarters admitted to being present. Esposito asked Kusumoto what officers were present at Western Army Headquarters on July 15. Inada was not, but Fukushima was. Yokoyama lost his command on August 20, 1945, and had been farming in Fuksukaichi ever since.

Esposito's questioning shifted from the facts Sato supplied to the colonel's role in the events. Up to this point, the CIC considered him a minor participant in the murders, a subordinate officer following the orders of his superiors. Kusumoto indicated that Sato was anything but a helpless subordinate, however, and was a staff officer at Western Army Headquarters. Yet aside from that, Kusumoto's testimony essentially supported the information the CIC possessed, mainly that Fukushima was Sato's superior and had the authority to issue orders.

Kusumoto's repeated references to Colonel Sato bothered Esposito. The CIC investigator deviated from his game plan momentarily and continued to inquire about his informer's credibility as a military man. Kusumoto indicated that Sato was a reliable officer and would not take action without having the appropriate orders or approval. As the officer in charge of POWs, this meant that Sato would have to have had orders from either Fukushima or Yokoyama—if not from both—in order to act.

Esposito returned to the subject of the beheadings. He discovered that Sato's name refused to go away.

"How many people attended the execution at the General Headquarters?"

"I don't know. Sato is whom you should ask."

Esposito paused when he heard Kusumoto's response. How much did Sato know? And if Kusumoto really didn't know about the number of people at the execution—meaning he did not attend them—then how did Sato know unless he was there? Moreover, why was Kusumoto so intent on placing blame on Sato?

"So on 15 August you knew that there were fifteen men to be beheaded?" Esposito asked after gathering his thoughts.

"Yes. I knew that some were executed before that." It was something Kusumoto hadn't mentioned earlier. However, when asked for specifics, he claimed that he couldn't remember many details.

"How did you learn about it?"

"Colonel Sato told me."

Esposito continued to press Kusumoto for information, only now an increasing number of questions related to Sato. Kusumoto consistently indicated that Sato had told him about all of the executions.

"Who ordered the execution?" Esposito asked once more.

"The commanding general."

Thus far, Kusumoto's testimony confirmed a portion of what Sato had told Esposito: Yokoyama issued the orders. One thing stuck out, however. The deeper into the story Esposito probed, the more Sato's role expanded from a passive participant following orders to an active accomplice. Could there have been more behind his eagerness to cooperate than a desire to see justice served?

Esposito questioned Lieutenant General Nishihara Kanji next. With any luck, the interrogation would go better than with Kusumoto. And while Esposito managed to gather testimony against Yokoyama, he failed to gather incriminating evidence against Fukushima.

Nishihara assumed command of Western Army Headquarters after Tokyo relieved Yokoyama of his duties. As Yokoyama's successor, Lieutenant General Nishihara played an obvious role in keeping the Western Army Headquarters murders as far away from the Prisoner-of-War Information Bureau as possible. He was the officer in command, and just as Yokoyama bore responsibility for the wrongdoings under his command, Nishihara did as well. In short, it was his role in the concealment plans that warranted questioning. Aside from admitting that thirty-one American prisoners had been executed at the headquarters, the interrogation yielded little new information.[5]

Esposito's next target was Colonel Akita Hiroshi. If the previous interrogations—Nishihara's in particular—were any indication of what to expect, there would be more lies. Nothing had been proven. Evidence against Fukushima had yet to surface. Yokoyama's guilt, while at least mentioned, needed more support. Still worse, Sato—the man Esposito had come to rely on during the formative stage of the investigation—came under increasing scrutiny. But for now, his attention fell on Akita.

Akita spent the majority of his early military years as a member of the Japanese cavalry. His first promotion after graduating from cavalry school made him a first lieutenant. After a brief stint as a cavalry instructor, he received orders to attend Military Staff College in Tokyo. Akita graduated in 1933 with the rank of captain but remained at the school for four more years as a special member of the Research Section. The following years saw Akita serving tours as a military attache in China, France, and Belgium. In 1941, he was one of General Yamashita's nine companions on a special trip to Nazi Germany. In the meantime, he was promoted to lieutenant colonel. As Japan entered the war, Akita joined the Air Corps and eventually served as both an instructor and a squadron commander in the South Pacific. Tokyo ordered Colonel Akita's transfer to Fukuoka in April 1945. Since then, he served as a senior staff officer at Western Army Headquarters until he was demobilized in March 1946.[6] A month later, the CIC arrested him, interned him at Dotemachi Prison, and questioned him.

Akita admitted that he had been stationed at Western Army Headquarters during the span of time that the executions occurred. However, he indicated that he was not present at Western Army Headquarters during any of those dates. On June 20, he was in Kagoshima, and on August 12 and 15, he was at the 16th Divisional Headquarters in Yamaya.[7]

Without much prodding from Esposito, Akita admitted that Sato's report regarding the disappearance of the Tokyo-bound plane carrying American POWs was a fabrication and that the fliers had been executed. The dates he cited—June 20, August 12, and August 15—corroborated Sato's account. Moreover, Akita claimed to have heard about the executions from Fukushima, indirectly implicating the major general.

Akita told Esposito that Oki informed him about the August 12 executions as well. He supplied the names of three officers he believed acted as executioners. He also mentioned the November 20 meeting held at Western Army Headquarters between several high-ranking officers, including Yokoyama, Inada, Fukushima, and Nishihara. Esposito was not satisfied and pressed for more information about Fukushima. Unfortunately, his efforts failed to elicit more information about the executions or concealment plans.

Esposito was done. Akita's testimony fell short of expectations. No matter how hard he tried to draw out proof of Fukushima's role in the beheadings, Esposito's efforts were not enough. The CIC investigator was forced to reconsider his view on Fukushima's degree of involvement, adding to the growing sense that Sato played an important part in the executions. Still, the CIC's secret informant claimed that he acted under orders. It remained a possibility.

Besides Lieutenant General Yokoyama, the CIC held Major General Fukushima Kyusaku responsible for the executions. Again, Sato's testimony placed an unrelenting spotlight on a fellow officer at Western Army Headquarters, and American investigators sought the general out like a pack of attack dogs. Esposito was determined to get him to confess that he had ordered the second and third executions. After identifying Yokoyama and Inada as his immediate superiors, Fukushima confirmed Lieutenant General Yokoyama's presence at Western Army Headquarters on June 1 and 20, 1945.[8]

When questioned about the executions, Fukushima maintained his innocence. He had nothing to do with them. He issued no orders. Fukushima repeatedly placed the blame for the beheadings on Colonel Sato. He did, however, readily admit to meeting with Colonel Sato and Major Kusumoto after the war and discussing plans for the concealment of the executions. More important, Fukushima indicated that for a while Sato played the primary role in orchestrating the concealment plans. As the interrogation continued, ignoring Sato's role became impossible.

Up until now, preceding testimonies indicated that Sato played a supporting role in the executions. Now, if Fukushima told the truth, it appeared that Sato played the major role. Why else would he try to assume such a large burden? Esposito remained skeptical. It was, after all, Fukushima talking—a guilty man with his life to lose. Why wouldn't he try to pin it on a subordinate? Fukushima's testimony alone would not do the trick.

"Who else played a part in the concealment?"

"Sato was trying to conceal this incident to all but himself," Fukushima explained. "During the latter part of September, he weakened, and that was when I jumped in and tried to conceal the incident with Sato. Kusumoto hadn't come into the picture yet."

Esposito pushed Fukushima for information about the June 20 and August 12 executions. Fukushima answered that he knew nothing about them and repeatedly implicated Sato.

Esposito confronted Fukushima about a letter he had written stating that thirty-one prisoners of war had been transferred to Tokyo and that the plane carrying the prisoners landed on August 18, 1945. He pulled out the letter from a folder, held it in front of the general, then slammed it onto the table. He ordered Fukushima to read it.

"That's a mistranslation," Fukushima cried indignantly. "In the letter, I stated that the plane hadn't reached Tokyo yet, and we were investigating it."

"Didn't you state that the plane had landed in Tokyo?"

"No, I didn't."

Esposito lost his patience and his composure and screamed: "I have the letter! Quit lying!"

"It isn't a lie. It's the truth."

"Well, you knew then that these thirty-one prisoners of war had been beheaded before, didn't you? In other words, you conspired to conceal the fate of these boys?"

"Yes."

"Do you know what happened to Yamashita and Homma?"

Fukushima offered a reluctant nod.

"Good."

Fukushima admitted that he and Yokoyama knew about the executions but only after being informed of them by Major General Ito. Esposito questioned him about the false report and letter he filed with the CIC. He read them back to Fukushima, who readily admitted that he wanted to hide the facts.

"All of the facts of the beheadings hadn't surfaced yet," Fukushima stated. "I wanted to hide the incident until I found out all the facts. I didn't know about the third set of decapitations. On August 15, before the emperor's speech came over the radio, all of the personnel in the Western Army HQ were gathered waiting for the speech. Colonel Sato came into my office to plan the third set of executions. I told Sato that it wasn't good, and after that I thought that Sato had taken my advice. The next day I found out that the execution had taken place. That is why I thought Colonel Sato was responsible for issuing the order."

"Could you have ordered Sato not to have committed the execution?"

"I don't have the power to order Sato to do anything."

"Why did you conspire to conceal the facts and why didn't you denounce Sato?"

"That wasn't my responsibility."

Esposito changed the subject abruptly. "Why were you surprised that the CIC was serious about the matter in Kurume?"

"I don't recall saying that."

"We have confessions from the executioners and they point their fingers at you."

"I don't know anything about that," Fukushima replied. He turned away from his interrogator and stared out the window.

"Would you like to jump out the window?" Esposito's voice dripped with sarcasm.

"No." Fukushima's response was flat.

Esposito continued pushing Fukushima about not stopping the beheadings.

"You were a general and Sato was a colonel. Why couldn't you stop the executions?"

"I told Sato not to do it and that it wasn't right. I thought that Sato would take my advice. I found out the next day that the men had been beheaded."

"Who gave the order for the first execution?"

"I think it was Sato." Sato again.

"And on August 12?"

"I think it was Sato." And again.

"August 15?"

"Sato again." And again.

"Why did you conspire to conceal the fate of the pilots?"

"It was a terrible thing."

"Why didn't you denounce Colonel Sato and tell the generals in Tokyo that Sato was responsible?"

"It was too terrible a thing."

"Aren't you as guilty as Homma and Yamashita?"

"I didn't have any relation to the incident. I am only guilty of trying to hide it. I had no way of stopping the executions, so I am not responsible."

"Why did you as a major general not disclose the facts to Tokyo if you were not guilty?"

"I didn't think that I was responsible. I realized that the incident was very serious and it was an international situation. I tried to keep it from the public."

"How do you think the pilots felt?"

Silence filled the room.

"They must have suffered."

Esposito repeated a few earlier questions, but the interrogation was essentially over.

At Western Army Headquarters, Lieutenant General Inada Masazumi answered only to Yokoyama. While he admitted that he was stationed at Western Army Headquarters during the first set of executions, he indicated that he had left town that morning and returned two days later. On June 25, Yokoyama split the Western Army command between Fukuoka and Yamae. He and Inada moved to the new headquarters, leaving Western Army Headquarters under the immediate command of his subordinates. Lieutenant General Yokoyama, however, continued to function as the supreme commander of the Western Army, and all major decisions required his approval.

With Fukushima's interrogation and the facts about Colonel Sato still fresh in his mind, Esposito questioned Inada about his role as Sato's superior. The colonel had become a prime suspect. The investigation shifted. It was no longer solely about Yokoyama and Fukushima. Now it was about Colonel Sato Yoshinao.

Inada admitted attending the November 22, 1945, meeting in Fukuoka. Unlike the other members of the Western Army staff questioned thus far, he placed Yokoyama at the meeting. In addition, he indicated that Colonel Sato was in attendance. Further interrogations continued pointing to Sato's considerable role in the affair. In fact, Inada suggested that it was Sato who gave the orders for the beheadings and not Fukushima or Yokoyama. It was a major shift in the case's direction. All the while, the CIC had been trying to pin the executions on the wrong people.[9]

Esposito and the CIC had been fooled. It was clear that Sato had played the entire Counter Intelligence Corps in Kyushu for fools. The story that Esposito reported to his superiors and the rest of his peers had been a clever attempt at sending the investigation astray. And Esposito ate it up. He bowed and barked for Sato, boasting of the colonel's honesty and eagerness to help. Now he knew the truth; now he looked like an amateur; now he screamed as loud as he could.

"Colonel Sato is going to hang before you do!"

Oki Genzaburo had been interrogated by the CIC on three separate occasions. He was not a suspect and was not being held at Dotemachi Prison. He represented a rarity: a person who had nothing to do with the executions and the concealment, and who had conducted a genuine investigation of his own. In that way, he and Esposito had something in common. On April 17, Oki requested a meeting with Esposito. He had information that he withheld during the previous discussions.[10]

"What does the colonel wish to tell us with reference to an atrocity?" Esposito scribbled in his notepad.

"It is a story that was related to me by a Captain Goiyama, a prison guard at the Western Army HQ."

"When was the story related to you?"

"In the middle of January."

"What was the story?"

Oki did not answer immediately. He needed to gather his thoughts. What he was about to reveal went beyond anything Esposito could ever imagine. Oki took a deep breath, then began speaking.

"On June 20, eight American prisoners were killed, but from the records, they show that there were five more. He found out that those five were sent to Kyushu Imperial University Hospital in Fukuoka with some sickness."

"Do you know what was wrong with them?" Esposito scribbled on his legal pad.

"No, but they never returned."

Esposito glanced up from the paper. He wore a perplexed and worried expression.

"Did you hear what happened to those five men?"

"I asked Colonel Sato about it," Oki replied. "He stated to me that he didn't want to relate this incident even to the American forces."

"Do you know what happened to them?" It had to be bad.

"I checked up and found out that they were used in experiments."

Used in experiments.

Esposito asked if there were any more incidents. Oki replied that there weren't.

"Who gave permission for these five men to be taken to Kyushu University for the purpose of experiments?"

Esposito should have known what Oki's response would be.

"Colonel Sato."

6

The Families: January–March 1946

As the investigation gathered momentum in Japan, Marvin drove thousands of miles. He traveled from Virginia to Pennsylvania, then to New York and New Jersey. His green Chevy cut through frozen daylight while strands of air whispered through slits in the car's body. Hard rubber wheels spun on their axles in even-paced intervals pushed forward by an engine pumping streams of spent fuel into the countryside. The road coiled and uncoiled in front of Marvin. Scenes of an America reborn flickered silently through the car's windows, framed neatly into front, side, and rear views. He passed through towns smaller than his own. He navigated across traffic-drenched cities. His metal carriage carried him on his lonely quest. It moved through space. It shifted through time. It held the world and its noise and its touch at a distance.

The country was no longer stable. After nearly four years of tense day-to-day existence, the American populace, still trembling with pent-up anxiety, needed to exhale. More important, they needed to know that everything they had fought for would bring a new peace-filled era. A generation of young men lost their lives or were injured or maimed. Americans wanted a new beginning, but the various celebratory parades following the Japanese surrender had not supplied that opportunity. When the final marchers faded away, people still found themselves stuck in a year dominated by war. That was why New Year's Eve meant so much. It brought a definitive close to their anxieties—one they could point to and say, "That is where it all ended." But celebration turned to mayhem, and after four days of heavy bacchanalian revelry, more Americans died. Nationwide, at least 492 people suffered violent deaths.[1]

Things did not improve at home. They only got worse. On January 2, 1946, meatpackers in Chicago, New York City, and most of the country threatened to go on strike. Western Union—owned by the American Communications Association—joined them, as did workers in other industries. Overall, two million workers in the telephone, telegraph, meatpacking, steel, and electrical industries threatened to walk off the job.[2] What Japan and Germany could only dream of doing—crippling America—its own citizens threatened. In the months to come, various labor unions from the auto, coal, railway, and steel industries continued to harangue President Truman.[3]

All the while, GIs continued to trickle stateside. Every day, newspapers carried lists of ships arriving in ports in New York City, Newport News, San Diego, and Seattle: 3,417 men on the USS *General Brooks*, 11,225 men on the *Queen Mary*, 1,571 men on the *Texarkana Victory*, 3,559 men on the *Saratoga*. They returned steadily, albeit slowly. And on January 3, 1946, the two millionth American soldier, Sergeant Irving Feldman, returned home from the Pacific aboard the USS *Carrard* in San Francisco. His happy-to-be-home smile graced newspapers all over the country.[4]

For the families of GIs killed in action, there was little to hoot and holler about. The daily reports served as constant reminders of their loss. It was cruel, and the black ink on the page seemed absolute and appropriate. Instead of waiting for loved ones to show up at their doorstep, families scurried to find out as much about their sons' fates as possible. What was saddest was the simplicity of their questions and the difficulty receiving answers. Where were they when they died? What were the circumstances behind their deaths? What became of their remains?

During the months after the war, the proper burial of soldiers became a priority. Mothers and fathers wanted their sons and daughters honored while wives needed to remember their husbands and know that their loss meant something. The process started with laying them to rest. All over Asia and Europe, the U.S. Army Quartermaster Corps oversaw the exhumation of the dead. They had been buried in local cemeteries or anywhere that was convenient at the time. Once a soldier had been located and identified, the Quartermaster Corps notified the next of kin and burial options were left to their discretion.

But others weren't even lucky enough to bury their beloved. Sometimes, they died deaths so violent that nothing remained to be buried; sometimes, their bodies got lost amidst the chaotic swirl of combat and calm. Whatever the circumstance, the drawn-out pain suffered by the families differed little. There was no burial ceremony to supply closure and ultimately no gravestone to give their memories form. It was as if even their ability to mourn and heal came under attack.

The bodies of the Watkins crew had not been found and they had not even achieved killed-in-action status. Yet, with each passing day after the war, the likelihood of a safe and happy return disintegrated a little more. It was only a matter of time until the U.S. Army gave up and changed the status from "missing" to "killed." The bodies would probably never be found.

Marvin could not bring closure to his crew members' families. He knew as much about their final fates as they did. He could, however, tell the families what he knew, and for families with little to go on, it meant a lot. His own experiences limited him and his knowledge. For some crew members, he'd be able to give enough information to supply hope; for others, he'd only be able to offer his guesses and hopeful predictions of their safe returns.

It had been months since Marvin saw his crew. Since then, they existed in his memories. But when he pulled up to the first house, that all changed. And as he spoke about their final moments together, the men became real again.

• • •

They were on their way home. The bomb bay doors slammed shut and Marvin Watkins started tuning in the coordinates for the trip back to Guam. Their role in the bombing raid of Tachiari Airfield on Kyushu proved to be a routine daytime drop. Not a cloud in the sky, nothing but a vast, ever-so-still ocean of blueness lay before them.[5] Sometimes, Japan's majestic landscape, with its godlike mountains, its perpetually ascending terraces, and its steamy lakes and rivers, made you forget that you were at war. The further you pulled away from the action, the more you could allow yourself to appreciate the country's natural splendor. But on May 5, 1945, things went terribly wrong.

"We had completed our bombing run and were ten to twenty miles away from the target when our plane was attacked by a twin-engine enemy fighter," Watkins later recalled.[6]

That was when a small explosion shook the plane. The crew members looked around and at each other in confusion. Watkins glanced out the window and his heart dropped. The number 4 engine, the farthest on the plane's right side, had been hit by enemy gunfire. There were holes, and threads of smoke starting to stream out. Making matters worse, they were still under attack.

Japanese Zeroes swarmed around the B-29 like vultures maintaining their distance until they swooped in unmercifully. They took turns diving toward the Superfortress that trudged along with three engines. Machine gunfire—bright like giant fireflies—sprayed in every direction from the enemy and from the B-29. The Watkins crew was gradually being isolated from the other B-29s, but even if another plane could come to their aid, it would be too late.

The motor burst into flames, transforming a portion of the wing into a fireball. Tar-colored smoke—a mixture of oil, melting metal, and burning rubber—pulsed out of the craft. All at once, it trailed behind the plane, filled the flight deck, and seeped into the remainder of the plane. The situation on the plane deteriorated and showed no signs of improving.

Marvin ordered the crew to get ready, just in case they had to bail out. He still hadn't made up his mind, however. It would buy him time until he made his final decision, and it would facilitate their exit in the event he decided that all was lost. He wanted the best for his crew. Currently, they were still over Kyushu. If they bailed now, they would be stranded in a very hostile land with no means of escape.

Finally, it became too much. Remaining on the plane guaranteed death. The best thing a lead pilot could give his crew in situations like this was a chance to survive. So Watkins said it.

"Bail out! Everyone bail out!"

The smoke-filled plane fell into a state of controlled chaos. No matter how many times they had practiced it, nothing could prepare them for the real thing. Unlike make-believe bails, this one was full of fear that led to confusion.

Positioned in the tail of the plane, Corporal Leon Czarnecki (tail gunner) was on his own and had to fend for himself. Most likely, he was the first to leave the ship. Corporal Leo Oeinck (gunner), Corporal Robert Johnson (gunner), Corporal John Colehower (lethal gunner), and Second Lieutenant Dale Plambeck (radar) all made it out of the plane safely, as well. Evacuation of the flight deck followed suit. Everyone but Watkins and Staff Sergeant Teddy Ponczka scurried about, readying themselves for the long and uncertain plunge into Japan. Second Lieutenant Howard Shingledecker (bombardier) was the first to evacuate, followed directly by Second Lieutenant Charles Kearns (navigator), Corporal Robert Williams (radio operator), and Second Lieutenant William Fredericks (copilot). Watkins and Ponczka, still checking the flight and engine instruments, remained on the plane for about another five miles.

The unrelenting Japanese attack continued to target the fatally injured B-29, peppering it with gunfire. All the while, the plane forged forward with its remaining two crew members. That was when a Japanese fighter decided to single-handedly destroy the plane along with himself. It shattered the glass nose of the bomber, sending it into a fatal spin.

Without one of the B-29's wings, there was no saving it. After being tossed around following the fighter plane's initial impact, Watkins and Ponczka left the plane. The pilot could not recall where the plane finally crashed, since he did not watch it go down. His main concern now was where the parachute would drop him and how he would survive. In less than thirty minutes, the lives of the Watkins crew had been irreparably altered. As he approached the ground, a fire in the woods below awaited him.

At about 0830, Watkins landed three hundred yards away from the limited but concentrated blaze. The plane must have caused the fire, he thought. But he did not know for sure. It just made sense. He was unable to investigate it, however. In a matter of minutes, the Kempei Tai, the civilian police, and local villagers would set out on their prospective manhunts. In the best-case scenario, nobody would find him; in a reasonable case scenario, the police would find him; discovery by an angry civilian mob would be the worst thing that could happen to him. It would guarantee his death.

Marvin removed his parachute and hid it in a small field. He ran for two hundred yards until he found a bamboo thicket where he could hide and regroup.

Civilian search parties combed through the shrubs and trees that filled the woodland surrounding the downed flier. Their silhouettes slid along the mountains of Kyushu that loomed in the distance. Those giant natural structures reinforced the desperate position in which Watkins found himself: he had never seen any mountain in Japan from the bottom up, always from the top down. His desperation doubled when a Japanese search party spotted him. Marvin sprinted into brush on the side of a hill three hundred yards away.

The cat-and-mouse game continued until late in the afternoon, but it could not go on forever. Eventually, a solitary old man straggling along stumbled on Watkins and called for help. Dozens of villagers wielding swords, clubs, pitchforks, and shotguns arrived at the scene. Resistance would have been futile and would only have led to Watkins's death. He turned over his gun and surrendered. And though he was struck a number of times by the civilian mob, Marvin got off lightly.

For the next two days, the local Japanese police transported Watkins from one town to another. He spent the entire time bound—first with metal handcuffs, then reinforced with rope—and blindfolded. While the material covered most of his vision, he was able to peek under it if he tilted his head back slightly. He needed to know where he was and who, if anyone, was with him. So slowly, deliberately, all the while expecting to be struck at any moment, Watkins arched his neck ever so slightly. He was not alone.

Second Lieutenant Fredericks sat nearby in silence. A blindfold covered his eyes. His hands were bound in front of him. His feet rested flatly on the floor and his back was stiff and upright. From what Watkins could see, Fredericks appeared in good condition. His broad forehead bore no marking of physical harm. His posture indicated that he was able to support himself. Small consolations during a desperate time. Fredericks sat close enough for Marvin to whisper to, but ultimately it was too risky. If he got caught talking to Fredericks, there was no telling what their captors would do to them both. The B-29 pilot would see his copilot a final time later in the day while being transported to yet another location.

Watkins arrived at an undisclosed destination at about 1700. A Japanese officer immediately transferred him from the train to a truck. The constant travel schedule wore Watkins down, but he maintained his composure the best he could. Once again, Watkins was able to tilt his head slightly so that he could peer under his blindfold. He scanned his surroundings. Had Fredericks been placed on the truck as well? To Watkins's tempered relief, he had been. As Watkins continued his survey, he chanced upon another of his crew members: Staff Sergeant Teddy Ponczka.

The engineer lay unconscious on a stretcher, still enough to be a corpse. A thick blindfold covered his eyes and a thin rope was wrapped around his wrists. Ponczka had the most developed physique of the entire crew. A sturdy athletic frame plus well-developed muscles made him an imposing figure. He wore his hair pushed back, clearing the way for a broad forehead. His facial features—slightly squinting eyes, a strong jawline, slightly pronounced cheekbones, and a perfectly centered mouth—always made him appear in control of situations. The feeble figure lying helpless before Watkins resembled the Teddy Ponczka he knew as much as the dead resembled the living. He was obviously injured. Was it the fall from the plane? Did the Japanese beat him so badly that he could not support himself anymore?

Whatever the case, seeing Ponczka motionless reinforced the gravity of their situation.

The final destination appeared to be a recruit training center of some sort. Watkins, Fredericks, and Ponczka were separated and placed in different cells. Their blindfolds and the rope were removed. The handcuffs, however, remained. They sat in darkness, swimming in silence so thick that if they opened their mouths their voices might simply drown.

Then a voice.

"Lieutenant Watkins?" A familiar voice whispered from the adjacent cell. "Lieutenant Watkins, is that you?"[7]

"Plambeck?"

"Yes, sir."

"Are you okay?"

"A little injured, but besides that I'm all right."

"Injured how?"

"I think my shoulder is dislocated, sir."

"The fall?"

"No, sir. I made it to the ground fine. Even avoided capture for a while. But when a civilian search party caught me, they beat me with a stick. It happened then. Are you injured, sir?"

"Just a little cut. Nothing more," Watkins replied. He knew that they could not talk for much longer, so he needed to make every question count. "Plambeck, what happened to the others? Did they get out of the plane in time?"

"Yes, sir. We all got out of the plane safe. I even had to give Colehower a little nudge before bailing. Everyone got out, though."

Just then, another familiar voice rang loudly.

"Toilet paper. I need toilet paper. Is anyone out there? Do you hear me?"

It was Colehower.

"Colehower," Marvin whispered. No response. "Colehower." Dead silence. "Colehower, answer me." It was no use. There would be no reply. The cell that seemed to brighten for a few minutes sank back into darkness. They spent the night in their cells and didn't say another word.

The next morning, the Japanese removed Marvin from his cell and brought him to a large nearby building for questioning. He remained there, blindfolded, until he was removed for interrogation.

Three Japanese officers interrogated Marvin and asked him questions about the Air Corps' strategies. He refused to answer, instead responding to their queries with his name, rank, and serial number. As a punishment, Watkins found himself locked in the stockade. It would not be his first time.

Ponczka's condition continued to deteriorate; when the Japanese placed Marvin in the cell with him, it did not look like the engineer would survive. He was still on a bamboo stretcher. A bandage was wrapped around his shoulder, and when Marvin raised it, he saw an infected wound between the shoulder blades. In addition, Ponczka suffered from partially paralyzed legs—the result of a blow to the groin. The Japanese ordered Watkins to nurse Ponczka back to health.

Immediately after bailing out, Ponczka found himself on the ground and surrounded by villagers. When he was apprehended, he heard numerous gunshots, one of which coincided with a sharp pain in his back. Soon afterward, he passed out and awoke on the stretcher. He believed he had been shot, but Watkins informed him that he had definitely not been shot. Rather, it looked like a stab wound.

For four days, Watkins tended to Ponczka—feeding him, washing him, consoling him—and they were allowed to speak freely. As much as they could, they made the best of the situation. Gradually, Ponczka's health and spirit returned. He was able to move about, albeit gingerly; the infection disappeared and the wound was healing. When Watkins was taken from the cell, Ponczka was feeling much better. That was the last time that First Lieutenant Marvin S. Watkins would ever see any of his crew.

Marvin knew for certain that four of the ten remaining crew members were alive: Ponczka, Fredericks, Colehower, and Plambeck. But what had happened to the others: Oeinck, Johnson, Czarnecki, Shingledecker, Williams, and Kearns? Had they been able to avoid capture? The forest where the plane descended was dense, and if they made it into the evening without being discovered, surely it would have been to their advantage. Did something go wrong during their descent? Drifting down in a parachute left you vulnerable to the relentless attack of agile fighter planes that could kill you any number of ways—gunfire to the body, gunfire to the parachute, or they could use the plane as a high-velocity battering ram. Then there was one last possibility that Marvin acknowledged with apprehension.

"Shingledecker made the remark that if one landed in Japan, he might as well kill as many Japanese as possible and save one bullet for himself."[8]

7

Sato and Aihara: June 1946

Case 420—Aihara Kajuro et al.—broke wide open, exposing one of the Pacific War's most gruesome events: eight young men murdered in cold blood under dim lights and dirty instruments and the gaze of curious onlookers hoping to witness a spectacle. Doctors, nurses, and medical students all partook in snuffing out lives that they should have been fighting to preserve.

For the time being, the investigation fell under two separate but related case names: Case 420 and Case 604. Case 420 dealt primarily with the military personnel responsible for sending the POWs to the university; Case 604 focused on the doctors at Kyushu Imperial University. The majority of both cases' grunt work belonged to two civilian investigators: Robert Tait and John Eglsaer. Aiding them in the interrogations were two other investigators: Henry Daty and Robert McKnight. Of the four, only Tait would see the case through to the end.

Eglsaer had a misleadingly soft-looking face, an illusion owing to its well-fed roundness. He had lots of cheek and forehead, and his ears clung tightly to his head and short, dark hair. It certainly was not a face that had struggled through the daily grind of infantry combat.

He had a medium build—neither skinny nor fat. A government-issued watch dangled from his left wrist, and he dressed neatly: creased pants, a crisp shirt tucked into his pants, and an army hat with a pin on the left side.

Tait, in contrast, looked the part of the intimidating investigator. It was not that his face was scarred or hard or mean-looking. In fact, his face had a certain roundness to it, and he was only slightly skinnier than Eglsaer. Tait, however, had one of those intangible swaggers that could bully a bully. His voice boomed without being loud. He wore dark semicircular sunglasses whether walking out under the Fukuoka sun or interrogating a noncooperative suspect in his office. On warm days, he often took off his government-issued khaki-colored shirt and blasted questions while wearing his white undershirt. He smoked and spoke, paced the room anxiously, and leaned over the table—knuckles resting flat on the tabletop—when he wanted to drive a point home. By all accounts, Robert Tait embodied the consummate investigator.

But the Legal Section had its limitations. They did not have the direct authority to arrest suspected war criminals, nor did they have the resources to track them down. As a result, they conducted business the same way as all other occupation offices. If they needed something done, they turned to the equivalent Japanese office to carry out their directive. In the case of the Legal Section, warrants of arrest actually came from local Japanese police forces that showed surprising efficiency in tracking down suspected criminals. Everything happened, however, under the Legal Section's guidance.

Captain Aihara Kajuro oversaw the detention barracks and prisoners at Western Army Headquarters. In addition to implicating Aihara for releasing the prisoners to the university, Sato indicated that the captain attended at least one operation. As a result, he was among the first officers to be questioned in relation to the Kyushu Imperial University vivisections.

Before joining the army, Aihara worked as an electrical engineer for a local company in Osaka. In May 1944, he reported to Western Army Headquarters to aid the faltering war effort. At forty-six, he was well past combat age and did not have to officially join the military.

But he did, anyway, receiving the rank of captain. His assignment placed him in the Staff Section, where he acted as an aide.[1]

In many ways, Aihara fell victim to being in the wrong place at the wrong time and not having the authority to do anything about it. For all intents and purposes, his role at Western Army Headquarters consisted of receiving new prisoners, maintaining the roster of POW names, and collecting any intelligence papers pertaining to the captured B-29 fliers. That was all. But it also put him in direct contact with prisoners, making him a strong candidate to identify them. At the rank of captain, a more decision-making role was unlikely.

In 1946, Aihara looked every bit his age. His face sagged at every crucial juncture. The wrinkles on his forehead, the corners of his eyes, the skin on his cheeks, and the edges of his mouth all drooped as if invisible two-pound weights had been fastened to them. He peered out of sunflower seed–shaped eyes, and his squint added to his aging appearance.

On June 30, 1946, the Legal Section questioned Aihara at the Fukuoka office. Nobody expected him to disclose everything he knew. He was simply being warmed up for later, more intensive questioning. Of course, the more Aihara volunteered now, the better.

As expected, Aihara proved uncooperative, volunteering as little information as possible. He admitted that he had witnessed an operation on an American POW and that the operation took place some time in May or early June. It became evident that Eglsaer needed to play a more active role. He shifted the questioning a bit, away from the operation facts and more toward identifying the people present.[2]

"How many people were in this operating room?" he asked.[3]

"About seven or eight people."

"What were their names?"

"I only know Komori and Ishiyama by name." Eglsaer took note of the names.

"Was the American brought in unconscious?"

"I think unconscious, as he was already on the operating table when I went into the room."

"Who operated on this American?"

"Komori and Ishiyama."

Aihara had witnessed an operation on the back of a prisoner's head but did not know why the procedure occurred. For now, it did not matter. Eglsaer got some facts and two names.

After the brief interrogation, Aihara was returned to his cell at Dotemachi Prison, where the Legal Section held him for the time being. When the Legal Section no longer needed him close by, he would be shipped north to Sugamo Prison in Tokyo, where almost all suspected war criminals awaited trial.

Aihara's refusal to cooperate surprised no one. To expect a demobilized Japanese soldier to suddenly discard his prejudices against his former enemy—even under normal circumstances—bordered on stupidity. For all intents and purposes, everything that mattered to the Japanese had been destroyed. The lack of cooperation facing Legal Section investigators not only reflected natural hostility, it revealed the extent of their emotional and spiritual trauma after returning from the ledge of annihilation.

By 1300 on June 20, 1945, conditions at Western Army Headquarters degenerated. A Staff Section messenger approached Captain Wako at the Legal Section. Colonel Sato wanted to speak with him. The two spoke in the air defense room just as Sato rose to leave.[4]

"I asked him what he wanted," Wako recalled. "He said that there had been a heavy air raid and that more were expected to follow. He said that the Operations Section was going to execute their enemy fliers and asked me what we were going to do with ours."[5]

The Legal Section had decided that they would do the same after getting permission from Yokoyama.[6]

When the discussion ended, Wako went directly to Yokoyama's office and informed him of the plans to execute the fliers without a trial. Wako reasoned that because of the increasing intensity of the Allied bombing and the threat of future air raids, there was no time to try the prisoners. According to Wako, Yokoyama agreed with his assessment.[7]

"Lieutenant General Yokoyama then said that it would be all right to execute the fliers without a trial."[8]

After that, Wako informed Legal Section Chief Ito about the plans. Again, Wako received the green light. The executions won the approval of the necessary people at Western Army Headquarters.

At 1400, Wako found Judicial Lieutenant Murata in the corridor between the main headquarters to the trial building. The Legal Section offices burned down the night before and temporarily moved to the trial building. Wako updated Murata about everything that had gone on since he met Colonel Sato earlier in the afternoon. He informed Murata that all of the fliers held prisoner at Western Army Headquarters would be executed later in the day and that Sato had told him to prepare for the executions. Murata wanted confirmation that Yokoyama had granted his approval. Wako dispelled the lieutenant's uncertainty.[9]

"The commanding general asked me where the plane crash survivors were kept during the air raid last night. I replied that they were kept near the guard house in front of the main gate. He then told me that it was because they were taken to a place where so many people could see them that such a commotion arose. Then the commanding general told me to execute all of the fliers today, as Colonel Sato had said."[10]

Wako's explanation satisfied Murata.

"Does that mean that the four fliers who were going to be tried by the commission are also going to be executed?" Murata asked.[11]

"Naturally."

"Where will the executions be held?"

"It would be better if the fliers were executed somewhere other than at the headquarters, but because of the disorder caused by the air raid, the executions would have to take place within the compound."

"Where?"

"A place where people can't see it. I think the yard behind the service company's kitchen would be a good place."

"Next to the girl's high school?"

"Yes," Murata said. "I will send some guards to dig a pit out there."

"Captain, have you informed Major General Ito about this?"

Wako's answer did not satisfy Murata; when the two parted ways,

Murata looked for Ito. Murata searched everywhere he could think of: the former Legal Section office, the quartermaster office, and the adjutant's office. Finally, Murata gave up and decided to check the status of the pit diggers outside.[12]

Wako supervised the guards digging what was to become a grave. Shovel pierced soil, overcoming the natural resistance that nature provided and eventually cutting through its surface. Soldiers tossed severed earth to the side into a growing mound. Meanwhile, the void grew until there was enough room for eight full-grown bodies. With the hole emptied to Wako's satisfaction, he, Murata, and the winded guards left for the Legal Section Detention Barracks. It was time to release the prisoners.[13]

The Western Army Detention Barracks lay behind the headquarters. POWs wasted away in their cells—three men pressed together in an 8-by-15-foot room better described as a glorified wooden box. Some rooms had a tiny bench; all had a modest container that functioned as a group latrine. There was no bed or hammock or cot, only tatamis strewn out over the floor. The Western Army denied their prisoners baths. Instead, POWs were allowed to pour water over themselves once a week. They subsisted on baseball-size rice balls, strands of pickled daikon, and water. In a month's time, they left their cells only once for five minutes.[14]

Wako ordered the barracks warden to release the prisoners from their cells.[15] He now acted with the authority of Commanding General Yokoyama and the legal chief Major General Ito behind him. His words, gestures, and demeanor reflected it. As the prison guards led the POWs out of their cells, Wako ordered them outside and lined up on the headquarters lawn. As the men marched outside, members of the Legal Section gathered around the yard and watched the spectacle unfold.

The young Americans struggled in the open air. Their eyes, accustomed only to the blight of darkness, burned. Under jagged yellow sunlight, their blotchy government-issued garments testified to a bitter captivity. Knotted beards, matted hair, and cheeks as sharp as mountain cliffs shrouded men who once looked down upon clouds. As their captors bound their hands immobile, wrapped their eyes closed, and bestowed one final drink of water, the men stood but a few footsteps from the ditch that would eventually embrace them.[16]

Everyone stood around anxiously waiting for Sato to arrive. Five minutes passed. Finally, Wako went to Sato's office to inform him that the executions were set to take place. He returned a few minutes later with Sato's orders: take the fliers to the pit and the colonel would meet them shortly.[17]

The guards guided the blindfolded fliers toward the grave. The crowd that had gathered to witness the spectacle shifted with the main participants. They whispered and speculated among themselves. For the prisoners, it was a cacophony of foreign and hurtful voices.

Once Sato arrived, the executions began. He stood close to the pit and watched his wishes materialize.[18] Wako ordered two soldiers—Ikeda and Onishi—to act as executioners.[19] When Lieutenant Onishi protested, Wako lashed out at the dissenter: "What you have just said is unpatriotic!" The shamed Onishi consented. Nobody wanted to be labeled unpatriotic, even if it meant murder.[20]

The time had come. Wako indicated that he was ready to begin and signaled to the guards to bring the first prisoner to the edge of the pit.

The American did not resist. He made no noise as he was made to kneel on a straw mat. Behind him, Wako stood erect, clutching the samurai sword he brought specifically for the occasion. Something was said in Japanese and the blindfolded prisoner began to say something.

"English—"[21]

But before he could finish, the blade of the sword sliced through the right side of his neck—a single stroke, and head, body, and soul drooped, then dropped into the ditch.[22]

Wako held his sword extended, and a soldier poured water over the blade in preparation for the next flier. The crowd watched silently. For some, the death of the enemy was still the death of a human being. You could only deny so much.

The second flier kneeled in silence. Wako stood over him, hand and sword held high in the air. He brought the sword down. One stroke. But it was not clean. Wako failed to cut through the entire neck; as the American's head dangled by a stretch of skin, his body tumbled into the pit alongside his countryman.[23]

Major Ikeda stepped forward while the third victim knelt at the pit. Ikeda looked down at the American's exposed neck, took aim, and brought the blade of his sword straight through.[24] The reluctant Onishi performed his patriotic duty immediately after Ikeda, decapitating a fourth prisoner.[25]

Major General Ito arrived after the fourth flier's execution and stood alongside Sato. At this point, a young officer pushed through the crowd and presented himself to Sato. He introduced himself as First Lieutenant Toji Kentaro. He wanted to execute the remainder of the prisoners. "My mother was killed in the air raid on Fukuoka this morning, and I think it would be fitting that I be the one who executes these American fliers." Sato agreed and said that it would be all right.[26]

Toji had no sword and borrowed Wako's weapon.

Murata later recalled the execution with a mixture of wonderment and revulsion:

"Toji stood behind the prisoner and raised the sword over his right shoulder. Then with terrific force and a loud cry, he brought the sword down across the right side of the flier's neck. He completely severed the flier's head with so much force that the head flew into the air before it fell into the pit."[27]

Toji swung so hard that he chipped a steel samurai sword. Toji's rage did not end until the final decapitated body lay lifeless.[28] On two more occasions—August 11 and 15—more American prisoners would be executed. In all, thirty-one men died.

Investigators speculated why the POWs died. Revenge for the air raids, the atomic bombs, and a lost war emerged as the final SCAP explanation. Perhaps the reasons held some degree of validity. Vengeance definitely dictated much of the Western Army Headquarters officers' actions. But they also acted out of a genuine and unconditional patriotism that was unyielding, unquestioning, and undeniably destructive—something never mentioned by investigators. The nationalistic aphorism—my country, right or wrong—supplied the executioners with all the moral justification they needed. It allowed them to see the helpless and the weak—their bound and blindfolded prisoners—as nothing but objectified manifestations of their own imaginations. They failed to live up to the responsibility of their power. Thirty-one young men died. There was no question that it was wrong. But that was war.

Eglsaer interrogated Colonel Sato the same day as Aihara. He confronted Sato with the false report he had filed, supposedly accounting for all of the American POWs held at Western Army Headquarters. It communicated to Sato that the Legal Section already possessed enough evidence against him to convict him, so being completely forthcoming with his answers worked to his advantage.

Eglsaer placed the document on the table and said, "You have just testified under oath that the report made by Major General Fukushima and submitted to us by you, titled, 'List of American

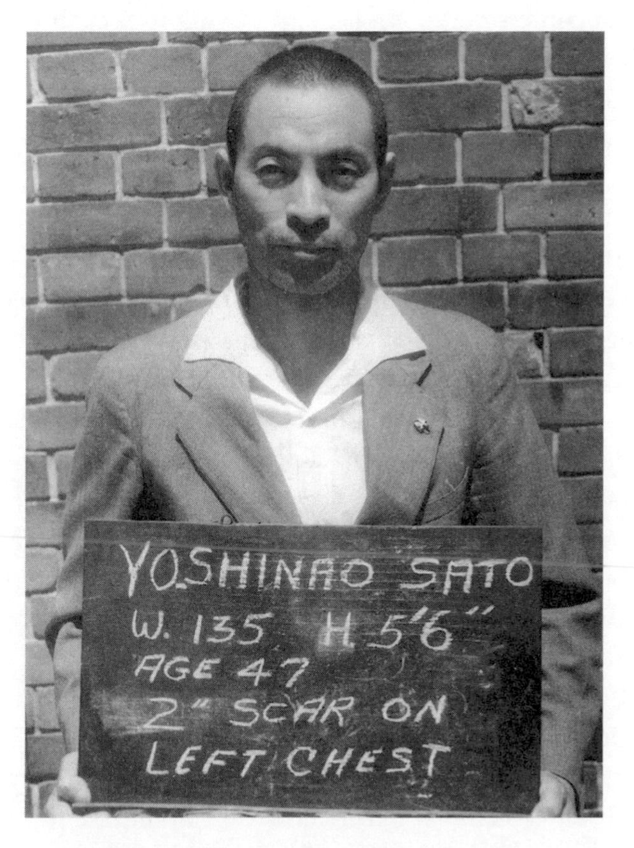

Colonel Sato Yoshinao, Imperial Japanese Army

Aviators Received, Sent and Held,' is accurate with the following exceptions. First, that the 18 August 1945 entry showing that thirty-one POWs were sent away should state that these men were beheaded. Second, that you believe there were two prisoners received during May 1945 which are not shown and that this accounts for the discrepancy between the number of prisoners received and the number of prisoners sent away."[29]

"Yes." Sato nodded. "That is correct."

According to Sato, the prisoners were sent to 2nd Central Area Army Headquarters at Hiroshima.

Eglsaer gave Sato a chance to correct himself.

"Sato, do you have anything more to say?"

The colonel stared at the paper in front of him and considered his statement.

"I must confess that it is a lie. I was trying to protect my country and fellow Japanese. I am only thinking of them." Sato took a deep breath, then continued. "I will tell you the truth. Actually, there were thirty-three persons beheaded instead of thirty-one. In addition to this, eight of the nine persons shown as being sent to 2nd Central Area Army on 31 July 1945 were killed."

According to Sato, he first met a medical probationary officer named Komori after being involved in an automobile accident. Although he had nothing to do with treating POWs, Komori told Sato that the Americans looked undernourished and sickly. He went on to tell Sato that the best thing to do would be to allow him to take the prisoners to Kyushu Imperial University for treatment. Sato consented immediately.

"Then I asked him what type of treatment he was going to give them. Komori explained to me that a professor Ishiyama of Kyushu Imperial University medical staff was experimenting with a drug extract from saltwater. When I heard this, I became suspicious as to what the POWs were going to be used for.

"On about 27 May 1945, Komori came to me and said that he was taking one of the POWs to the Kyushu Imperial University Medical Department for treatment. He asked me if I would like to witness the treatment, and since I was not very busy, I consented to go."

Sato claimed that he doubted Komori's intentions. When he arrived at the university, his fears were substantiated. The POWs would be used as guinea pigs.

"We arrived at the autopsy building of the university at about 1400. When we entered, I noted that there were about ten persons in the room that had been prepared for operating. I recollect that these persons were there: Ishiyama, Ishiyama's chief nurse, a Torisu, and a Hirako. I believe that a person named Hirao was there, but I am not sure."

Sato witnessed an operation in which an entire lung was removed. Komori claimed that it gave them an opportunity to determine the effectiveness of a new saltwater drug being developed at the university. When the operation was finished, Sato approached Komori regarding the status of the prisoner.

"Komori then told me that even if the patient did live, he would have to be killed later, because if he was later returned to the United States, they would prove by X-ray that the POW's lung was removed unnecessarily in a medical experiment."

Sato continued: "As I was preparing to leave, I noticed that one of the surgeons, I believe Torisu, took a scalpel and reopened the POW's incision. At that time, the gas mask was off the POW's face. One of the surgeons then put his hand inside of the POW's chest. I believe this was to stop the POW's heart action. I then noticed that they brought a coffin into the room and placed it in the corner."

A total of three sets of operations took place between the end of May and early June. In all, eight American prisoners died. Sato attended each operation.

Unlike Aihara, Sato had volunteered all the information without being prompted. He supplied names—Ishiyama, Komori, Torisu, Hirako—and their roles in the operation. Moreover, Sato described the experiments in considerable detail. The investigators now had weapons to use against the other suspects. Sato's account might not have been the complete story, but it was enough.

8

University Suspects: July 13–17, 1946

On July 11, 1946, SCAP issued a memorandum to the imperial Japanese government by way of the Central Liason Office in Tokyo. The subject heading read: "Apprehension of Suspected War Criminals." It listed each suspect, his rank and title, and information pertinent to each person's arrest. The memorandum requested that the suspects be "apprehended as suspected war criminals and delivered to the Commanding General, EIGHT ARMY, at Sugamo Prison (Tokyo Detention Camp) at the earliest possible date."[1]

The Case 420 interrogations of the doctors responsible for the vivisections promised to be brutal, nonstop mental beatings. Questioning would be designed to weaken the suspects' wills, both to deceive and to live. Now that the suspects were in custody, the Fukuoka Legal Section needed to get them talking. There was no doubt as to their guilt. The challenge that lay ahead of the investigators had to do with establishing each person's degree of involvement and ironing out the exact sequence of events that culminated in the surgical executions of eight American prisoners.

The campaign to break the Kyushu Imperial University suspects started the day the Legal Section assumed custody of them: July 13,

1945. The sooner they achieved their goal and weakened the resolve of the doctors, the sooner the facts would begin to emerge. Then they could begin stringing facts together and compare them with Sato's story. To date, the Western Army colonel's version of the murders was all the Legal Section possessed. Alternate versions needed to be constructed. On one level, this allowed the investigators to use one suspect's statements against the others. Once the common facts were parceled out, the people contradicting them were most likely being deceptive. The accumulation of data would also allow the investigators to assemble a working version of the murders by using the common facts as definite points in the narrative. From these established points, it would be possible to determine the roles and degree of involvement of each of the suspects.

The process, however, entailed more than interrogating the suspects already in Legal Section custody. In time, the investigators would have to speak with university employees and military officers from the highest decision-making levels to common university servants.

Then there was the issue of the remains of the murdered fliers, which were still missing and had to be found. Locating their bodies would be ideal, but that possibility seemed unlikely, since Japanese custom dictated that bodies be cremated when possible. Even with nothing to hide, the corpses would have been cremated. With an active concealment plan being implemented, the probability of not cremating the bodies hovered at around nil.

The day the suspects arrived at the Legal Section, they were paraded into the office in front of army cameramen. Documenting a case of this magnitude—experimental operations on American soldiers—held a high priority. Even then, the historical significance of the case was understood.

Once the essential information like name, age, and address had been noted, each suspect endured an extensive strip search. Coarse gaijin hands pushed the suspects' bodies into humiliating positions, exposing intimate areas ordinarily protected. Woolen pants, cotton shirts, white undergarments, and coarse footwear struggled to retain their prior shape after being twisted and probed mercilessly. The shelter their clothing provided—physical and emotional—lay in crumpled heaps where they could not help anyone. In every sense, the suspects stood in isolation.

The suspects from the university represented a wide range of medical backgrounds, from neurology to pure research. Some of them boasted decades worth of service to the university, whereas others were still engaged in postdoctorate research. Together they formed the intellectual core of one of Japan's premier surgical clinics: the Ishiyama clinic, also known as Kyushu Imperial University's First Surgical Clinic.

Hirao Kenichi no longer held a position at Kyushu Imperial University, where he finished his eleven-year stint serving under Professor Ishiyama and conducted blood substitute research. Until his arrest, Hirao had entertained thoughts of opening a private practice that promised greater financial reward than an Imperial University salary.[2] More money meant being able to give his family—a wife and two young children—things that other occupied Japanese families couldn't even imagine, things like meat and milk.

Chief Nurse Tsutsui Shizuko graduated from Kyushu Imperial University in 1935. She was a veteran of the operating room, assisting in over a thousand operations during her decade-long career. Until her arrest, she had served in the Ishiyama clinic for four years. She was the chief nurse and oversaw a staff of twenty-four nurses. In addition, she acted as a secretary for Ishiyama and handled his daily correspondences. This made her an ideal witness. Not only could she provide insight into the operations themselves but also the behind-the-scenes maneuvering that occurred in order to procure the American prisoners from Western Army Headquarters. Unfortunately, she proved less than cooperative.[3]

Torisu Taro graduated from Kyushu Imperial University Medical School in 1932. He was twenty-six years old. From February 1941 until he joined the Kyushu Imperial University staff in 1943, Torisu served in the Imperial Army. While he specialized in surgery, his most recent work revolved around the use of seawater as a temporary blood substitute.[4] During the war, this type of research was given the highest priority level by the government and universities because of the shortage of blood for injured soldiers. As it stood, his testimony was essential on another front as well. Sato had identified him as the man directly responsible for a soldier's murder.

Hirako Goichi was sixty years old, by far the oldest suspect interrogated by Tait or Eglsaer. For seventeen years, he supported his wife and two children by teaching anatomy and neurology.[5] He had a long, gangly body and wore his pants too high with a white shirt tucked into them. His torso seemed to start at most men's shoulders. With all of his hair shaved off, his lanky gait, tubular head, and sagging stare, Hirako was a pathetic figure.

Morimoto Kenji, a thirty-five-year-old doctor, had worked on and off at Kyushu Imperial University since graduating in 1935. He lectured on sterilization techniques and also served as Ishiyama's assistant when Mori and Torisu left the university in early June 1945.[6]

From left to right: Morimoto Kenji, Hirao Kenichi, Ishiyama Fukujiro, Hirako Goichi, Torisu Taro

Mori Yoshio served as an assistant surgeon at Kyushu Imperial University from April 1936 to May 1939 and again from August 1943 to May 10, 1945. Like Morimoto, Mori worked under Ishiyama as his assistant. After leaving the university, Mori left for Kagoshima but returned to Fukuoka several times, the first of which was a one-week stay on June 2. Mori also worked in Kyushu Imperial Univeristy's Tropical Communicable Disease Laboratory.[7]

Senba Yoshitaka's testimony would be crucial. Above all else, he bore the responsibility of the use of seawater. It was his key field of research, and he worked closely with Hirao and Torisu in developing a functional blood substitute. Though a recent graduate, Senba received a special research grant from the Education Department for his research in seawater blood substitutes.[8]

From the first question, the suspects refused to cooperate and feigned a confident ignorance.[9] It was something the investigators would encounter for the duration of their efforts. The doctors had a plan: admit as little as possible; and, when left no other choice, blame Komori. Whether they would carry it out successfully was a different and difficult question. Fear of the unknown—what did the other suspects say—worked against the individual suspect and in favor of the investigators. If the others discussed the operations and one person refused to say anything, it would place him in an awful position. In the end, they tried their best to offer noncommittal answers but ultimately admitted more than was safe.

After each interrogation, Tait and Eglsaer summarized the outcome and significance in written reports. They were left with scattered lies supported by disparate half-truths, all of which needed to be pieced together.

Certain core questions emerged during questioning that needed to be addressed in order to lay a foundation for more involved interrogations: Did the operations take place as described, and if they did, when and where? Did those questioned participate in the operations? More specifically, what role did they play? Who was present during the procedures? What type of operations took place? Was seawater or a related extract injected into the POWs? Each question needed to be addressed for each POW who died.

Legal Section investigators already had Sato's account to use as a foundation for their questions. Facts drawn from subsequent statements would be held up against his and contradictions on both sides noted. Sato's penchant for lying automatically relegated his statements to a weaker position. Yet, if the doctors' accounts showed basic similarities, the strength of Sato's entire statement would be increased. Sato's statement regarding the operation did have one immense strong point. He had already admitted to his culpability in the beheadings of the thirty-three POWs at Western Army Headquarters and had also admitted to sending the eight POWs to Kyushu Imperial University, where they were subsequently murdered. Sato had nothing to lose. The doctors, however, had admitted nothing and had everything to lose if their roles emerged. Because of this fact, Sato's account was gospel—at least for the time being.

After sufficient prodding, each suspect admitted that operations on American POWs took place in the university hospital autopsy room. None pinpointed exact dates, but the general consensus placed the operations between mid-May 1945 and early July 1945.

Problems occurred when asked to identify the other doctors and nurses present during the operations. Understandably, nobody wanted to implicate someone who might have been able to escape prosecution. More importantly, all of the suspects obviously went out of their way to protect Professor Ishiyama and the reputation of Kyushu Imperial University. For the First Surgery staff—and anyone past and present whom the Legal Section would interrogate—it was a question of saving face.

When the suspects eventually came around and named the people whom they remembered being present during the operations, the same names recurred: Ishiyama, Komori, Hirako, Torisu, Hirao, Morimoto, Tsutsui, Senba, Mori, Tanaka, and Sato. The various accounts also placed unidentified army officers—Aihara and Yakumaru—and an additional nurse as key participants. They also agreed that a number of spectators were present.

Establishing an exact number of operations and dates proved more difficult, as did getting an idea of the type of operations. According to Hirao, six POWs died in the course of three days. He specifically cited

Chief Nurse Tsutsui Shizoku being escorted into SCAP Legal Section for interrogation.

a lung operation, two brain operations, a stomach removal, and a liver operation. Torisu admitted to knowledge of operations on at least three separate occasions. Six POWs perished. He could only recall two lung removals. Both doctors made positive statements to the use of a seawater extract, however.

The most important phase of the interrogations involved the facts behind the operations themselves. Surprisingly, once the suspects opened up, they shared significant amounts of information in great detail. In contrast with the initial attempts at establishing who was present, Tait and Eglsaer found themselves with a glut of facts to sift through. In this case, the challenge facing the investigative team involved matching consistent facts and excluding noncorroborated testimony.

In recalling the types of operations that occurred, none of the testimonies matched. A number of factors contributed to this and did not necessarily indicate a cover-up. The most likely reason for the discrepancies was the passage of time and the fact that not all of the doctors were present for each operation. This made establishing exact correlations between the type of operation and when it occurred a messy undertaking that would never be definitely resolved. Finding out about the procedures that occurred was a less daunting task.

A lung operation emerged as the most corroborated procedure mentioned by the suspects—excluding Tsutsui, who chose to issue blanket denials regarding the operations and the participants. Hirao, Torisu, Morimoto, and Mori admitted to playing some role in the operation but noted that Ishiyama and Komori actually performed the lung removal. Hirako claimed that he was not present for the lung operation but had heard about it. Hirao, Torisu, Mori, and Senba admitted knowledge about a complete stomach resection, making it the next most corroborated operation. They also admitted to participating in a liver operation. Hirao, Hirako, and Senba recalled a brain operation taking place. Only Hirako mentioned a heart operation, while Senba remembered participating in neck and gallbladder procedures as well.

Senba, aided by Torisu and Hirao, was the main culprit in establishing the use of seawater as a blood substitute. All of the doctors eventually acknowledged that it was used and hinted at the person responsible for administering it. Senba eventually took credit for it, though he did attempt to partially deflect the blame by suggesting that he acted under Ishiyama's supervision.

Hirako Goichi emerged as the person who assumed responsibility for the remains of the American prisoners. As head of the anatomy department, he was responsible for autopsies and the subsequent disposal of the remains. Under normal circumstances, bodies were cremated, identified, then claimed by the families of the deceased. Hirako admitted to having the POWs' bodies cremated, but their ultimate fate shocked the Legal Section investigators.

Hirako: "The ashes of the first four were brought to my office. There were no records, so I numbered the paper bags that they were in from one to four. I was told by Ishiyama about March 1946 to throw

Anatomy Section Chief Hirako Goichi being interrogated by Robert Tait.

the ashes away. I then emptied the bags on an ash pile in back of the crematory. I wanted to make a grave for the ashes, but Ishiyama had told me not to leave any proof, so I threw the ashes away."

After weeks of interrogations, the basic facts of the case still lay buried. It would take time and luck to draw out a complete chronology. But it had to be done. Moving on to the next phase of the investigation hinged on having a working picture. Only after cementing the facts could the arduous process of identifying the victims and searching for their remains begin.

The most disturbing aspects of Case 420, however, had already emerged from the suspects' mouths. They admitted that the operations were experimental and conceded that the procedures were unnecessary and that the soldiers should have survived.

9

Ishiyama: July 15–17, 1946

On July 15, 1946, Ishiyama Fukujiro pleaded his case to SCAP Legal Section investigator Henry Daty, a Japanese-American. Ishiyama looked nothing like he did prior to his arrest. During the war, Ishiyama strutted through the hallways of Kyushu Imperial University wearing his immaculate medical garb on top of a faux military shirt and pant set. Now, he wore the same white dress shirt and slacks every day.

Because Ishiyama refused to cooperate and maintained a stubborn silence, Daty decided to ease Ishiyama into the questioning by asking for information about his experiments with blood transfusions and substitutes. Initially, the conversation dealt with animal experiments, but once Daty felt confident that Ishiyama felt more comfortable, he shifted the questioning to the topic of human experimentation.

The seawater experiments on dogs and rabbits proved so successful that Ishiyama began experimenting on human subjects in February 1945. The procedure was a success, and the patient survived both the near fatal drop in blood pressure and the novel substitute employed during the operation. A second experiment proved equally successful.[1]

Daty knew that discussing successful trials would only draw him further from the American POWs who died at the university. He needed to focus on the failures. Moreover, he needed to broach the subject of the prisoners. The time for babying Ishiyama was over.

"Have you ever in your stay at the university operated on any American POWs?" Daty asked.

"Yes," Ishiyama replied.

"Tell me all about the operations, beginning with the first."

Ishiyama's professional medical career spanned over a quarter of a century. A graduate of Kyushu Imperial University in 1916, he served as a university surgeon until 1928. At that point, Ishiyama shifted his focus toward medical research pertaining to surgery. Ishiyama eventually assumed the position of chief surgeon for the First Surgical Clinic at Kyushu Imperial University. What was the Akaiwa Surgery Clinic now adopted the namesake of its chief surgeon and became the Ishiyama Surgery Clinic.[2]

With Ishiyama's new position came increased opportunities to push forward with his various fields of research. His interests ran the gamut of human anatomy and physiology. He did extensive research into the nature and formation of gallstones; he speculated and experimented on different ways of treating stomach cancer; he searched for the cause and a viable treatment of epilepsy; and he attempted to solve a major problem afflicting nations around the world, particularly those involved in armed conflicts—finding a viable and cost-effective blood substitute to maintain blood pressure.[3] He vice-chaired the local scientific society and participated in numerous scientific debates, always being among the last to leave.[4] As a man of science, Ishiyama's dedication, curiosity, and zeal could not be questioned. It was his integrity that proved to be lacking. When presented with the choice between knowledge and morality, he chose the former.

During the 1930s and 1940s, the scientific community in Japan, with the backing of the government, enjoyed a great thrust toward scientific inquiry and discovery. An unfortunate side product, however, was Japan's biological experimentation program that included Ishii's Unit 731 and numerous similar outfits spread throughout the Imperial Japanese Empire. At some point, Ishii Shiro, the founder of Japan's biowarfare program, realized that recruiting the top minds from throughout Japanese academia could only strengthen his operation. With that in mind, he campaigned throughout Japan, offering top university scientists and doctors the opportunity to conduct research that could not be performed in a typical university setting. Ishii extended the bait and the scientists bit freely. What resulted was a revolving door–type of operation in which scientists from various universities took up residence at bioexperimentation centers like Pingfan or Harbin for a certain amount of time. They were supplied with a laboratory, assistants, and materials—the most valuable yet expendable were human beings. When their research was complete or their time expired, the scientists returned to their respective institutions, making room for other researchers to take their place. The degree of contact between the military and the civilian sector was unprecedented and extensive. According to one former Unit 731 member, almost all of Ishii's researchers were civilians.[5]

Ishiyama's position at Kyushu Imperial University granted him great power and influence. It also meant that he became a prime candidate to spend time in Unit 731's revolving door system of bringing in civilian researchers for limited tenures. Although Ishiyama never directly indicated that he had served in Japan's underground biological experimentation program and Legal Section investigators inexplicably failed to pursue a line of questioning pertinent to it, certain facts about Ishiyama's research indicate a strong possibility that he had spent time in this program.

One of Ishiyama's main fields of research involved gallbladders and gallstones. For nearly twenty years, Ishiyama dedicated a portion of his time to analyzing various medical and chemical aspects of gallstones. One interesting line of research involved comparing the chemical composition of the stones with respect to nationality. He compared the gallstones of Japanese, Korean, Chinese, Taiwanese, Siamese, and Malaysian people, among others. But where did he get direct and unhindered access to research these stones at his convenience? Malaysia (Indochina), Siam (Thailand), Korea, northern China, and Manchukuo.[6] Each place Ishiyama indicated as a source of research material also contained a major bioexperimentation center:

Indochina had a site in Singapore; Siam had a site in Bangkok; northern China had Hailar; Manchukuo had Harbin, Changchun, and Mukden. A few hours southwest of Mukden was Peking (Beijing), another major Unit 731 site.[7] This would account for all of the nationalities—Koreans and Chinese in the northern sites and the remainder coming from the southern sites. Ishiyama personally went to Manchukuo and northern China; he sent his assistant, Mori, to Siam and Indochina.

Ishiyama stared across the table at Investigator Daty and began relating his version of the operations. He explained that Komori had called him early on the morning of May 10, 1945, urging him to operate on American POWs who had been seriously injured. Though he initially refused, Ishiyama cited a sense of duty in finally conceding to help the injured men and operated on them later that day. However, because the injuries to the two POWs were so bad, he was unable to save their lives.[8]

Dr. Ishiyama Fukujiro being interrogated by Henry Daty.

Ishiyama named all the people present during the operations: Komori, Torisu, Tsutsui, Hirao, Sato, Hirako, Miki, and Yakumaru.

"Now tell me exactly what each person did in the first operation. I shall name the persons as we go along. First will be Tsutsui."

"She passed the equipment, I think, but Miki might have done it."

"Please make up your mind."

"Miki passed the surgical equipment to me."

"Now tell me what Tsutsui did."

"She felt the patient's pulse, brought the ether from another table, and helped out where she was needed."

"How about Hirao?"

"He was my assistant. He stood next to my other assistant, Komori. He wiped the clogged blood from the patient."

"What did Komori do?"

"Komori stood directly across from me. He handled the ligature, which prevents unnecessary bleeding. Also, he handled the pincett when I made the incision."

"What did Hirako do?"

"He was an observer. In fact, I think he was not there throughout the operation."

"Then who injected the seawater into the patient?"

"Torisu."

"Were any other serums injected?"

"No. Usually when we use seawater, no other injections are given."

"Now tell me what the following persons did in the second operation. First Tsutsui."

"She did the same thing as she did in the first operation."

"What about Miki?"

"She passed the surgical equipment to the surgeons."

"How about Hirao?"

"I cannot say clearly what he did, but I believe he did the same as in the first operation."

"And Torisu?"

"He didn't handle the ether nozzle in the second operation because I am pretty sure we used a local anesthetic on this patient.

Komori gave the local anesthetic. Torisu injected saline and Ringer solution."

"Who injected the seawater?"

"We did not inject seawater into this person."

"According to these answers, then Miki was present at both operations?"

"Yes."

Daty's questioning continued the following day, July 16. He began by pressing Ishiyama about Komori and who granted permission for the operations to take place.

"Around the 10th of May, you stated that Komori had one prisoner who he wanted to bring to the autopsy room, but that afternoon Komori had three POWs. How do you account for this?"

"I did not know he was going to bring three prisoners. I found three POWs at the autopsy room."

"Did you see the three POWs when you arrived in the autopsy room?"

"Yes."

"What was said when you met Komori there?"

"Komori stated that he had brought three POWs instead of one and further stated that the other two would be operated on. I agreed to this."

"Who was there when you met Komori?"

"Torisu, Hirao, and Tsutsui."

"What else was said in the conversation?"

"I asked Komori under whose orders he brought these POWs. Komori stated that he had permission from the Western Army commandant, Lieutenant General Yokoyama. Also, the man in charge of POWs. I asked Colonel Sato about this matter when he made his entrance to the autopsy room. Sato replied that it would be all right to operate since the Western Army commandant had given permission to do so. In November 1945, I learned for the first time that these POWs were members of the group that were executed in June or July 1945."

"Who did you hear this from?"

"From Colonel Sato at Dr. Tanomachi's home. Since all the operations of the POWs resulted in death, I told Colonel Sato it would jeopardize my position greatly; therefore, Colonel Sato said we must keep this secret. I asked Colonel Sato if the POWs that were brought to the University were included in the thirty-four that he had mentioned were executed. Colonel Sato's reply was no. I stated then in that case I must report these operations to General MacArthur. Colonel Sato in return asked that no such report be forwarded because we have those POWs listed as having been sent to Hiroshima."

"Tell me exactly what had happened to the bodies that had been operated upon," Daty asked.

"The bodies were cremated at the hospital, and the bones and ashes are in a vault in the pathology building."

"Are the remains still there?"

"Yes."

"Now you mentioned that in November you had found out how the army was going to cover up the story and also the fact that thirty-four POWs were executed. Don't you think the army had a different objective other than saving the lives of the POWs that were brought to the hospital?"

"In May and June, when I took part in the operation, I had no purpose other than saving their lives, but in November at Tanomachi's residence Sato explained more thoroughly about the POWs. I then realized there must have been another meaning and another objective other than saving their lives."

Daty attempted to draw out more information from Ishiyama by returning to the first series of operations, and while he was able to establish that little, if anything, was wrong with the POWs, he failed to get an admission of guilt. For all of Ishiyama's cooperation, he would never tie himself to the military and would need to be prodded.

"Please tell me more about Komori," Daty asked.

"Komori was a medical student of mine around 1928. After he had graduated, he served under my staff until about 1935. He then went to work for the Wakamatsu Isolation Hospital. From there he transferred to the Fukuoka Miyagi Hospital, and later when the war came, he entered the army and became a medical officer. He was stationed at Beppu and then transferred to the Fukuoka Hospital in 1944. In June 1945, during an air raid, Komori was wounded in the leg. This necessitated an amputation. I performed this. Komori did not recover from the operation and subsequently died. At the death bed, Komori stated that it was orders from higher officials that made him bring the POWs to the university to be operated on. Therefore, he called me by phone to notify me that he had injected some seawater as I had suggested, but the patient turned to the worse, so he brought the POW to the anatomy ward. He said, "I'm sorry that I have caused you so much trouble."

"Who else was present at Komori's death?"

"Colonel Sato, Yakumaru, another soldier whose name I do not know, Torisu, and Tsutsui."

"Did you have any connections with the Western Army?"

"I used to visit the Western Army for two years for the purpose of instructing young medical officers in techniques of operations and use of injections such as seawater, blood serums, polyphenyl alcohol, and ether. Instructing medical officers was a request throughout Japan by Lieutenant General Kambayashi from Tokyo. This order came from the director of the Bureau of Army Medical Officers in Tokyo. A copy of this order should be at the university in the care of Nunio Shimizu."

Daty leaned back in his seat and looked up at Ishiyama.

"There is one more point that I want to discuss with you now. Did you and Komori take the initiative in operating on the POWs or were you under orders of the army to operate?"

"I cannot answer that question."

"Colonel Sato testifies that he did not give such an order, and as for Komori receiving orders from higher officials, he knows nothing about it. Ishiyama, I am asking you whether you had an order from Komori or had Komori and you decided to perform an experimental operation?"

"I cannot give an answer to such a question because the operations were not experimental. You can ask me anything, but I want it known that I did all I could to save the lives of the POWs."

"Tell me what was wrong with the gastric operation or the brain operation."

"That is outrageous," Ishiyama cried out. He grew increasingly hostile and incoherent as the questioning progressed. "I admit I have performed gastric operations on Japanese nationals; in fact, I perform such operations as the stomach, brains, and various other types daily. On a POW I have never performed a gastric operation or removed a stomach. There is nothing unusual about a brain or a stomach operation."

"As I have stated before, we are going to clarify this point—that is whether or not you operated on the POWs on your own initiative."

"If there is a request to treat a POW, I cannot refuse."

"Who ordered you to perform this operation?"

"I was asked, not ordered."

"Then it was not an order from the Japanese army to perform the operation?"

"I do not know. I had received a phone call as I have stated before from Komori to assist him to operate on POWs."

"Then you were not ordered explicitly on paper or by any army officers. It was just a request from Komori."

"There were no written orders and I cannot say whether Komori received any written orders from his superior officer."

"Then all you received was a request from Komori, a probationary officer, to operate?"

"There were no written orders from higher officials of the army. Komori happened to be a former student of mine, and since he was only a probationary officer, I refused to operate, as I have stated before. Since Colonel Sato was at the operation, I figured he was representing the army."

"Why didn't you refuse to operate the second time?"

"Komori had brought the POWs, so I could not refuse to operate. According to the doctor's oath, I cannot refuse to treat a patient."

"We know all about the experimental operations and how they were performed," Daty stated. He leaned forward, placed his pencil on the lined legal pad, and stared into Ishiyama's downcast eyes. "What have you to say to this?"

"You are trying to get unreasonable answers from me."

The following day, July 17, Ishiyama described a second set of operations he participated in: a heart operation and a brain operation. Again, he maintained the operations were necessary because the

POWs were seriously injured. Both patients were injected with seawater. Both died.[9]

That was Ishiyama's story.

At 1730 hours, Ishiyama sat alone. There was not much in the 8-by-6-foot cell. The walls dripped with chipped paint mixed with filth. A lidless toilet protruded from the left corner of the room. An amorphous discolored patch—more so than the rest of the room—marked the area where scores of prisoners pressed their backs. A thick metal grill sat alongside the toilet; the hiss of rising steam slipped into the room. Directly above the heating duct, the only opening to the outside world floated tantalizingly, its five vertical bars and one crossbar teasing openness while restricting freedom. The bars, framed by wood and cement, ran high, almost to the ceiling. A hand, forearm, or elbow could fit between them. But that was all. Ishiyama could literally touch the outside world; he just could not be a part of it.

The third day of interrogations ended with an admission that a second set of operations took place. Ishiyama admitted to the brain operation he previously denied performing. The stories, facts, and lies all shifted and melted into one another. Seawater here, seawater there—was there seawater involved? Yes. And the way that the interrogator insisted—all those operations, the bodies, the blood—the other doctors must have said something. Perhaps they all divulged everything.

Ishiyama's eyes scanned the cell, passing over the same objects countless times: the toilet, the grill, the bars, the white enameled bowls. Articles of clothing the prison authorities allowed him to keep were strewn about the cell: a white shirt, a blue-gray suit, various undergarments, and a pair of shoes. He continued surveying the room, his mind and imagination desperate for escape. All he had were his clothes and the prison cell, no matter how much time he spent surveying his surroundings. Of course, he also had the robe and tie, and just like that, he had found it—a way out.

Ishiyama picked up a pen and smoothed out a piece of paper. He started writing. After completing his escape, he wanted everyone to know that he was innocent.

• • •

On the morning of July 18, 1945, the tin ring of a telephone shrieked through the Legal Section office.[10] At 0810 hours, most of the staff still hadn't straggled in yet, and the ones in the office were still groggy with sleep. People wake up at their own rate, at least when given the opportunity. This morning was not one of those times.

Eglsaer fielded the call. A rigid voice—monotone enough to be military—spoke through the receiver. The caller, an officer from the Office of the Provost Marshal, 24th Division Artillery stationed in Fukuoka, wasted no time. Something had happened at Dotemachi Prison overnight. One of the suspects under the Legal Section's custody had hanged himself. The caller did not identify the prisoner in question, nor did he indicate any other details pertaining to the suicide. That had to be done in person by a Legal Section staff member.[11]

Eglsaer slammed the receiver down and darted out of his office. Wasting no time, Tait, accompanied by a Legal Section photographer, gathered his things together and left for Dotemachi Prison.

Ever since the suspects had been taken into custody and interned at the prison, the Legal Section insisted that round-the-clock attention be allotted for their prisoners. Three times they asked the local provost marshal to provide a military police officer; three times they were turned down. According to the provost marshal, the understaffed MPs did not have the manpower. Talk to the 24th Division Artillery, he said. Eglsaer took it upon himself to contact the executive officer at the 24th, Lieutenant Colonel Walters. No definitive response was given. Walters expressed doubt that his commanding officer would approve the request but added that he would get back to Eglsaer the following day—1600 hours on July 18. The prisoners went unwatched.[12]

The situation did not bode well, regardless of who had died. Losing someone this early threatened to cripple the entire investigation. The suspects showed signs of breaking, the cracks in their resiliency widening into fissures, and shared more information with each passing hour. The facts had just started coming out, sprouting through the layers of lies like sunflowers in a field of weeds. With one key suspect, Komori, already dead, losing another made a daunting task insufferable.

Immediately after Tait's departure, Eglsaer got back on the phone. He called the 118th Station Hospital. The situation warranted the presence of a doctor. There were many things that would need to be addressed that only a medical professional could do. An estimated time of death needed to be assessed. Any signs of foul play had to be investigated, particularly on the deceased's body. The doctor would not arrive at Dotemachi Prison until almost an hour later—0908 hours.[13]

By 0820 hours, Tait arrived at the prison. The assistant warden, Private First Class Kenneth Knowles, greeted them at the gate.[14] Even before they entered the building, Tait pressed for information.

"Which of the prisoners hung himself?"

"The person in Cell 64," Knowles replied. "I don't know his name."

Rather than proceeding directly to the holding cells, Knowles brought Tait into the prison's administrative office. The prison records would indicate definitively who the deceased was. With the prison roster spread out before him, Tait scanned the cell assignments. He passed over names he had heard all too often during the past month. As he reached the sixties, his heartbeat jumped from rushed to rapid. Cell 62: Aihara Kajuro. Cell 63: Sato Yoshinao. Cell 64: Ishiyama Fukujiro.

10

Marvin: Spring–Fall 1946

Marvin stood in the lobby of the Central Bank Building waiting for his cousin, Thelma.[1] It was noon, and the coming and going of lunch-hour traffic bustled around him. Packs of men and women in twos, fours, or tens circled in every direction. A cacophony of sound—frantic chatter, slamming doors, and clumsy footsteps—swirled through the vestibule. Large crowds and loud noises no longer bothered him.

Since Marvin's return to Virginia, he had rediscovered his confidence. Something wonderful had happened to him during his trip, and now he spent his nights sleeping rather than staring into the past. The final vestiges of captivity—a cocktail of guilt, shame, and fear—diminished to the point of tempered insignificance. The feelings never went away, but Marvin managed to relegate them to a nagging discomfort. And that, he could live with.

The lobby elevator unloaded and picked up Central Bank employees at regular intervals. Marvin inspected each new face to disembark. When Thelma finally emerged, Marvin found her immediately, then lost her. His attention drifted to the young lady walking beside Thelma. Her long, dirty blond hair—pushed back and away from her slender face twisted from head to shoulders like satin Christmas ribbons. She had snowflake-soft eyes supported by a delicate nose and mouth. She cut a streamlined figure, and the fringe of her dress swished and swayed as she swept through the crowd. Thelma turned and said something to the young lady. They were together. She was a friend of Marvin's cousin, and she was beautiful.

Marvin greeted Thelma, but little lay behind his enthusiastic words. He struggled against the distraction his cousin's young friend represented. Thelma said something—who knows what? The only thing that mattered was the phrase "Marvin, this is Beatrice." It took forever to come out, but when it did, nothing in the world sounded better.

Beatrice Astley liked Marvin immediately. He was six feet tall, in uniform, and terribly handsome. Though this was the first time meeting him, she knew all about him. While Marvin was in the service, Beatrice had already met most of his family through Thelma. And when the Japanese took him prisoner, she shared in the Watkins family's despair. In many ways, she had emotional ties to Marvin even before he ever met her.

Marvin invited Beatrice to join him and Thelma for lunch. Though she wanted to accept, she declined. Marvin and Thelma had catching up to do and Beatrice did not want to get in the way. There would certainly be a next time, and the three parted ways.

Marvin badgered Thelma about her pretty friend for days. A week after first meeting Beatrice, Marvin had Thelma call her. He wanted to take her out and talk to her. Thelma relayed the message, and Beatrice accepted his invitation this time. For their first date, Marvin and Beatrice went to the movies, then had burgers at a local soda shop.

Over the next few months, Marvin and Beatrice shared many more evenings. They went on double dates with Marvin's old friends from before the war—John Smith and Hank Edwards—and their girlfriends. They went on picnics in various public parks in Richmond where they grilled burgers, franks, and an assortment of vegetables. Sometimes, the group drove out to the Blue Ridge Mountains; other times, they opted against altitude for the rushing waves, saltwater breeze, and shifting sands of Virginia Beach. And when Marvin and Beatrice weren't with friends, they saw more movies or just enjoyed each other's company at Beatrice's home. Wednesday nights and weekends were their days together. Her parents loved Marvin so much that they even allowed him to stay over on occasion. Beatrice would give him her room and she would sleep in the guest room. It was that kind of relationship from the start—even, compromising, and giving. They brought out the best in each other.

That was how well things were going when Marvin received a telegram—dated September 6, 1946—from the adjutant general of the army. The army requested to be briefed on everything he knew regarding his missing crew.[2] It would take him over two weeks to rake through the memories he had subordinated to the recesses of his psyche and put them on paper. Fredericks, Plambeck, Colehower, Ponczka, Johnson, Williams, Czarnecki, Oeinck, Shingledecker, and Kearns—names, faces, and lives—all came rushing back.

They were still missing.

11

One Step at a Time: August–December 1946

By the time Tait filed his Report of Investigation Division (RID) on August 19, 1946, he had names; among them: Second Lieutenant William Fredericks, Sergeant T. Roracka, and Corporal Robert B. Williams. He did not know who they were or whether they were real people or how they died. But he had a hunch. They probably died during their captivity and possibly belonged to the group of eight POWs who died at Kyushu Imperial University.[1]

Arriving at the victims' names involved months of intense research. With nothing more to go on than the helter-skelter testimony of the Western Army officers collected by the CIC, the task was a painful exercise in referencing, cross-referencing, and cross-cross-referencing. The fact that the accused constantly hurled counteraccusations at one another—a terribly effective means of concealing the truth—made the task that much harder.[2]

Tait took note of his efforts: "It was felt that the only practical approach to the investigation was to make an intensive study of all the interrogation reports forwarded to the Legal Section by the CIC. Although a slow and laborious process, this was done."[3]

One line at a time, Tait dissected each answer, then consolidated the facts in a file dedicated to each person. He took note of every response and checked it against similar responses. He compared dates and events to check that they matched. All answers involving a second person were cross-referenced against other statements concerning him. The process took a month and a half total.

As a result of Tait's thoroughness, SCAP investigators concluded that Colonel Oki Genzaburo had "no direct connection with the atrocities" and was released from Sugamo Prison on July 28, 1946.

With an orderly collection of facts at his disposal and a partial story evolving each day, Tait embarked on the next phase of the investigation. "It was then felt that the identification of the POW victims should be attempted."

Interrogations of Colonel Sato yielded more half-truths than pure facts. Adding to the investigation's difficulties, all specific records concerning POWs at Western Army Headquarters had been destroyed at the war's end by order of the War Ministry in Tokyo. Proving the validity of most of his claims depended on further interrogations with Sato and with other parties involved in the atrocities.

Yet, possibilities existed. Sato divulged the names of a number of POWs that could be checked with records through Air Corps channels. At the worst, they narrowed the collection of questionable facts and indicated how frank Sato was being. But if even a few names checked out, the leap in progress would be immeasurable. They would lead to more names, which in turn could trigger something in the memories of other Western Army Headquarters officers being questioned. Plus, Legal Section investigators would have faces to show. Most importantly, they would finally have hard facts—real pieces of the puzzle.

With the aid of Colonel Horace B. Neely, A-2 of the 5th Fighter Command, Fukuoka, Tait studied the information from the Air Corps. The names Sato supplied checked out and Tait had his facts.

A number of conferences between Tait and members of the Western

Demobilization Office revealed that a handful of records pertaining to POWs still existed. The documents indicated that between August 24, 1944, and early May 1945, no Allied prisoners were captured and sent to Western Army Headquarters. However, during early May 1945 to early June 1945, POWs had been received and processed—sixteen total. Moreover, from late June 1945 until the end of the war, more prisoners went through Western Army hands—twenty-six in all. The documents even broke down the prisoner tally by date, type of plane, number of survivors, and place of capture.

Date	Type of Plane	No. of Survivors	Received From
5/45	B-29	1	Kusu-gun, Oita-ken
5/5/45	B-29	3	Naori-gun, Oita-ken
5/6/45	B-29	2	Aso-gun, Kumamoto-ken
5/6/45	B-29	3	Shimoki-gun, Oita-ken
5/7/45	B-29	1	Umibe-gun, Oita-ken
5/14/45	B-29	4	Miyazaki-ken
5/27/45	B-29	1	Moji City, Fukuoka-ken
June 1945	B-29	1	Naku-gun, Miyazaki-ken
		Total: 16	

Tait noted at the bottom of the chart: "It is known that between middle May and 20 June 1945, sixteen POWs were killed. Eight of these were sent to Kyushu Imperial University and killed by medical experimental operations and eight more were beheaded at Western Army Headquarters on 20 June 1945."[4]

With that information at his disposal, Tait concluded that "every effort" must be extended to identify the POWs. He requested that separate investigations be conducted at the scene of each crash. With any luck, interviews with local residents, doctors, police, and Kempei Tai would yield more information that could help establish the identities of the captured airmen.

Further interrogations with Colonel Sato and Captain Yukino yielded more names. Unlike the previous set, these came with circumstances.

- On 5 August 1945 a B-24 crashed. . . . There were five survivors. Information indicates three of the survivors were: 1st Robert Neal, Navigator Robert Coulet, and an engineer last name of Light. They were sent to WAHQ on 8 August 1945.
- That seven of the survivors of the B-29 crash at Yokoyama-mura, Yame-gun Fukuoka Ken on 27 July were: Second Lieutenant or Corporal Hayward; Flight Officer Apply; Corporal Sterns; S/Sergeant Thornton; Capt. Nelson; Capt. Hewitt; fnu. Nosun.
- That three survivors of the B-29 crash at Takeda-machi, Oita-ken were: 2nd Lt. William Fredericks, Sergeant T. Roracka, and Corporal Robert B. Williams. They were sent to Western Army Headquarters on 5 May 1945.[5]

Hopefully, these names would lead to the names of other crew members. With accurate information, Tait would have the names he needed within days of filing his report. By then, his request for the Missing Air Crew Reports for all planes shot down over Japan during the May–August time span would be complete.

Tait concluded the report with tempered optimism, a touch of frustration, and an appeal for aid: "The reporting agent feels that sufficient information has been gathered concerning the atrocities to conduct direct interrogations of the suspects. And that this information will enable the investigators to break through and stop these men from lying and attempting to deceive the investigator. Since the suspects have had some eight months to coordinate their 'stories' it is believed that proving their guilt will still be a slow process. The speed with which this case is completed will depend upon the number of investigators assigned to this case."[6]

Copies of Tait's report landed on Colonel Alva Carpenter's desk. The head of SCAP's Legal Section—MacArthur's legal counsel—wanted to be kept apprised of the Kyushu Imperial University atrocities case.

Tait worked diligently toward identifying the POWs who perished at Western Army Headquarters. With the Missing Air Crew Reports

(MACRs) at his disposal, he continued to reap the rewards of his efforts. The MACRs furnished the names and serial numbers of every American air force member shot down over Kyushu during the final months of the war. Indirectly, the reports opened the possibilities of finally contacting the families of the POWs. Until now, the status of the Western Army Headquarters POWs had been listed as MIA. The families lacked closure. Once Tait completed his investigation and matched names with crimes, the closure would come.[7]

For all intents and purposes, the Watkins crew had been found. The MACR for their plane indicated that they had been shot down over Kyushu while returning from a mission on May 5, 1945. This matched the second entry in the chart of downed airmen supplied by the Western Demobilization Unit. Now, Legal Section investigators knew where the story began after the crash—Takeda-machi, Oita-ken—an area just outside of Fukuoka.

The MACR also supplied a positive ID on the members of the crew that crashed on May 5, 1945—the Watkins crew. Two names matched perfectly: Second Lieutenant William Fredericks and Corporal Robert C. Johnson; a third matched indirectly: Sergeant T. Roracka was most likely Sergeant Teddy Ponczka. Three names for three survivors.

The separate investigations of the various crash areas supplied Tait with more information that could help him determine the fates of the POWs. Teams of investigators visited crash sites and conducted intensive interviews with the local townspeople, who would have witnessed everything from the fight in the air to the crash and subsequent apprehension of any surviving crew members. Local police officers were also interviewed, since they would have been in charge of the primary searches for the downed Americans. Finally, the investigators questioned the Kempei Tai units responsible for the crash sites, since they assumed custody of captured Allied airmen.[8]

Tait turned to a variety of sources in order to complete what he termed the "composite picture" of the crashes and the fates of the surviving airmen. He combed through the interrogations of suspects and witnesses for each of the fourteen B-29 crashes, matching facts for each flier with testimony. Anything that could help identify the crew members with actual events was considered: hair color, wounds, or any other distinguishing features. In addition, Tait conducted further investigations of Western Demobilization Unit records for any other reports that might indicate the fates of the POWs more definitively. Finally, Tait turned to the records of the 108th Quartermaster Graves Unit, U.S. Army. They were responsible for disinterring and documenting the graves of American soldiers buried in Kyushu. They, if anyone, would be able to affirm the deaths of any downed airmen. Nothing—not even deaths during bailout—could be taken for granted.

During the investigation, three tremendous and related discoveries emerged. Each concerned the Watkins crew. The first discovery involved Marvin himself. Up until now, Legal Section investigators worked under the impression that every POW held at Western Army Headquarters had died. Technically, they were correct. What they hadn't considered was that a POW might have been sent to Tokyo, as was the case with Marvin. An interrogation with Yamanaka Fumitoshi revealed that unlike the other B-29 crew members, Marvin was seen as an intelligence asset and sent to the General Staff Headquarters in Tokyo for further questioning. In this way, he escaped execution.[9]

Yamanaka's testimony contradicted what Tait learned from the Western Demobilization Unit's records. While official documents indicate three survivors, Yamanaka stated clearly that four B-29 fliers were captured. Japanese civilians apprehended three Americans at Kusumoto-ken while another was taken prisoner in Oita-ken. At the time of capture, two soldiers bore injuries—one a shoulder wound and the other a leg injury. On appearances alone, it seemed that the leg injury was the more serious of the two.

Yamanaka's testimony went on to supply the Legal Section with the first indication from a witness that members of the Watkins crew had been sent to Kyushu Imperial University and killed at the hospital. He recalled an incident on or about June 1, 1945, in which a member of the local Kempei Tai, Major Enatsu Tokuji, called him into the major's office at Western Army Headquarters. When the two were alone in the room, Enatsu divulged that because Yamanaka belonged to the Intelligence Unit, he should be aware of the exact number of prisoners held at Western Army Headquarters. He did not stop there. Enatsu informed Yamanaka that he was going to share something very secret with him. He indicated that what was going to be said was to remain in that room. It was at that point that Yamanaka learned that all of the crew members of Lieutenant Watkins's plane—mentioned specifically—had been sent to Kyushu Imperial University and died there.

On September 21, the adjutant general received Marvin Watkins's response to the inquiry regarding the fate of his crew.[10] For Marvin, it simply rehashed events he needed to get past; for the adjutant general and Legal Section, it was firsthand testimony from the only American lucky enough to survive capture and incarceration at Western Army Headquarters. It was invaluable. A copy of Marvin's response was forwarded to the Legal Section on October 6.[11] For the record, the first full contact—a question and a response—between the SCAP and Marvin Watkins occurred. Soon, the former crew chief from Church Road would be pulled back to a world he never dreamed of revisiting.

The monstrous report that Robert Tait struggled to compile entered the official record on October 15, 1946. Months of frustration paid off. The Legal Section now had the names of all of the POWs held at Western Army Headquarters and the identities of the prisoners who had been beheaded. Most important, he discovered the identities of the American boys used in biological experiments at Kyushu Imperial University. Copies of the report were sent to every SCAP Legal Section branch in Japan, the prosecutor's office, numerous record-keeping sections, and Colonel Carpenter.

Four days later, a request for photographs of each Watkins crew member was sent to the Zone of the Interior.[12] The time had come to discover the truth.

Sometime during the first week of October 1946, Hirako Goichi completed a short testimonial in his Sugamo Prison cell and handed it to the Legal Section in Tokyo. Choppy English sentences filled the manuscript, reminiscent of university test booklets, with lined pages and fragile paper. In dividing his work into separate headings, Hirako essentially broke down each line of Legal Section questioning according to the information they sought to elicit. Hirako's contents read as follows:

I. Why and how our Institute [was] used?
II. Who participated with the operation when I attended?
III. How I advised the brain operation and my behavior?
IV. On the personality of the late Prof. Ishiyama with reference to the Japanese building.
V. On my connection with Prof. Ishiyama.
VI. How kept the secret? And Ishiyama's confession.
VII. The victims post mortem, and the crematory.
VIII. Who is the prime mover?
IX. Conclusion and Summary.[13]

On first viewing, it appeared that Hirako had little to add to the information he had already shared with the Legal Section interrogators. The first half of Hirako's document rehashed information divulged during his initial interrogations. The first three sections amounted to an elaborate effort to downplay his culpability in supplying the autopsy room, which was under his control, to Ishiyama for the operations and in participating in the brain operations.

Hirako claimed that Ishiyama made a request to use the room but never mentioned POWs. Permission was granted. However, when the time came to use the autopsy room, Ishiyama never showed up. After a week had passed, Ishiyama used the room without Hirako's permission. The following day, Hirako "called Professor Ishiyama on [the] telephone and condemned his moral impurity using our institute without any asking." To this Ishiyama replied, "There was no time yesterday to ask you, because the military transport of the patient took place suddenly." Hirako then forbade Ishiyama from using the room in the future. Each time a subsequent operation occurred, Hirako claimed in his statement that it was against his wishes and by order of the Imperial Japanese Army. He added very little regarding his role in the operations he witnessed and reiterated the claims made during interrogation.

Hirako's account took on significance when dealing with issues not directly involving him, and they posed serious questions for investigators—issues they would not have considered had it not been for the manuscript. In this sense, it did contain important morsels of new information that the investigators could pursue as leads. For example, Hirako divulged that after the operations concluded, the military held a celebratory dinner at Kaikoasha Military Restaurant honoring the university and the doctors responsible for the biological experiments with seawater—the Ishiyama clinic. "The reason for celebration of medical men upon the completion of operations which resulted in one hundred percent fatalities will be explored."[14]

Other issues arose after reading the entire manuscript. During Hirako's initial interrogations, he claimed that while he had come into possession of the fliers' ashes, he received direct orders from Ishiyama to discard the remains. Since there were no records remaining, it would destroy all evidence. To the investigators, it seemed as if Hirako possessed the ashes for such a short time that further inquiry was not needed. The truth differed slightly.

By his own admission, Hirako returned to the site where he threw out the ashes the following morning. He collected the ashes and placed them in a wooden box. "With purpose to be hidden from sight of Ishiyama, I laid it based on a piece of white paper not in my room but in another small room attached to the lecture hall, where at the moment was not a personnel."[15] The room functioned as a provisional holding place for ashes waiting to be claimed by the families of the deceased. The ashes were held there for seven months. It made little sense that Hirako would hold the ashes for no reason when they could even implicate the university. The Legal Section needed to explore "why he [Hirako] kept the ashes of American victims on the table in his room for seven months after American armed forces were in control of Fukuoka, and did not report the location of these remains; also, why, after Ishiyama had thrown out the ashes, he did not report the desecration of these remains to the United States Army."[16]

In addition to probing deeper into Hirako's intentions, the Legal Section would need to identify the university employees responsible for all phases of handling the fliers' remains postmortem. Who brought the bodies to the crematory? Who performed the cremation?

They already possessed some information, however. They knew that the person ultimately responsible for the ashes was Hirako, who in turn identified the person who delivered the ashes to him as Takeda. He would need to be questioned as soon as possible.

The most intriguing aspect of Hirako's written statement lay in his consistent references to the role the Japanese military played in the operations and in daily university affairs, in general. Time and again, he referred—sometimes, directly; other times obliquely—to the military's influence. He repeatedly connected Ishiyama with the Japanese army: "I dare to say, that the prime mover should be the military authority which made a profit by Prof. F. Ishiyama, an instructor of the military surgery."[17] Moreover, Komori served as the liaison between the army and the university. Hirako went on to blame the military for ultimately forcing Ishiyama to use the anatomy section. Blame "must be laid upon the military because Ishiyama's behavior was under command of the military authority."[18] Hirako's insistence on the military's role and the apprehension he showed regarding the Japanese army prompted Legal Section investigator L. H. Barnard to note: "Will ascertain the nature of the 'military compulsion' exerted over Hirako that would enable him to hold counsel with the other murderers concerning the keeping of the murders a secret and Hirako's continued denial of knowledge of these matters after he was in the custody of the United States Army and beyond any attempt on his life which might be attempted by the demobilized Japanese Army."[19]

Rather than alleviating the pressure placed on the anatomy section head, the Hirako manuscript exposed him to greater scrutiny. Investigators questioned his role in the operations and cover-up more than ever and hoped he would lead them to further discoveries. He was nervous, and the Legal Section hoped he would reveal more. It did not take long for this to happen. On November 4, 1946, the Civil Censorship Detachment (CCD) in Kyushu intercepted a letter sent from Hirako to Takeshige Yukio at Kyushu Imperial University. It was immediately processed, copied, and duplicates were sent to the Legal Section and the Criminal Records Division (CRD).[20]

The letter explained how Hirako had hidden the ashes in the small room next to the lecture hall "for fear that it would be discovered by

Ishiyama again."[21] He did so in secret. When he returned to the room in June 1946, he could not find the ashes but decided to conduct a more intensive search when he returned from a trip. "Unfortunately, I was interned in Sugamo Prison and couldn't do anything about my intentions."[22] Hirako asked Takeshige to complete the task he could not: locate the ashes. "I didn't put any identification marks on it. For this reason someone might have transferred it to the ossuary. Please locate it and send it to me as it is my most important evidence."[23]

Hirako's letter proved that the remains of the victims still existed. What once floated around the Fukuoka office as a hunch now became a fact. The Legal Section even had a location. With any luck, they would be able to identify the remains.

On November 26, Captain Joseph Sartiano followed the lead set out by Hirako's letter and conducted a search of the Kyushu Imperial University anatomy section, crematory, and ossuary.[24] With any luck, the investigation would yield the ashes of the four vivisection victims mentioned by Hirako.

Exterior of the anatomy building, Kyushu Imperial University (1946)

A member of Hirako's staff, Dr. Mori Masaru, led Sartiano through the anatomy section lecture hall into an adjacent room. It was the room mentioned by Hirako in his letter to Takeshige. Broken bottles lay scattered, their glass dulled by layers of dust. Waste materials and other unwanted odds and ends filled the room. There was no sign, however, of any ashes.[25]

Mori brought Sartiano to the room on the opposite end of the lecture hall. White-boned skeletons and numerous medical charts dangled from the walls. The room was definitely used more often and recently than the refuse room. Sartiano walked through the room, carefully taking note of its contents. Then he saw them—four boxes with Japanese lettering. Sartiano rushed to the containers and opened them. Ashes. For a moment—a very short one—fate seemed to be on Team 420's side. If only things had been that simple. As it turned out, university records showed definitively that the ashes belonged to four Japanese nationals who had been cremated recently.

Ossuary pit behind crematory building

Undeterred, Sartiano—accompanied by Takeshige—took his search to the ossuary. Tucked away in a far corner of the university grounds, the building stood alone against a backdrop of a chain-link fence topped with barbed wire. In the distance, Fukuoka Bay and a cloudy horizon hovered like the scene from a Japanese painting.

The ossuary's interior carried the stale and sterile aridity of a crypt. Microscopic flakes of dust and ash floated and swirled with whatever movement invaded the area. A network of dense and darkened wooden shelves climbed from floor to ceiling, each holding a set of modest-size boxes big enough for the ashes of one person. Sixty-four boxes filled the ossuary.

One at a time, Sartiano inspected the containers. Each box had Japanese lettering on it. The more he inspected the more futile the procedure became. A sweep of the eyes could have told him that all the boxes were the same size—made for the ashes of one individual. And when he finally stumbled on an unlettered box—a box that bore possibilities—it, like the others, held the ashes of an individual, not a collective.

Outside the ossuary, there was an unassuming pit. Sartiano asked Takata Haruso, a university employee in charge of cremations, about the hole in the ground. According to Takata, unidentified ashes were disposed of in the pit. Though Taketa said it outright, Sartiano could figure out that it would be impossible to distinguish the remains of specific individuals from the heap of gray ash. No records had been kept of the ashes in the pile or of the four American soldiers vivisected at the university. Sartiano left the Kyushu grounds empty-handed. He later conceded, "In view of the fact that it is impossible to distinguish the American ashes from the others, a further search is considered useless by this office."[26]

On December 3, 1946, Hirako passed a supplement to earlier statements and written testimony. What he labeled as additions and corrections to his previous stories were simply rehashes of the same themes: Ishiyama's belligerence and dictatorial nature; Hirako's obliviousness to the operations until they were already in progress; and Hirako's moral disapproval of the procedures.[27] This was nothing new and a disappointing way to end the investigative year for Team

420. But it did not mean that the year was uneventful. On the contrary, they made considerable progress in their journey. With the names of the victims in their possession, the investigation changed. The victims were no longer faceless soldiers. They were men with families who deserved to learn the truth about their loved ones' fates. They had stories, personalities, likes and dislikes, hopes and dreams. In a strange way, they came to life.

12

Synthesis to Schism: January–April 1947

Any hopes that a new year would lighten the tensions between the United States and the Soviet Union that had developed frightening venom during 1946 dissipated like steam in a snowstorm. It took exactly one week for Soviet officials to make the next move in the Cold War chess game.

On January 7, 1947, a member of the Russian Prosecution Section, Tokyo, Colonel Leon Smirnov, approached D. L. Waldorf of the International Prosecution Section, the office responsible for overseeing war crime trials, in particular the International Military Tribunal—Far East (IMTFE) currently in progress. Smirnov made a request on behalf of the Soviet government. They wanted access to Ishii and one of his aides, Colonel Ota Kyoshi, to question them regarding atrocities committed in Manchuria during the war. The Russians claimed that testimonies of Japanese military men currently in Soviet custody indicated that Chinese and Manchurian prisoners died as a result of the Japanese biological experimentation program. Specifically, Smirnov referred to the research centers located at Pingfan and Anda.[1]

"Shortly after cessation of hostilities, General Kawashima, 4th

Section, Manchu 731, and his assistant, Major Kurasaba, were interrogated." Smirnov spoke through the Soviet interpreter, Alex Kuniv. The American officials listened closely to the names but could not be definite on their spelling. However, rather than tip the Russians off to American interests, they chose not to inquire into the exact spelling of the Japanese officers. Instead, they allowed Smirnov to continue.

"The Japanese carried out extensive experiments in Biological Warfare at Pingfan Laboratory and field experiments at Anda, using Manchurians and Chinese bandits as material. A total of two thousand died as a result of the experiments. Facilities for producing typhus-carrying fleas in quantity, and two conveyor systems for producing cholera and typhus cultures in quantity, existed at Pingfan. Forty-five kilograms of fleas were produced in three months. One conveyor could produce one hundred and forty kilograms of cholera culture or two hundred kilograms of typhus culture in a month."[2]

As Smirnov outlined the Japanese operation, the American contingent listened attentively, discerning and decoding everything they heard, taking each Soviet sentence and contemplating its implications. It was an indirect way of gauging the extent of Russian biological warfare knowledge and how much they really wanted Ishii for legal reasons. Their guess, however, was that their interest in the Unit 731 commander was for purely intelligence purposes.

On the subject of Pingfan and the allegations of the extensive program housed at the location, Smirnov reported: "The information was so preposterous to Russians that Russian BW experts were called in. They reinterrogated the scientists, checked the ruins of Pingfan, and confirmed information."

Lieutenant Colonel Robert P. McQuail stopped Smirnov and backtracked. "The colonel said 'ruins of Pingfan.' Was it bombed or destroyed as a result of fighting?"

Smirnov responded, "Pingfan was completely destroyed by Japanese who attempted to cover up all evidence. All documents were also destroyed, and our experts did not even bother to photograph the ruins, so thorough was the damage."

As the Russian colonel continued to lay the case for interrogation, he pointed out the similarities between German instances and

Japanese. "At the Nuremberg trials, a German expert witness said spreading typhus by fleas was considered the best method of BW. The Japanese seem to have this technique." Smirnov concluded by proposing that both the United States and the U.S.S.R. benefit from the Japanese biological research program. "It would be of value to the U.S.A. as well as the U.S.S.R. to get this information. It is requested that these three Japanese [Ishii, Kikuchi, and Ota] be interrogated without being told they are liable to be war criminals, and that they be made to swear not to tell anyone about the interrogation."

The Russian suggestion was a strategy that American scientific and military officials would use to their sole advantage, much to the behest of the Soviet government. And even though the two parties had come to a temporary impasse, the Soviet Union made it clear that for the United States there was more at stake than just Ishii and the secrets he held. American credibility and that of the American-controlled IMTFE lay close to crumbling should the world discover that it prosecuted criminals according to convenience and not guilt. The best thing the United States could do in response to the Soviet threat would be to somehow take that option away from the Russians without conceding any of the advantages they had worked for over a year to procure. It meant countering the Soviet propaganda attack with one of their own. They needed to seize the initiative from the enemy.

By January 1947, a larger Legal Section investigation, of which Case 420 formed but a fraction, began to develop a momentum of its own. Although the Kyushu Imperial University case initially appeared to be an isolated incident of scientific depravity, time proved it to be more than a moment of madness. It was part of a carefully orchestrated, government-sanctioned biological research program that stretched from the ministry level—a war and education tandem—down to the local university laboratory and military unit.

Four separate cases—excluding Case 420—comprised the bulk of the Legal Section's investigative thrust. Each case came into being because at some point a charge of war crimes emerged against someone involved. Case 330[3] went under the name of Motoji Yamaguchi but focused on Lieutenant General Wakamatsu Yujiro's biowarfare research operation (Unit 100) at the Kwantung Army Quarantine Stables in Changchun, Manchuria. Case 91[4] focused on charges against Lieutenant General Ishii and his notorious Unit 731 operation, labeling him an "enemy of humanity." Case 1117[5] also involved Ishii, but this time identifying him with the Densenbyo Kenkyusho (Infectious Disease Research Laboratory) that functioned as the primary biowarfare research center in Tokyo. Along with Ishii, the investigation also named Naito Ryoichi and Abe Yasuo as second and third in commands at the center. Case 997[6] charged that Dr. Ariyama Noboru of Niigata Medical College illegally used Allied POWs as guinea pigs during blood substitute research similar to what went on at Kyushu Imperial University's First and Second Surgical Clinics.

While on the surface the cases appeared unrelated to each other—with the exception of Cases 91 and 1117, which shared Ishii as a suspect—a common thread of accountability ran through them all. Eventually, the Legal Section consolidated Cases 91, 330, and 1117 due to the commonality of the various names and elements. In time, Cases 997 and 420 would be associated with the biowarfare units—both by suspects and the Legal Section.

On January 24, 1947, Legal Section investigator Neal Smith interrogated Naito Ryoichi regarding his association with Ishii and what was referred to as his "BKA [Bacterial War Army]." In particular, Naito was questioned about the Unit 731 operation at Pingfan.[7] It would prove to be the Legal Section's first glimpse into the man and operation already terribly familiar to the U.S. intelligence community. For the remainder of the occupation and war crimes trials, G-2—with Colonel Carpenter's aid—would stay one step ahead of the Legal Section. The simple fact that Smith interrogated Naito in 1947, almost a year and a half after Naito greeted Murray Sanders, an American microbiologist sent by Washington to investigate Ishii, in September 1945, testified to the lack of cooperation between the two levels, except between the highest positions.

Naito knew Ishii well. As a member of the Tokyo Army Medical College faculty, he served under Ishii from 1939 to 1942 and from 1943 until the end of the war. The Medical College functioned in conjunction with Tokyo Imperial University and its Infectious Disease Research Laboratory, where Ishii acted as the head and Naito as his assistant.[8]

"Were you ever connected with Lieutenant General Ishii Shiro?" Smith asked.[9]

"Yes," Naito replied. "I was at the Tokyo Army Medical College, which was under the supervision of Ishii."

"What was Ishii's mission?"

"Ishii's chief mission was bacterial warfare, and it was divided into two sections, offensive and defensive."

Under the auspices of defensive research, Ishii's program concentrated on ways of attacking germs in their various natural media. Water purification—the cover for the entire organization—entailed the obvious and had long been a major thrust of the Japanese army's scientific program of improving hygiene for soldiers fighting in the front lines. Ever since the turn of the twentieth century, top Japanese scientific minds concentrated on this goal because of the problems that disease had been known to create among warring armies. For centuries, pathogens killed more combatants than bullets and bombs.

The knowledge that resulted from defensive research led to a deeper understanding of ideal methods of infection and what pathogens infected humans most easily and devastatingly. They were two sides of the same coin, and Naito admitted as much. He detailed Ishii's operation: "Ishii was chief of the Harbin troops and also chief of the Army Medical College. He would be at Harbin for three-fourths of the year and at Tokyo Medical College for the other quarter. Whenever he returned to Tokyo, he tried to hide his real purpose by saying that his experiments were being conducted in secrecy. The only way we could learn about Ishii's work was when his men from the Harbin unit would return to Tokyo. Rumors that circulated all through Japan were such that it led us to believe that he was using humans for his experiments. Ishii was very famous among the professors in Japan, and they also heard these rumors. The experiments were being conducted in bacterial warfare and could and probably did include most every kind of disease. Other animals used were goats, dogs, cats, pigs, cow, horses, etc."

Rumors also circulated among members of the scientific community in Japan that Ishii's research subjects included human beings. The notion that a vaccine, treatment, or theory concerning human beings was not complete until tested on a human being resurfaced in its most gruesome form.

Naito stated that Ishii assumed an alias—Major Togo Hajime—while running the Harbin operation and that his older brother, who was Ishii's personal assistant, assumed an alias as well. In fact, Naito asserted that most of the officers associated with Ishii went by different names during their times at Ishii's Manchurian laboratory.

Naito declared bluntly that Japan's aggressive pursuit of biological weapons originated with one person: "The idea of bacterial warfare was solely that of Ishii. He came back from Europe in 1930 and immediately initiated steps for financing BW, both offensive and defensive."

Then Naito admitted something so basic yet so stunning in its vastness that it implicated the entire Japanese scientific and academic community:

"Most microbiologists in Japan were connected in some way or another with Ishii's work. He mobilized most of the universities in Japan to help in research for his unit. In addition to the Tokyo Medical College, Kyoto Imperial University, Tokyo Imperial University, the Infectious Disease Research Laboratory in Tokyo, and other universities were involved."

Naito supplied an extensive and detailed list of the major officers and researchers involved with the Harbin research laboratory—sixteen in all. He then named eleven key members of Ishii's Tokyo Medical Army College water purification unit, including himself, and designated their field of research. The areas ranged from bacteriology to serology and included more benign-sounding fields like disinfection and water purification.

Naito listed the eight designated sections of the Harbin operation: general research, offensive bacterial research, defensive vaccine manufacturing, water purification research, administrative, education, clinical, and supply.

Naito's cooperation appeared limitless as he volunteered the names of several Ishii associates, most notably Ota Kyoshi—one of the men the Russians sought to question.

Naito added, "General Kitano Masaji, successor to Ishii when he was removed to be chief surgeon of the 1st Army, must be able to tell you everything regarding the organization, equipment, and general setup of the Harbin unit."

As the interrogation drew to a close, the investigator asked the usual question: "Do you have anything else to add that might be of value to the statement?"

"Nothing," Naito stated matter-of-factly, if not sanctimoniously. "But if Ishii was guilty of using human beings for his experiments, I think that he should be punished."

Meanwhile, photos of the Watkins crew began filtering through the Legal Section transom. On January 23, a black-and-white photo of Dale Plambeck arrived from the Zone of the Interior.[10] With the first glimpse of the victims behind the names, Tait and his men discovered a man wearing a military cap tilted to the side and sporting a dazzling smile so genuine that it was hard not to imagine that someone had been standing behind the camera saying something funny. Plambeck's expression communicated happiness, pride, and confidence.

The following week on January 28, Norman Tracy, a new addition to Team 420, brought the picture of Plambeck with him to Sugamo Prison. The photograph would be shown to Aihara, Mori, and Sato.[11] After Tait's initial identification of the Kyushu Imperial University victims, this represented the next significant step in definitively establishing the identities of the B-29 fliers who had been experimented on.

Soon after showing Plambeck's picture, a photo of William Fredericks arrived. His smile was every bit as heartfelt and idealistic as Plambeck's. Once again, Tracy brought the photo—along with Plambeck's—to Sugamo Prison. This time, however, he did not limit his questioning to Aihara, Mori, and Sato.[12] All of the key Kyushu Imperial University suspects saw the photograph. Their responses, however, were even more uneventful than the initial display a week prior.

• • •

Upon being shown Dale Plambeck's photograph—

Hirao: "I do not remember seeing him."
Torisu: "I did not see this face there. All the POWs were blond."
Hirako: "I didn't see the face of any of them. They were all blindfolded."
Senba: "All the POWs were blindfolded. I did not see their faces. They were all blond."
Tsutsui: "I did not see their faces. I didn't look at them. I only handed the instruments to the doctors."[13]

Upon being shown William Fredericks' photograph—

Aihara: "I do not recall that face. I do not remember the name Fredericks."
Sato: "I believe I saw him when he was being interrogated at the headquarters."
Mori: "I suppose I have seen such a face before."[14]
Hirao: "I never saw him."
Torisu: "I did not see this face there."
Hirako: "I didn't see the face of any of the POWs."
Senba: "They were all blindfolded. I did not see him. There was one first lieutenant operated on."
Tsutsui: "I did not see this face there."[15]

With each negative response, the attempt at identifying the victims appeared to hit a continuous string of roadblocks. The cultural differences between Westerners and the Japanese—the root of the Pacific conflict—arose again, this time in a less deliberate manner. To the Japanese, especially those unable to travel extensively and study abroad, all Westerners looked alike. The faces of dead men must have been as recognizable as they were unrecognizable.

While the Legal Section struggled to simultaneously identify the American soldiers who died at the hands of the Japanese biological research program and piece together a bottom-up view of the extensive system, senior-level American and Soviet delegates continued to jockey for the secrets of the same program they saw from the top down. The IMTFE prosecutor for the Soviet Union increased his efforts to gain access to Ishii, and, as a result, on February 7 SCAP sent a memo to Washington requesting instructions.[16] The Soviet threat of bringing war crime charges against Ishii could not be blocked much longer.

By February 11, the JCS requested that the State-War-Navy-Coordinating Committee (SWNCC) subcommittee to the Far East to formulate a policy to deal with the Soviet requests.[17] For nearly a month, during which Soviet prosecution requests became a daily event, a draft of the policy bounced back and forth between members of the subcommittee. For each round the document made, major and minor alterations were applied in order to fine-tune the document. Each modification came with a rationale supporting it. In the end, on March 3, 1947, an official policy came into existence regarding Soviet prosecution requests, and a carefully worded telegram for SCAP with instructions on how to proceed was attached as an appendix.[18]

Washington's rationale revolved around the notion that they had more to gain by allowing the Soviet prosecutors controlled and supervised access to Ishii than by denying their request. With Ishii under SCAP custody, he could be coached beforehand and instructed on what type of information to share and what not to share. In addition, he could not document the entire program himself—the implication being that he was only a part, albeit integral, of the larger entity—and Soviet scientists could not get a significant amount of novel information from him as a solitary source. While Ota and Kikuchi Hitoshi had not been interrogated at the time of the policy's issuance, it was suggested that they be questioned, then coached in a manner similar to Ishii, should they possess additional information.[19]

Granting Soviet access would allow the American officials present during the interrogation to infer what information the Russians already had access to through a careful analysis of their questions. In addition, the gesture would alleviate the risk of bringing the issue of biological warfare and Ishii's capture into the open. According to the subcommittee, "Since there is no clear-cut war crime interest by the

Soviets in acts allegedly committed by the Japanese against the Chinese, permission for the interrogation should not be granted on that basis, but rather as an amiable gesture toward a friendly government."[20] In other words, since Soviet soldiers were not involved in the experimentation, the U.S.S.R. would not introduce the subject in the ongoing IMTFE.

Of all the Kyushu Imperial University doctors held at Sugamo Prison, Hirako Goichi continued the most aggressive campaign to exculpate himself. On February 24, the anatomy professor wrote another document elaborating on, among other things, the role of the military in the Kyushu Imperial University experiments. As in previous statements, Hirako chose, perhaps to his detriment, to express himself in a tattered English that often bordered on unreadable. His main points, however, were clear enough to add to the growing sense that Ishiyama's operations were closely coordinated with the Japanese military and by extension the Ministry of War and the biological research program.[21]

According to Hirako, the Imperial Japanese Army exercised considerable influence at the university. As the third most prestigious academic institution—behind Tokyo and Kyoto Imperial Universities—a military presence, in one form or another, would be expected, even without making assumptions about their participation in the top-secret program. However, Kyushu Imperial University became increasingly martial, so much so that a "student battalion and Zaigogunsinbunkai (district battalion of the not enlisted student[s] and retired soldiers and officers) were set up."[22]

In a manner reminiscent of Ishii's heavily protected facilities in Pingfan and Mukden, Imperial Army soldiers were stationed around the medical clinic building and a machine gun was installed on the roof. The need for such measures indicated that the Japanese army deemed whatever proceedings were occurring within the confines of the medical clinic to be so secret and sensitive that lethal force would be taken against unauthorized intruders if necessary. The fact that both the Ishiyama First Surgery and the Second Surgery Clinics resided in the building was another point of consideration.

During the waning months of the Pacific War, when Kyushu came under constant and intense bomb attacks, it was the Japanese army that took charge and directed the relocation of select university departments. In March 1945, the pathology department joined the pharmacology department in the same barracks. The two later shared space with the department of forensic medicine.[23] In essence, experts from the key bacteriological warfare fields were brought together under one roof where incubation, vaccination, and autopsies could sbe performed conveniently. Eventually, material—and presumably personnel—from the anatomy, physiology, and chemistry departments were brought to the "safe" building. Even more suspiciously, the Japanese army, in conjunction with members of Kyushu University, destroyed the biochemistry laboratory in the Medical Section after conducting the relocation—again reminiscent of Ishii's modus operandi.

The links between the Japanese military and Kyushu Imperial University continued with appalling openness. For whatever reason, after freeing Arakawa—the former president of Kyushu Imperial University—the Legal Section failed to investigate his successor. Hirako, however, made sure his identity came to the investigator's attention. Rather than having a career academic administrator assume control of the university, the Ministry of Education, in conjunction with members of the university board, installed a career military man in the presidency. And they did not just install any military man, they placed a man named Hyakutake Gengo in charge of the school.[24] His credentials would soon come to light.

Though recently retired, Hyakutake was one of a handful of admirals in the entire Japanese navy. In 1941, he was the third highest-ranking naval officer in all of Japan and was an influential member of the Tojo cabinet that initiated, planned, and executed the attack on Pearl Harbor. Because during wartimes many senior officers of Hyakutake's status retained their rank and prestige, he still held great power and influence. On the island of Kyushu in March 1945, when he assumed the Kyushu Imperial University presidency, Admiral Hyakutake even outranked Lieutenant General Yokoyama, who was in charge of the entire island's military. As a result, the university enjoyed a closer relationship with the Japanese military establishment, which meant increased funding and equipment for government-approved research.[25]

Described by Hirako as "a surgeon in charge of the military,"[26] Ishiyama benefited directly from the university's affiliation with the military, both pre- and post-Hyakutake. In addition, because his blood substitute research was a major area of interest for the military, he was able to enjoy the same perks as other Ishii-recruited researchers, only he did not have to leave the comfort of his own laboratory. "During the war, there were a few professors in charge of the military who were given much more facilities in expenditure and material than any other not-militarized investigators."[27] As it turned out, those additional "materials" would include live human beings for experimentation.

Ishiyama also benefited from Kyushu Imperial University's proximity to Western Army Headquarters and its Medical Section. As one of Kyushu's most respected surgeons, Ishiyama often found himself summoned to the Medical Section and its hospitals to give lectures to the staff. He developed a relationship with members of the Medical Section.[28] In addition, Komori, a former student of Ishiyama's, was stationed at the Medical Section and was in charge of the Officers Hospital. With these factors in place, the situation in Fukuoka was ideally suited for experimenting on POWs. The Medical Section needed to act as a liaison between the Staff Section and the university. In addition, with Komori acting as the liaison between the university and the Medical Section, Ishiyama had a personal friend inside Western Army Headquarters to promote his case.

As Team 420's investigation progressed, the collection of facts indicated that Ishiyama needed the close cooperation between every facet of his university and the military. Their job was to prove it.

The Soviet Union's threat of introducing the subject of biological warfare into the tribunal forced Washington to address the damage that publicity would cause should the international community be made aware of their attempts to procure biological warfare information as well as sheltering criminals from justice. The current legal proceedings going on in the Tokyo IMTFE represented an ideal vehicle for introducing the topic into the public forum.[29] And while one disaster might have been averted by partial appeasement of Soviet wishes, there were a number of variables that needed to be monitored and controlled. Among the thousands of cases being investigated by the SCAP Legal Section, a number of them involved the very same individuals under U.S. government protection. Should any of those cases came to trial, it would undoubtedly blow up in Washington's face.

In order to avert unwanted publicity, ongoing investigations related to the Japanese program needed to be stopped. But wholesale silencing might arouse too much suspicion, particularly in legal circles. Selectivity, therefore, needed to be practiced and only the most sensitive cases pulled from Legal Section control.

The easiest cases to classify were the ones most obviously associated or not associated with Ishii and his counterparts, most notably figures like Lieutenant General Wakamatsu. Case 330 represented as obvious a threat as they came. The Legal Section had already figured out that the Kwantung army stable's major objective was to develop and test viable means of disseminating bacterial weapons. That alone posed a threat. Moreover, during the course of the investigation, Ishii's name surfaced repeatedly as a major figure in the case. If it ever went to trial and Ishii was tried for war crimes, the issue of bacterial warfare would definitely arise and the secret information that Washington labeled as having direct bearing on national security would slip through their fingers.

The Densenbyo Kenkyusho case also represented an investigation that held the potential of leading directly to Ishii. It bore every indication of being a major bacterial warfare development center. Anonymous tips named him specifically, and the further that Legal Section soldiers probed, the larger his role was guaranteed to become. At the case's current point, however, Ishii's association was tenuous at best. With the opportunity to keep any prosecutorial information at a bare minimum, immediate action by Washington, G-2, and SCAP—all of whom were aware of the true nature of the DK and Ishii's involvement—became a prudent means of intelligence prophylaxis.

The Niigata Medical College case existed on the opposite end of the security spectrum. Unlike the DK, the blood research initiative—while a definite branch of the Japanese biological research program—did not directly deal with bacterial warfare research and as such appeared to be an entirely safe case for the Legal Section to investigate. Proof of POW atrocities—the basis for any Legal Section action—disappeared with each passing day. Moreover, upon inspection by American scientific experts, the research conducted at the Medical College adhered to valid paths of inquiry and the test trials followed accepted methods.

Somewhere between the Densenbyo Kenkyusho and Niigata Medical College cases lay the Kyushu Imperial University case. As the case developed and facts revealed themselves, Case 420 continued to prove increasingly unwieldy. Because of its close association with the Western Army Headquarters atrocities, coupled with the overwhelming and well-circulated proof of wrongdoing against American POWs, the case was harder to conceal if the need to do so arose. The risks outweighed the benefits, particularly taking into consideration that the Kyushu case bore more similarities to the Niigata Medical College case than to the DK case. The differences, however, made Case 420 more of a potential Pandora's box.

POWs were killed as a result of the Japanese biological research program—something that could be cited as a precedent for other allegations of wrongdoing at facilities like Pingfan, Mukden, and Harbin. In addition, the more suspects testified and the more facts emerged, it became clear that the Kyushu case could easily be tied to the Japanese military and by extension to Tokyo and the emperor. Also, military aspects of the Kyushu case led to Ishii and others. The leap was not a very big one to make. It did, after all, belong to the same umbrella program. They were simply different branches of the same tree, sharing a common body and being fed by the same roots. Stifling the investigation, for all intents and purposes, could not happen. Another line needed to be taken. The case and investigation needed to be controlled and sanitized. The Legal Section and subsequent trial officials could be "advised" as to how far to probe into certain aspects of the case. By concentrating on safer aspects of the case—investigative tunnel vision—such as the murders, and not probing into their causes, the Kyushu case could proceed without issue. In fact, with enough vision, it could aid in efforts to deflect Russian pressures.

On April 18, 1947, Case 330—an amalgam of Cases 91, 1117, 2239, and the original Case 330—was officially classified as secret, falling off the prosecutorial radar permanently.[30] The Niigata Medical College case was going nowhere. All that remained was Case 420—the Kyushu Imperial University vivisection case.

13

From Tokyo to Kyushu: April–June 1947

With Case 330 safely hidden behind the opaque wall of intelligence channels, the onus fell on the Legal Section and its prosecutors to devise a strategy for trying the Kyushu Imperial University atrocities case. The chief architect of the prosecution would be Paul K. Von Bergen. Acting in supporting roles, George T. Hagen and Richard O. Baird also contributed to developing a strategy. While the resources and level of Japanese cooperation appeared to heavily favor the prosecution, assembling a solid argument challenged the legal team.

The first thing that needed fixing was the Legal Section's case organization. Because the Kyushu Imperial University case developed as a result of the Western Army Headquarters atrocities case—the actual Case 420—they shared many of the same suspects as well as investigators. However, they technically existed as separate cases, with the Kyushu Imperial University atrocities case labeled Case 604. That would change; the Legal Section consolidated both cases under the umbrella of Case 420.

Von Bergen made it clear that exploring, understanding, and

exploiting the blood substitute aspect of the case would play a key role in his presentation. He cited a Report of Investigation Division (RID) referencing an article entitled "Blood Substitute from Seaweed" from the *Kyushu Times*. According to Von Bergen, "It is very desirable that a certified copy of this article be obtained and, further, that this matter be traced."[1]

In addition, Von Bergen wanted a clear explanation regarding the formula of various experimental blood substitutes including "argin acid" from Japan, "Periston" from Germany, and any American versions of synthetic blood substitutes currently under research.[2]

Great emphasis would be placed on locating and identifying the fliers' bodies, as well. According to Von Bergen, the "ephemeral"[3] nature of the case made it essential that the remains be traced successfully, not only for identification, but also in order to establish the fact that "said individuals are dead."[4] The prosecution, however, did not hold out much hope for the discovery of the bodies, particularly considering the numerous attempts already made by Team 420.

Without the remains in Legal Section possession, the prosecution had no choice but to build a case on completely circumstantial evidence. That meant that careful and close attention needed to be paid to taking statements, "since the case will be based only upon statements of Japanese involved."[5] Every detail needed to be expressed as clearly, comprehensively, and succinctly as possible. Any holes in written statements meant similar deficiencies in the court case.

Accumulating admissible statements pointed to a larger problem. The prosecution needed more weapons. Von Bergen went so far as to outwardly admit that "there must be evidence of the corpus delecti, other than the confession itself."[6] The limitations of presenting a case purely based on statements were obvious at an early juncture. Moreover, strict rules of court martial forbade the use of confessions of conspirators against one another. The people who actually participated in the atrocities—university employees and Western Army Headquarters staff members—could not implicate each other, though they were allowed to testify in each other's defense. As a result, Von Bergen conceded, "It cannot be taken into Court until we can satisfy the Commission that we have exhausted every possibility of evidence."[7]

Anticipating the defense further complicated matters. Countless hours of testimony indicated that the Japanese used the blanket charge of indiscriminate bombing as a justification for the mass executions. Most likely, it would comprise a major portion of the defense's argument. If they could even instill a sense of doubt regarding bombing campaigns and their subsequent precision, it would certainly cripple any attempt at convincing the military commission that the executions were acts of pure, unprovoked, and unjustified barbarism. Admittedly, the defense would have to do more than establish indiscriminate bombing to win the case—there was, after all, the inexplicable lack of a trail—but considerable damage would still be inflicted to the prosecution's argument.[8]

One final problem loomed before the prosecution: separating fact from fiction when dealing with Komori's role in the atrocities. From the outset of the investigation, it quickly became apparent that Komori represented a convenient scapegoat for the members of Kyushu Imperial University and Western Army Headquarters. For starters, he was dead and could not contradict anyone. The fact that he held major ties to both parties undoubtedly contributed to his appeal and made it all that much easier to place most of the culpability on him. He was a member of the military and was a former student of Ishiyama. He was an obvious fit for both suspect and prosecutor. Too obvious. Von Bergen cautioned against accepting the Komori-as-coordinator too readily. "It is impossible to believe that Komori, a mere probationary officer, was the important link between the Medical College and the Army."[9]

Yet, for all of Von Bergen's anticipating and strategizing, he never indicated the desire to place the Kyushu Imperial University experiments in their proper context, choosing rather to concentrate on the immediate small picture. While limiting the investigation solely to the murders, the direct circumstance surrounding the operations, and the subsequent desecration of the bodies as a theoretically sound and acceptable approach, Von Bergen's reluctance to probe further provided Washington all the wiggle room it needed with regards to Ishii.

While Washington and SCAP coordinated their efforts to muzzle any legal investigation into the biological research program, more information continued to surface. Case 997, Niigata Medical College, appeared to be a safe case that would burn itself out, since there had been no substantial evidence of atrocities against POWs beyond the initial mention. However, as Legal Section investigators continued to interrogate scientists involved in the case, aspects of the Japanese biological research program began to surface and become clearer. More importantly, the first clear link between blood substitute research and an Ishii institution was made.

On the same day that Case 420 became a unified whole, a Legal Section investigator interrogated Miyazaki Goro, a former lieutenant commander in the Imperial Japanese Navy. A graduate from Tokyo Imperial University in 1937, he spent his entire medical career in the military, serving aboard various naval hospitals on land and ship. During his two-year tenure (1943–1945) at Tsukiji Hospital, Miyazaki participated in numerous experiments using artificial blood.[10]

Miyazaki's interrogation yielded the first link between artificial blood research and major institutions associated with Ishii. According to Miyazaki's testimony, the Densenbyo Kenkyusho oversaw much of the pertinent artificial blood research. Some artificial blood samples were even tested with various diseases. Throughout Japan, the three main research centers experimenting with artificial blood substitutes were Nagoya Imperial University, Niigata Medical College, and Kyushu Imperial University. Each research facility conducted its own experiments and pursued different types of substitutes. They only needed to report their data and conclusions to the Densenbyo Kenkyusho.[11] In that sense, each university and research laboratory functioned semiautonomously. Although Miyazaki could not elaborate on the experiments at the three universities, he supplied a major lead that linked the two subdivisions of the general Japanese biological research program—bacterial warfare and general medical research—with each other.

For the first time since the Kyushu Imperial University atrocities emerged, the avenues between Ishiyama and higher authorities opened up. Miyazaki's testimony established a link between the vivisection of the Watkins crew and Ishii's Unit 731 by way of the Densenbyo Kenkyusho. Furthermore, because the Densenbyo Kenkyusho fell under the jurisdiction of the Ministry of Education, a link between the murders and Tokyo could be drawn as well. Taking it one step further, because of Ishii's support from the Ministry of War, Ishiyama's support from the Densenbyo Kenkyusho—Ishii's Tokyo operation—meant that he had the support of the Ministry of War as well. If any of the prosecutors trying the Kyushu Imperial University case wanted to ride the prosecution ladder up to members of the emperor's cabinet, the proof lay at their disposal. All they needed to do was act on it.

In May 1947, Team 420 turned their attention to placing the experimental operations in context. There were several questions that needed to be addressed. Where in the Kyushu Imperial University administration did Ishiyama get the authority for his research? Who among Ishiyama's superiors bore the responsibility for the operations? How did Ishiyama's research fit in with other work being done at the university and around Japan in general? One obvious starting point dealt with blood substitutes and the links established as a result of the Niigata Medical College case and the Miyazaki interrogation. The two cases shared more than superficial similarities. They were essentially pieces in the same puzzle.

On May 14 and 15, Special Investigator Tracy interrogated Tomoda Masanobu.[12] Miyazaki identified him as being involved with the blood substitute research program at Kyushu Imperial University. The most immediate goal of the interrogation was to determine whether Tomoda played any role in the vivisection experiments and whether he ever conducted similar experiments. As Ishiyama's equal of sorts, Tomoda's testimony could shed light on how the blood substitute research program was organized and functioned. With any luck, the Legal Section would be able to establish who funded and sponsored Ishiyama. If that could be established, then the next step could be proving that the supervising party probably knew about the vivisections and could also be held responsible.

Tomoda was forty-six, and his medical career had taken him around the globe. After graduating from Kyushu Imperial University in 1927, he immediately joined the university surgery clinic and after four years became a lecturer at the university. In 1937, Tomoda, like so many other members of Japan's scientific community, went abroad to study and observe Western medical institutions. His ten-month whirlwind tour took him to Europe and the United States. Among the notable institutions he attended were the Mayo Clinic in Rochester, Minnesota, and Mount Sinai Hospital in New York City.[13]

Tomoda was the director of Kyushu Imperial University's Second Surgery Clinic, opposite Ishiyama, who ran the First Surgery Clinic. Although designated first and second, neither clinic held a more prominent position than the other. Tomoda conducted his research independent of Ishiyama. Both clinics applied for their own grants; each clinic functioned with complete autonomy from the other. The only key element both clinics shared was exploring different means of developing blood substitutes.[14]

"What accomplishments have you made on your experiments of a blood substitute?" Tracy asked.[15]

"Alginic acid is a viscous colloidal substance extracted from the cell membrane of seaweed. It is dissolved in physiological NaCl solution and injected into a person needing a blood transfusion."

Tomoda explained how he believed the alginic acid was extracted from seaweed by members of the biochemistry department and that he could not give exact details as to how the extraction was performed since he was not a biochemistry expert.

"When did you first start your experiments with alginic acid as a blood substitute?"

"I believe it was in the fall of 1944."

"On whom did you use this new blood substitute?"

"The patients in the hospital [Second Surgery Clinic]."

As Tracy continued to question Tomoda, it became evident that the doctor knew little about Ishiyama's research, or at least refused to divulge any information for fear of implicating himself in some related affair. But one significant piece of information that emerged from the questioning reinforced the link between Tokyo and the vivisections.

According to Tomoda, the Ministry of Education sponsored and financed a scientific research conference for doctors and professors interested in blood substitutes. Tomoda admitted to attending two meetings and remembered seeing Ishiyama in attendance at one meeting. The conference was run by Dr. Miyagawa Yoneji, director of the Contagious Disease Institute attached to Tokyo Imperial University. It was yet another fact that tied the Kyushu Imperial University atrocities with Japanese government officials.

While Tracy conducted his series of interrogations with Tomoda, Special Investigator Robert Miller worked to establish the exact structure of Kyushu Imperial University's administration for April to July 1945. His main objectives were to get the exact information on (1) the president and dean of the university, (2) the president and dean of the medical school, and (3) the identities of the professors in charge of each section of the medical school.[16] Establishing the school's organization would help to clarify the flow of culpability from Ishiyama's subordinates to his direct and ultimate superiors.

On May 15, Miller began setting out flowcharts of the various Kyushu Imperial University sections. He summarized the roles and relations of the different departments as well as the faculty belonging to them. He broke his work into six categories: high-level chain of command, KIU Medical College, KIU Attached Medical College, KIU Hospital, the Anatomy Clinic, and First Surgery (Ishiyama Clinic).[17] By ascertaining the personnel and their functions, a clearer sense of the university's chain of command and culpability emerged.

During the time of the murders, Hyakutake Gengo sat as the head of Kyushu Imperial University. He succeeded Arakawa Bunrioku as president of the university in April 1945 and held the post for a little over three months. During his brief tenure, the military's presence increased significantly, due in part to his presence but also to the Allied bombing raids.

As president, Hyakutake oversaw the affairs of the university. The deans of each college reported only to him. He also directly controlled the three administrative offices at the university. He did not, however, exert an omnipresent and omnipotent power; the amount of day-to-day paperwork for one college alone would have taken up his entire day. Instead, a system was worked out in which the general affairs office functioned as an everyday administrative conduit with the office of the president. Under normal circumstances, everything went through the general affairs office. Only under certain circumstances—matters of secrecy or extreme urgency—did the president deal directly with the individual deans or members of a specific college.[18]

Excluding the various administrative divisions, Kyushu Imperial University consisted of five independent colleges: medical, agriculture, technology, laws and letters, and natural science. In addition, the university had an official hospital that operated independent of but in conjunction with the Medical College. They shared many of the same doctors, who swung back and forth between the two, functioning as traditional doctors when under the hospital and lecturers under the Medical Section.[19]

Kyushu Imperial University Medical College created and nurtured some of Japan's most promising doctors. Dr. Ohno Yukizo headed the college, at the same time holding the chair of the pathology department. Like all higher-learning institutions, the Medical College was divided along official lines according to departments. Hence, the anatomy, bacteriology, pharmacology, and pathology departments, to name a few, formed de facto sections. Unofficially, the Medical College was broken into three major sections. An administrative section tended to the paperwork, a basic course section taught the medical basics, and an advanced/practical course section—of which Ishiyama's surgical section belonged—instructed students in specialty areas.[20]

The hospital was also under Hyakutake's control. Everything about the organization functioned separately from the Medical Section. It had its own administration and its own director, Dr. Nakashima Yoshida. Its structure, however, mirrored that of the Medical College's setup. Making the distinction even blurrier, the staff of the hospital and Medical College overlapped in many instances.[21] So, in essence, there was no official continuity between operations, but there was a definite but unspoken relationship.

Later on May 15, Miller joined Tracy in the interrogation of Jinnaka Seichi.[22] A professor of orthopedic surgery at Kyushu Imperial University for twenty-one years, he was held in high esteem at the university and ascended to the deanship of the Medical School in September 1945, holding the position until July 1946. While he was not a direct or indirect participant in the bioexperimentation operations, he presided over Ishiyama during the period immediately after the events. As such, he could testify to the steps taken, concealment or otherwise, to deal with Ishiyama's conduct. In addition, he could shed light on government-subsidized research at the university because of his experiences as the dean and also as a government-subsidized researcher in prosthetics. It was hoped that Jinnaka's testimony could be used to show that Ishiyama's and Tomoda's research originated in similar areas.

During May 1945, Jinnaka attended an assembly of surgeons at Kyushu Imperial University. The meeting was designed to allow local surgeons to share and discuss new information concerning surgical techniques, rare illnesses, or any other medical concerns they had.[23]

"Do you remember who lectured and what they spoke about at that meeting of May 1945?" Tracy asked.[24]

"I remember that Tomoda lectured on the use of alginic acid, which was extracted from seaweed, and the research which he had conducted in using it as a blood substitute in transfusions."

"Do you remember any other important lectures or discussions which were carried on at this meeting?"

"I think it was during the discussion following Tomoda's lecture that Ishiyama said that it was also possible to use diluted seawater as a blood substitute. I also recall that Komori stated he knew from experience that an injection of seawater into the arteries, not as a blood substitute but as treatment, would relieve neural pains."

"Was Ishiyama also studying blood substitutes at that time?"

"Yes, he should have been because he was interested in the use of seawater as a blood substitute."

"Which doctors at the university were conducting research in the use of seawater as a blood substitute?"

"This research was directed by Ishiyama, and working with him in this research were Senba and Torisu. I believe that these three were the only ones conducting this research."

The questioning returned to Tomoda's work. As the other major doctor involved in blood substitute research, he represented a back-door to the workings of Ishiyama's clinic. The Legal Section would do its best to draw parallels between the two research teams.

Jinnaka indicated that Tomoda received funds and reported to the Medical Section of the National Research Council, which belonged to the Ministry of Education. Though he could not state definitely whether the blood substitute research was ordered by the army, Jinnaka claimed that it received approval by the army and that the military maintained constant contact with Tomoda in order to keep track of his progress.

Jinnaka was not certain of any specifics, unfortunately. He did not know how initial contact was made or to whom Ishiyama reported the results of his research. Neither did he let on whether he knew where Ishiyama's orders emanated from. If they had been from the army, the university president could theoretically have been bypassed; if they had been from the Tokyo Ministry of Education, the orders would go through either the president's office or the dean of the Medical School's office. When questioned about Ishiyama's funding, Jinnaka maintained his air of ignorance, stating the increasingly infamous, "I don't know." According to him, he did not even know about the operations until fall 1945.[25] At least that is what he indicated.

The Jinnaka interrogation bore better fruit when the subject turned to his own research. Jinnaka received direct orders from the army to carry out his research. He was chosen by professors of the Army Medical College and his area of research was assigned by them. Because of the violent realities of war—arms ripped from their sockets, legs splintered into fleshy and useless appendages—the need for functional prosthetics became as much a medical necessity as blood substitutes. Finding something viable and affordable that could help injured soldiers back to a productive level would be a tactical advantage. In January 1944, Jinnaka received written orders from the Medical Section of the Ministry of War. He was to carry out research on artificial limbs and would receive funding from them. Most major decisions regarding his research data came from Tokyo. However, he also received orders from the Western Army Headquarters Medical Section—specifically, General Horiuchi.[26]

Because his research in prosthetics also emanated from an army–government mandate, the same way the blood substitute research did, matters regarding his own subsidizing, reporting, and accountability could be considered a model for Ishiyama's work.

On May 16, Tracy set his sights on Ohno Yukizo, the dean of the Medical College at Kyushu Imperial University, and began making inquiries into his background and history.[27] Three days later, the two men sat down in Tracy's office at the Fukuoka Legal Section. The interrogation spanned a week, with Ohno returning to the office daily.[28]

Tracy continued trying to establish the exact protocol involved in government-sponsored research. With Ishiyama gone and every participant in the murders withholding information for fear of implicating themselves, the most obvious strategy entailed drawing similarities between Ishiyama's project and other government-approved programs. As Von Bergen's memorandum indicated, the bulk of the case would have to be proved indirectly. This represented a single phase of the larger task.

"What authority did you have as dean of the Medical College over the professors under your jurisdiction?"[29]

"The dean takes care of the academic administration of student education. Any professor when acting as an instructor to the students comes under my authority. Those professors actually conducting operations in the surgery and orthopedic clinics come under the jurisdiction of the hospital. Also, all other professors in sections connected with the treatment of patients come under this jurisdiction."

"What person were you responsible to as dean of the Medical College?"

"The president of the university," he replied. "Arakawa Bunrioku until March 1945, then Hyakutake Gengo until I retired. Hyakutake was an army man."

Tracy could not understand how an army man could be appointed to an educator's position. It made no sense from an academic standpoint.

"Who appointed Hyakutake president of Kyushu University?"

"All the professors voted and elected him."

"Was he an old university professor?"

"No. He had nothing to do with the university. He was an army man."

"Why was Arakawa removed and a military man elected to the most coveted position at Kyushu Imperial University?"

"Arakawa's term of four years ended in March 1945, and because we were having a lot of trouble with the military, it was decided to elect a military man as president, so we could get the supplies and funds necessary to continue to operate the school efficiently."

Ohno explained the university election board's rationale for appointing a career military man with no educational background to an educator's position. The army and navy had all of the supplies, causing a shortage in other sectors of Japanese society. In addition, he pointed out that because the army seemed to be drafting all eligible professors into service and tearing them away from their research, they felt that a military man at the head of the university might be able to prevent more faculty members from being drafted.

Hyakutake Gengo assumed the university presidency in April 1945. The twenty-five-man board of elections chose him over two other candidates, both of whom were career educators. Members of every department of Kyushu Imperial University were represented and cast their votes by secret ballot. The secrecy, however, was more of a formality than anything else. Ohno's earlier comments indicated it had been agreed that a president with a strong military history would benefit the university. An even likelier scenario was that the entire vote was more of a token and symbolic gesture designed to validate Tokyo's choice of a university president.

Ohno indicated to Tracy that the Ministry of War and the Ministry of Education entered into an agreement that professors conducting "certain experiments" would not be drafted into the army.

"What type of experiments would exempt a professor from being drafted?"

"Not any particular type of experiment was necessary. Any that was recognized by the university would be recommended to the Ministry of Education, and they would discuss it with the Ministry of War."

"What actual specific experiments were being conducted by men on whom the university did ask deferment?"

"The university submits a list of experiments thought suitable to be considered by the Ministry of Education for approval. At the university, they are classified into the following four categories before selection: (A) number one priority in which results are needed quickly, (B) second in importance, (C) no immediate results necessary, and (D) nonessential. The Ministry of Education consults with Lieutenant General Kambayashi, head of the Medical Bureau of the War Ministry and also the vice admiral of the Ministry of the Navy. If they approved, we were instructed by the Ministry of Education how many persons we can assign to each approved experiment and to what departments."

"It looks as though the military completely controlled the university during the war."

"Yes. That was the national policy to some degree for graduate students. They controlled types of new research experiments and personnel to conduct these experiments."

Ohno described the procedure for choosing which professors received a temporary pardon from military service. After a given research topic gained the approval from the Ministry of Education, students and younger professors' names were assigned to the experiment and the list was sent once again to the Ministry of Education for their approval or disapproval. If someone failed to meet the government's standards, he became eligible for the draft. Approval meant a two-year deferment from the military. At the end of the period, the researcher reported the results of his research to the Ministry of Education for inspection.

"What experiments were approved and what professors supervised them?"

"In September 1944, we received approval and began work on eight experiments. Professor Toda worked on tropical contagious disease; I worked on tropical disease as well. Professor Fukuda conducted his inquiries into air and submissive fatigue and its medical treatment. Professor Sasaki explored the effect of changes in altitude on the nose and ears. Professor Ishiyama conducted experiments on brain abscesses and epilepsy resulting from external injuries. Professor Minami tried to find the optimal way to treat burns, while Professor Tomoda explored the influence of high external temperatures on the body. Finally, Kusunoki focused on airplane fatigue and alternate ways of treating it without medicine."

While immediately acknowledging that Tomoda conducted blood substitute experiments, Ohno was slow to mention Ishiyama and his research.

"Were these types of experiments, as conducted by Ishiyama and Tomoda, under your supervision and jurisdiction?"

"No. They conduct their own experiments within the limits of the subsidy."

Hirako had mentioned Ishiyama receiving additional money for his laboratory and research from the government. Shaky assertions were beginning to turn into stable facts.

"What experiments were getting special subsidies and who was in charge of them?"

"Those in the A classification needing immediate results."

Tracy shifted the focus of his questioning.

"Did you know Komori?"

"Yes, he graduated from the university as a surgeon. He was a graduate student at the university before the war and worked under Ishiyama in his clinic. I did not see him at the university at any time during the war."

"What did Komori do during the war?"

"He was not at the university. I believe he was with some other hospital. I heard he was drafted into the army and served at Western Army Headquarters."

"Was Komori a good friend of Ishiyama?"

"I don't know whether they could be called good friends or not. It was a relationship of teacher and pupil."

Ohno considered Ishiyama one of the foremost surgeons in Japan as well as a dedicated and "conscientious" researcher. He called Ishiyama an asset to the university, a "very valuable man." He portrayed him as an ideal professor who cared as much for his students as he did for his research endeavors.

Tracy attempted to establish just how much Ohno knew about the vivisections. He approached the subject from different angles—direct questions pertaining to the facts about the operations, questions about Ohno's handling of the atrocities after he became aware of them, and questions about who had the power and jurisdiction to approve of Ishiyama's experiments—but eventually came up empty on every attempt.

Ohno repeatedly tried to mislead Tracy. Throughout the interrogation, he repeatedly claimed ignorance but said that whatever information he did not know offhand could be gathered from the university records, knowing full well that immediately after Japan's surrender, a government directive had been issued ordering the destruction of all wartime documents. And when asked who at Western Army or higher headquarters could command Ishiyama to conduct illegal experiments, Ohno's response summed up an attitude that had been expressed already—though not in words—and would become frustratingly prevalent: "I do not know; I did not ask; and he did not tell me."

Special Investigator Robert Miller ended the month by interrogating Tsurumaru Hironaga. During the time of the interrogation, he belonged to Tomoda's Second Surgery Clinic. However, during the war, Tsurumaru served in the Western Army Medical Section under Brigadier General Horiuchi. Miller questioned Tsurumaru about the Medical Section and its relationship with both Western Army Headquarters and Kyushu Imperial University, using the testimony to piece together the chain of command and roles of each member of the Medical Section. Once he had the structure and general function of the Medical Section established, Miller shifted his questioning in an attempt to place Komori's role in its proper place.[30]

"Was Horiuchi a superior of Komori?"[31]

"No," Tsurumaru replied. "Komori was in charge of the Kaikosha Hospital, which is an army hospital for the dependents of officers. It is a Western Army Hospital, but for Horiuchi to give any orders to Komori, he would have to go through the chief of staff of the Western Army."

Miller rephrased his question. "Was Horiuchi indirectly a superior of Komori?"

"Yes. What I meant was that for Horiuchi to give orders to Komori, he would have to go through channels and could not do it direct."

"What were Komori's relations with the university during the time he was in the army?"

"He was a probationary medical officer in the army and had been away from the university for some years. I understand that he was on call at the university and could be called out there to lecture if it is requested through army channels."

"Was this a usual practice?"

"No."

Miller asked Tsurumaru to explain the relationship between Komori and Horiuchi.

"I know of no real relationship between the two since the Kaikosha Hospital and Medical Section of Western Army had no connection, though both were under Western Army jurisdiction."

Miller spent the remainder of the interrogation trying to gain more insight into the Komori-Horiuchi relationship but with little success. If Tsurumaru's testimony was truthful, the two had little to do with one another, making it that much more unlikely that someone as low in the chain of command as Komori could wield enough influence to act as the mastermind, setup man, or even liaison between Ishiyama and the Imperial Japanese Army. Komori, it seemed, would remain an enigmatic figure able to accomplish the impossible while having little, if any, real influence. His reputation would only grow more distorted.

The month of June was relatively slow, information wise, for the Legal Section. Tait and McKnight interrogated several Kyushu Imperial University professors regarding the post-op treatment of the POWs' bodies. Allegations that the corpses had been desecrated were continuing to accumulate and deemed worthy of investigation. The professors, however, staunchly denied any wrongdoing.

Miller met with similar futility but of a slightly different sort. He was in charge of searching for the remains—ashes or otherwise—of the American victims. Where Esposito failed, it was hoped that fresh eyes and an alternate outlook might result in a positive finding. In addition to conducting the obvious visual sweep of the crematory and ossuary, Miller interrogated members of the Kyushu Imperial University staff responsible for handling all postmortem bodies from the operating room to the crematory. The interrogations, however, left much to be desired, for unlike the well-educated professors, nurses, and medical assistants previously interviewed, the "University servants" consisted of minimally educated and often semisane simpletons unable to recall the same fact twice. In the end, an exasperated Miller proclaimed, "It's a hell of a mess and they can't read or write."[32]

Crematory building on university grounds

Crematory ovens

The only redeeming factor that June offered concerned the Komori mystery. An investigation into Goiyama Shinji that started at the end of June and eventually carried into the first week of July shed considerable light on Komori's role and supplemented the few facts already available.[33]

By all accounts, Komori Taku was an average surgeon. Unlike Ishiyama, who was regarded as one of Japan's most prominent surgeons, Komori was simply proficient. His credentials could not keep him out of the army, and though he acted as the director of Kaikosha Hospital, he did not command considerable responsibility. Kaikosha, after all, was a small operation in support of Western Army Headquarters officers' families. It was not a major research center, nor was it a hospital attached to a medical college, nor was it even an outfit involved in wartime casualties. Most of the patients at Kaikosha Hospital suffered from everyday ailments: colds, stomach problems, perhaps some broken bones, and banal infirmities that come with age.

In terms of military influence, Komori ranked as a probationary, not even a full, officer. The release of prisoners of war from military prisons often required the approval of at least the chief of staff. In most cases, the commanding general's consent was required. To assume that a probationary officer—or even a full Colonel like Sato—carried enough authority or influence to procure the release of not just one but eight prisoners of war for biological experimentation was plain silly. It showed a willingness to accept prima facie facts out of pure laziness, unforgivable denial, or convenience.

From most reliable accounts—testimony from those not facing prosecution who had nothing to lose and had not been instructed on who to blame—Komori seemed to have acted more as a lackey for whomever pulled the strings. As the man on the front lines, so to speak, he was the most exposed, making him a prime candidate to take the blame.

Because of the agreement to place the majority of the blame on Komori's shoulders, investigators ran into problems similar to those they encountered after Ishiyama's suicide—separating fact from fiction. The fact that Komori had been dead for so long and a thoroughly planned conspiracy to blame him had been months in the making—rather than the impromptu accusations heaped on Ishiyama by his staff postmortem—meant that everyone's testimony regarding Komori tended to support each other. Other times, however, when personal interests were at stake, stories diverged considerably. In the end, everything known about Komori and his role emerged from hearsay, nothing more.

Whatever the case, Komori clearly played a central role, though probably not as a decision maker. At best, he functioned as a common and convenient point man between the university, namely Ishiyama, and the Medical Section of the Imperial Japanese Army on Kyushu. In turn, the Medical Section played a supporting role between the Ministry of War and Kyushu Imperial University. All the while, the government-approved research at the university fell under the jurisdiction of the Ministry of Education, which acted in conjunction with the Ministry of War.

Komori and Sato supposedly met at Kaikosha Hospital, where Sato was receiving treatment for a leg ailment. According to Sato, he mentioned to Komori that a number of the POWs under his custody suffered from various ailments, some a result of their plunge from the sky and others from their imprisonment. At that point, Komori informed Sato that he would pay a visit to the detention barracks and take care of the prisoners. According to Goiyama's testimony, after seeing the prisoners, Komori insisted that their conditions needed treatment at a hospital: Kyushu Imperial University's hospital. And on four separate occasions, Komori and Sato supervised the transport of prisoners from Western Army Headquarters to the Ishiyama clinic. Not once did any of the prisoners return.

While admitting the unlikelihood of the scenario, the Legal Section reluctantly acknowledged Komori as a prime mover in the affair. Prior to the war, Komori served under Ishiyama, first as a medical student, then as a member of the Ishiyama clinic. A mentor-student relationship developed. It would never go away. As such, Komori would be intimately aware of the kinds of research taking place at the First Surgery Clinic.

On his own, Komori, a mere probationary officer, could not even dream of masterminding a plot like the vivisections. He simply did not have the authority or influence. In the military, he was a probationary officer; in the academic world, he was Ishiyama's subordinate and student. Even Ishiyama, for all his power and prestige, could not do it alone. The transfer of POWs had to be approved at the highest levels—in the immediate sense, this meant the commander in chief of the Western Army, the president of the university, and the dean of the Medical College. On a broader level, Tokyo had to be involved to a degree. While they might not have played a role in day-to-day affairs, they issued the various directives that set the tone for the researchers functioning under the biological experimentation umbrella. Research on healthy human beings had already been employed by Ishii's Unit 731, the darling of Tokyo's biological experimentation program. A precedent had been set with the tacit approval of the Ministries of War and Education. Perhaps even the emperor knew. Whatever the case, the sanctioned use of POWs for biological experimentation was a systemic, not localized, practice that stretched from the murky corridors of Mukden to the hallowed halls of the Japanese Imperial University.

When the time came to deliver the first test subjects to Ishiyama,

Komori played the liaison role for the Medical Section while Sato did the same for the army. Accompanied by Aihara—a claim he denied—Komori decided which prisoners he wanted to take. Aihara then checked the names off on his prison roster and brought it to Sato for his approval. Sato, most likely with the authority of Yokoyama's approval, ordered Aihara to release the American fliers, since he was directly responsible for them. Aihara, in turn, ordered his subordinate, Goiyama, to release the prisoners into Komori's custody.

During the third and fourth incidents, Komori began drugging the prisoners prior to their release so that they were already asleep upon their arrival at the university. It was a way to avoid any messiness and to facilitate the depersonalization of the act that was more emotionally draining when the POWs were conscious, coherent, and very often talkative.

A number of witnesses recounted a bizarre incident concerning Komori and his erratic behavior after one of the operations. Komori took part in each set of operations, usually acting as an assistant to Ishiyama, but never distinguished himself one way or another. He simply supported whatever experiments Ishiyama indulged in. When the experiments finished, however, Komori displayed a penchant for the macabre.

Komori removed giant portions of a murdered American soldier's liver, then dumped it into a tin pan. Blood quickly spilled out of the organ and into the pan like an oversoaked sponge made heavy and unable to hold its contents any longer. On his way out with the pan tucked under his arm, Komori turned to everyone in the room and boasted of his grand plan for the liver and its blood. One doctor present during the operation later recalled, "I heard Komori saying to Ishiyama, 'I am going to put poisonous medicine in this blood and make a poison for bedbugs.' I noticed a tray which contained the extracted left side of the liver and some blood on the floor in the middle of the room. As I remember, Ishiyama simply nodded."[34]

Inexplicably, Komori wandered through the halls of the Medical School carrying the liver. He cradled it like a trophy, boasting to anyone who would listen that he would develop a powdered bedbug poison from the liver and its blood. He passed professors, who studied him and his container curiously. Komori's demeanor almost begged inquiry from people with whom he came into contact. And when he was questioned about his prize, Komori's responses bordered on glib and playful. Kishi Tatsuro recalled one such incident.

"One day early in June I was in the surgery room when Komori walked in with a covered pan in his hands. When he removed the lid I knew that what I saw was a human liver, and in the pan was a great deal of blood. From what I could see there was nothing wrong with the liver. Even though I knew that what he had in the pan was a human liver, I said to Komori, 'What is that?' Komori answered, 'This is a pig's liver.' I replied, 'That's no pig's liver.' Komori simply said, 'Hummmm.' "[35]

Komori was even seen outside the hospital carrying the liver. Matake Shichiro, a Kaikosha nurse, testified, "While at the Officers' Club Hospital, I recall having heard Head Nurse Shiokawa telling someone in a loud voice, 'Probationary Officer Komori brought back a big ugly liver; oh how horrid.' At that time I did not know that this was a human liver—Shiokawa simply called it a liver."[36]

The mystery of the liver's fate would reveal itself in a matter of days. The Kyushu Imperial University atrocities case had one more deranged twist for Team 420.

14

The Liver Case: July 1947–February 1948

Team 420's investigation took an abrupt detour after the facts about Komori's erratic behavior emerged. The notion of someone carrying around another human's liver and boasting about it was a revolting thought—another gruesome aspect of a trial that tumbled from surreal to unreal. There was no way to ignore the allegations. If they proved true, it would be yet another charge against the Kyushu Imperial University doctors. By allowing Komori to remove the liver, they engaged in active desecration of a soldier's body.

While conducting interrogations regarding the Komori liver incident, Case 420 changed direction one final time, and the Kyushu Imperial University atrocities investigation would forever be associated with one thing—a human liver.

Tsurumaru Hironaga sat on the rigid metal folding chairs in the Fukuoka Legal Section. A table separated him from his interrogator, Robert McKnight, and the interpreter. It was Tsurumaru's second visit to the Legal Section. Early in May, Miller questioned him regarding the vivisections.

"Do you remember making a sworn statement before Captain Miller at the Legal Section between 20 and 25 May 1947?"[1]

"I remember most of the statement."

"Did you knowingly make any false statements or knowingly hide any matter from Captain Miller?"

"I did not knowingly make any false statements, nor did I knowingly hide anything from him. Recently, however, I have recalled a few incidents that would have been of interest to him. Had someone said something about what happened at the Officers' Club Hospital, I would have remembered more."

There was little time and McKnight had little patience to allow the facts to come out on their own. The investigation grew long and tiring and nobody wanted to waste time. He pushed Tsurumaru for an immediate answer.

"Tell me in detail what happened at the Officers' Club Hospital dining room." It was not a question. It was a command.

Tsurumaru drew a breath, then began to relate his story. All through the month of July, there would be others like him with similar tales to tell. Their combined stories would test the limits of both the imagination and humankind's willingness to accept the depravity of the "other."

In the days following the initial operations, Komori's behavior grew increasingly erratic.[2] He became foolish and boastful, and his arrogance would eventually strip the dignity from the doctors associated with Kyushu Imperial University. Assisting in the operations emboldened Komori, and he sought to impress those around him by shocking them into revulsion. His actions would turn the Kyushu Imperial University atrocities case from an ordinary, albeit gruesome, investigation into an archetypal tale that would transcend the Yokohama trials, SCAP, and the Pacific War.

The day after Komori's postop whirlwind tour of the university, a lunch party celebrating the promotion of a local officer was held in Kaikosha Hospital's dining hall. For all intents and purposes, it made the most sense to hold it there, since Kaikosha handled only officers and their dependents.

Komori and Kishi Tatsuro arrived at the dining area before the other partygoers, also members of Kaikosha Hospital's medical staff. It was around noon, and soon the hall would be more crowded. Komori, however, did not come to the party empty-handed. He revealed to Kishi that he had brought the liver he previously intended on drying and converting into bedbug poison. He never indicated what caused the change in heart. Whatever his reasoning, Komori decided that bringing a human liver to a celebratory luncheon was the right thing to do.

"Why don't we serve this liver to the guests?" Komori asked Kishi, both of them fully aware of the organ's origin.

"That seems like a good idea," Kishi said.

"Let us tell the others that we have already eaten some of the liver. That way they will feel more comfortable eating it."

A short time later, Head Nurse Shiokawa, Kanehisa Takuya, Ito Akira, Shinno (full name unknown), and Kamata (full name unknown) arrived at the dining area. The party was set to begin and they gathered around a Western-style table, sitting atop wooden stools that suspended them high off the ground. Each place at the table was set with a number of tiny plates and a sake bowl.

With everyone seated around the table, Shiokawa poured sake for each of the guests. Once a serving of sake sat at each guest's fingertips, Kishi directed their attention to the two plates of meat on the table. Each held what appeared to be broiled liver soaked in sharp black soy sauce. The chunks of meat differed, however. They had been cut into slices of differing thickness, with the contents of one plate lighter than the other. Clearly they came from different animals. The question for the diners was which animals.

"Please, help yourselves," Kishi said, gesturing to the table like a host presiding over a dinner party. His theatrics must have made Komori proud.

The guests picked up their chopsticks and passed the two servings of liver around. They stabbed, gripped, and dropped the liver onto their plates. Soy sauce splashed and splattered. Meat had become such a scarcity during the war that the sudden presence of two types of liver—a delicacy—must have seemed like a treat. It should have been terribly suspicious as well.

"What kind of liver is this?" a Kaikosha doctor named Momota asked Komori.

With a smile, Komori declared, "The liver is from an American prisoner of war. It is a human liver."

A consensus regarding the allegations of cannibalism during the span of madness at Kyushu Imperial University never solidified. Too many questions arose; the evidence, while solid and passionate, lacked the conclusiveness to persuade.

A cursory glance at the collected Legal Section testimonies conveys the impression of logic and consistency. The chronology of the revelations builds momentum in a clear and steady fashion—first a trickle, followed by a flow, culminating in a geyser-like gush of admission. The suspects display an initial and understandable reluctance to divulge the facts. The entire fact-gathering process spans an entire month, and only at the end the complete story emerges. Who, after all, incriminates themselves on first questioning?

Initial facts about the liver-eating incident emerged during a May 25 interrogation with Tsurumaru on a completely unrelated incident. At some point after the official testimony had concluded, he mentioned that a luncheon had been held at Kaikosha Hospital and that the liver removed by Komori that investigators had tried to track down ended up being served that afternoon. It was not until July 1 that Legal Section investigators—in this case, Special Investigator McKnight—followed up the lead set by Tsurumaru's statements by conducting an official interrogation aimed at establishing the facts about the lunch party. His statement proved to be the foundation for the entire story and the subsequent investigation. The people he named became primary suspects and targets for interrogation.

Tsurumaru implicated a number of Kaikosha Hospital doctors and nurses. Besides Komori, whom he identified as the person responsible for supplying the liver, he identified Kishi, Kanehisa, Ito, and Matake as participating in the incident.[3] On July 10, the SCAP Legal Section summoned Kishi, a doctor at Kaikosha Hospital, to the Fukuoka office. McKnight conducted the interrogation.[4] Ito was the next to be interrogated, being summoned to the Legal Section on July 11.[5] Matake, also a doctor at Kaikosha Hospital, arrived on July 14.[6] Their testimonies implicated additional members of the Kaikosha staff: Miyamoto, Shinno, Kamata, and Oda. During the month of July, they would all meet Tait, McKnight, or an addition to the Legal Section, Daniel Resendes.[7]

From Tsurumaru's July 1 statement to Miyamoto's July 30 statement, several consonant facts emerged. Unfortunately, they established little more than time, place, and tenuous proof that a human liver had been eaten.

Everyone agreed that the celebration took place during lunchtime at the Kaikosha Hospital dining room. Kishi stated that he and Komori arrived at Kaikosha at noon. Matake recalled reaching the dining area at about the same time. Ito said a few minutes later than noon—he left the dentist's office at 12:05—but not much. Tsurumaru arrived toward the end of the gathering, a fact corroborated by both Kishi and Matake, and he put his time of arrival as 12:50. Even the interrogees who denied that liver had been served agreed that the incident occurred during lunchtime, most likely around noon. That the suspects had congregated at some point for lunch at Kaikosha Hospital was certain.

Among those who conceded that the Kaikosha doctors consumed human liver, all agreed that Komori supplied the liver and seemed to orchestrate the affair. Oda, Tsurumaru, Matake, Ito, and Kishi indicated that Komori was the one to inform the party that human liver sat on the table. And when the lunch guests expressed reluctance, Tsurumaru recalled: "At this time Komori said, 'Can't any of you eat the human liver?' He also made some remark about the rest of us being weak, and he continued to eat the human liver slices. Komori said something about how good the human liver was."[8]

Komori offered the initial suggestion that it be served as part of the meal. According to Kishi, "Komori and myself were in the dining room by ourselves before the others arrived; at that time, Komori said to me, 'Since that liver has been cooked, let us feed it to the others.' "[9]

Yet, with all of the testimony indicating that human liver had been served at the lunch, only by the loosest of standards could it be said that the testimonies proved conclusive. Close scrutiny of the facts and documents reveal discrepancies that weaken, if not altogether destroy, any credibility that the blunt admissions of guilt might have. Inconsistencies inexplicably glossed over by an entire section of more-than-competent investigators abound; at times, the flow of information between question and answer defies logic and reads like a legal drama script pieced together pell-mell; and if that is not enough, the pure timing of the incident's discovery—a month after the Ishii files disappeared into intelligence channels—and its subsequent prominence in the international media begs several questions. The overall weakness in the prosecution's case was so glaring that it emerged as the one area in an otherwise clear-cut case that the defense could mount a respectable counterattack.

Problems arose once the suspects made their own statements in the presence of their defense council. By that time, the Kaikosha doctors accused of eating an American POW's liver had been arrested and taken straight to Sugamo Prison in Tokyo. Each defendant immediately retracted his statement, stating definitively that the Legal Section did not seek the truth so much as its version of the truth. In particular, Tait and McKnight were implicated in using intimidating tactics that often degenerated into violence.

One after another, the suspects supported one another's claims of coercive tactics on the part of investigators. The accusations typically included some form of simple verbal badgering—something entirely acceptable and understandable:

Tait: 3 June was the date. It happened during Matake's welcome party on 3 June 1945. Now do you remember?

Oda: I don't recall the date of the occasion nor what was served on that occasion, but I do know definitely that no such thing as human liver was served.

Tait: You are lying because you were there and you knew that human liver was served. You had better admit it if you know what is good for you.

Oda: That is not so. As far as I know, human liver was not served on this occasion or at any occasion.

Tait: Don't lie. We have proof that human liver was served on that occasion, and, furthermore, we have proof that you ate some of it yourself.

Oda: You must believe me when I say I know nothing of such an incident.

Tait: Yes you do, and everything is known to us. If you confess right now, we will protect you.

Oda: I cannot confess because it is not true. Such a thing is inconceivable to me.

Tait: We know all about it. There is no point in your trying to deceive us.

Oda: As far as I know, I never ate human liver at any time.

Tait: No, you're lying. If you persist in lying, do you know that you can get five years imprisonment at hard labor? [10]

Sometimes, however, the interrogation escalated to threats of physical torture and punishment—a borderline offense if anything:

Tsurumaru: He [McKnight] asked if I had eaten it [human liver]. I answered that I recalled putting the strange food in my mouth, and upon finding it distasteful, taking it out. Mr. McKnight then asked me if Komori hadn't said that it was the liver of an enemy flier and if I hadn't taken it out of my mouth upon hearing this. I had no recollection whatsoever of this and so stated. After being questioned on this point for about fifteen minutes, Mr. McKnight left the room and came in with a rubber hose, saying, "Do you know how the Japanese Kempei Tai conduct their interrogations?" I remember hearing or reading that in order to get people to talk, rubber hoses were inserted in their mouths, their noses were held, and water was turned on until their stomachs expanded. I felt very frightened thinking that Mr.

McKnight intended to use this water treatment on me. I, therefore, told him that Komori might have said, "This is human liver," even though I had no memory of Komori having said that.[11]

Occasionally, interrogators resorted to actual, albeit brief, beatings:

> Oda: At one point, Mr. Tait pointed his finger at me and waved it menacingly at my face while talking. . . . The more I denied the false accusation, the closer his finger came to my eyes . . . he grabbed hold of my hair and shook my head viciously from one side to the other until I felt as though my hair was going to come out by its roots. Holding me in this position, he said, "Now speak up—did or didn't you eat it?" I was terrified and could not answer for a while. . . . He also struck me on the jaw and on both sides of my face with his fists. I felt dizzy all over and felt as though I would faint. In an effort to escape from this physical violence, I said, "Do whatever you please with this case." Mr. Tait then said, "Then you admit that you ate the liver," and I could do nothing but remain motionless and speechless.[12]

Many times, the interrogators even resorted to the classic silver-screen gimmick—good cop/bad cop—with an overly enthusiastic Robert Tait playing the heavy and a steadier, more soft-spoken but no less stern Daniel Resendes playing the compassionate role.[13]

Admittedly, the testimony of the Kaikosha suspects alone held as much weight as the investigators' story. Some of Tait and McKnight's tactics were inadvertently corroborated in the transcripts of the Kyushu Imperial University doctors, particularly the tactic of bringing in one witness to pressure another into making an admission of guilt. Ultimately, however, it was one word against another. Both parties had reason to lie or at least stretch the truth to their advantage; for the investigators, a conviction was at stake; for the accused, their innocence. In the game of accusations and counteraccusations, there was nothing but a stalemate.

Another facet of the interrogation process that left much to be desired was the transcription process itself. Working off a tight military budget simply did not allow for luxuries like individual tape recorders.

As a result, interrogators also acted as impromptu secretaries, transcribing verbal testimony into longhand written form. When the interrogation finished, a summarized—not verbatim—version of the testimony was read back to the interrogee. He was informed as to the gist of the document written in English, then asked to sign it as being his verbatim testimony. The system was neither efficient nor genuine. It was cynical in the worst ways, understanding the nuances of language yet feigning ignorance. In reducing a twelve-page document into a fistful of general sentences, countless meaningful sentences disappeared into the translator's editorialized synopsis. Even worse, the documents read like a unified whole when they were in fact the result of a multiday, sometimes weeklong ordeal. They were temporally misleading because the time between two adjacent questions could be anything from five minutes to five hours to the following day. There is no way to tell what happened in between.

Making matters worse, the finalized version of any given transcript experienced so many revisions—cutting, pasting, rewording, and organizing—that the resultant document represented less of the suspect's actual testimony and more of the interrogator's editorial skills. Many times, the redraft process resulted in logical leaps that seemed terribly contrived. For example, when Kishi was questioned at the Fukuoka Legal Section, McKnight asked him numerous times whether he wanted to add anything to prior statements. The first time the question was put forward, Kishi told a story about a conversation he had with Komori regarding the use of anesthetics during the POW operations. Immediately after the story concluded, as if fishing for a specific response, McKnight asked again, "Is there anything else you would like to add?" This time Kishi related a story about a conversation he had with Komori and Sato at Kaikosha Hospital. McKnight brushed it aside and asked again, "Do you have anything further you would like to add?" Finally, he received the answer he had hoped to hear—an admission that Komori had served human liver at the Kaikosha Hospital dining hall.[14]

The eventual admission by Kishi deems a closer look because the questions that arise can be applied to the majority of the Kaikosha Hospital suspects. If Kishi were being genuine and did not know what information McKnight wanted to hear, the failure to discuss the liver-eating incident right away could mean three things: (1) Kishi did not think it a very serious affair—something highly unlikely considering the fact that an American prisoner's liver had been devoured: or (2) he was hiding it—which raises the question of why the sudden willingness to implicate himself by simple "Do you have anything else to add" type questions; or (3) the incident did not happen and the answer represented a coerced and doctored response—keep in mind the "process" of taking down statements.

The truth probably lies somewhere between the Legal Section's and the Kaikosha Hospital doctors' versions. Interrogations are not social calls, nor should they be. One must go on the assumption that the interrogee will not be entirely cooperative and forthcoming. In this case, a simple please won't suffice. All it will get you are denials. That is why it is safe to assume that there had to be some degree of heavy handedness on the part of Tait and McKnight. It is equally safe to assume that they did not allow things to spiral out of control. On the doctors' end, it is safe to assume that had they been guilty, they would not have come clean immediately, and that considering the fact that they felt the initial pressure of being under suspicion, any Legal Section tactic would feel a hundred times crueler. The one thing that must not be assumed is that innocent people under unrelenting questioning will not go to extraordinary lengths to end an ordeal. Herein lies Case 420's liver-eating aspect's complication. It never happened.

While there is no doubt that a luncheon occurred in which most, if not all, of the accused attended, the charge of cannibalism and the circumstances surrounding it do not hold. Too many factual gaps and inconsistencies exist, even after transcript editing. The suspects who conceded guilt—Tsurumaru, Kishi, Kanehisa, Matake, Ito, and Oda—all told similar stories but only after a considerable amount of leading questions. And even then, their stories never matched on key issues.

One such issue was that not one account of the guests matched perfectly. In fact, from Tsurumaru's initial testimony until the final interrogation, the list consistently grew. With each new interrogation, a new set of suspects had to be brought in for questioning. Tsurumaru named five people, including himself. By the time Matake made his statement, the list had mysteriously grown to eleven diners, including himself. What sticks out most, however, is that initial testimonies failed to mention two figures integral to the evening's action: Shiokawa and Sasaki. The accounts that mention Shiokawa have her serving sake and in some cases the human liver itself. Sasaki's omission raises questions because Matake—the guest of honor at the lunch party—supposedly made a toast in his honor.

Not only were the doctors unable to recall who was present, they failed to reach a consensus regarding the seating plan. In fact, people who supposedly sat next to each other don't even remember sitting next to each other. Tsurumaru drew a seating diagram in which he sat next to Ito Akira. Ito, however, fails to mention that Tsurumaru—the man who sat next to him at the gathering—was even present, though he does offer a decidedly longer list of suspects than Tsurumaru.

Another unresolved fact revolved around the meal itself. Tsurumaru stated definitively that two serving plates sat on the table: one containing thin slices of pig's liver and another with thick slices of human liver. Both dishes were soaked in soy sauce. Matake recalled a single "special" meat dish being served in addition to bowls of rice. Oda remembered sitting at the table with two separate plates in front of him and a sake bowl. He stated that a dish of liver in soy sauce had been served. He also claimed that vegetables were served with the liver. Finally, Kishi, Komori's supposed partner in crime, stated without a doubt that liver and only liver was served at the lunch.

Yet another major fissure in the liver-eating story regarded Matake. His presence at the gathering functioned as a key temporal indicator. As the guest of honor, his appearance was one of the few testimonial constants in a sea of inconsistencies. According to Matake, himself, he attended the luncheon during late May or early June when he had returned to Kaikosha Hospital for a visit. All but one statement corroborated this. The only dissenting opinion belonged to Tsurumaru.

Then there were the little things that cumulatively added up to a big thing. Everybody had different versions of how, when, and to whom Komori first said that human liver was being served. Surely, something as significant as this could be corroborated by at least two people. Kishi stated that everyone first sampled the liver after he prompted them to eat. Komori informed the guests about the liver's origin only after they ate. Kishi went on to say that when Tsurumaru arrived, Komori offered him liver, which he subsequently ate. After being told what the meat was, Tsurumaru continued to eat, unfazed by the gruesome revelation. According to Ito Akira, the liver had already been served when Momota queried Komori as to the meat's origin. Komori responded that it was from a POW. Matake offered yet another version. He stated that Komori announced that the liver was from an American POW. After hearing the truth, everyone ate, knowing full well where the meat came from.

Still another point of contention laid in the role played by Shiokawa, the Kaikosha Hospital head nurse, during the course of the evening. Tsurumaru left her out of his story. Kishi stated that she was not present, though she might have shown up after the meal. Oda remembered Shiokawa being present and serving sake. Finally, Ito and Matake corroborated each other when they declared that Shiokawa not only served sake, she also carried the plate of sliced human liver around the room, holding it like a priceless artifact, and served each guest—a terribly macabre image.

How do you account for the inconsistencies? More significantly and equally puzzling, how do you account for the facts? Corroborated facts and inconsistent fictions accumulate as the testimony goes on and the story grows more robust. They indicate a steady attempt at constructing a story with a definite goal in mind. The number and roles of characters grow with every testimony. The transcripts inadvertently chronicle how the liver-eating story evolved from Tsurumaru's stripped-down version into an elaborate, bacchanalian orgy of Oriental savagery embodied in an act of cannibalism.

As a stand-alone text, the liver-eating story builds on itself the way many of literature's great tales come to fruition—from a slim ur-narrative to an overweight story. In time, discerning the original story from the final product becomes impossible. The old story builds on itself to produce a new one that quickly turns stale until someone adds something that makes it fresh again. The constant interrogations provided the ideal milieu for the evolutionary process. A "fact" discovered in one interrogation became a leading question posed to the following suspect, which he acknowledged and added to create a new and slightly fattier fact. This new rendition underwent a similar process with yet another suspect, ad nauseam. Shiokawa's emergence in the narrative and the Kaikosha dinner guests' discovery of the liver's source exemplify the process.

Shiokawa's presence at the lunch party emerged midway through the liver-eating investigation. The earliest account (Tsurumaru's) failed to mention her completely. While the possibility existed that Tsurumaru's tardy arrival at the affair caused him to miss her, that notion was quickly dispelled during the course of the very next interrogation. After initially failing to mention Shiokawa, he reneged and raised the possibility that she attended the affair. However, he stated that if she was present, Shiokawa showed up toward the tail end of the luncheon, well after the meal had been served. If she arrived that late and Tsurumaru arrived during the end of the meal itself, logic suggests that they would have seen each other—that is, if they had in fact been present. It seems entirely plausible that Shiokawa was not there at all. Not until Ito Akira's testimony on July 11 does Shiokawa play a significant role in the narrative. According to Ito, Komori informed her of the meat's origin ahead of time, then coaxed her into acting as the luncheon's waitress. From being a literal nonpresence, she magically becomes the omnipresent dispenser of human flesh. Subsequent interrogations appear to corroborate Shiokawa's presence and her role.

The emergence of Shiokawa gave the liver-eating incident a credibility boost. For a culture steeped in ritual, protocol, and propriety, a celebratory luncheon without a hostess figure made no sense. Tsurumaru and Kishi's early versions, therefore, carried a significant weakness that could eventually negate everything else. Something as basic as having someone serve the sake and food needed to be included. Its absence called the existence of the entire lunch party into question and offered the defense a possible point of attack. It was essentially a hole that needed to be filled. Ito's testimony did just that.

Shiokawa's presence buttressed the prosecution's case on a subconscious level. All at once, Shiokawa became the nurturing mother-wife figure tending to her family, serving and feeding them, perhaps at some sacrifice to her own well-being. From that point, Shiokawa's character mutates slightly into that of the Edenic Eve. Though still a nurturer, she becomes the temptress dispensing the forbidden fruit—in this incarnation the taboo of human flesh cooked and seasoned in soy sauce—to the naive party of men. Like Eve and the serpent, Shiokawa's actions stem directly from Komori's influence. Komori, the serpent, and Satan—orchestrators of evil deeds—unite under the liver-eating narrative. It is a tale that Legal Section investigators, members of the International Prosecution Section, and ultimately the War Crimes Commission had been weaned on since their childhoods and had internalized since then. With or without their conscious acknowledgment, Shiokawa's presence bolstered the case's credibility. They'd heard the story somewhere before, just in another form and with different characters. It made perfect sense.

The evolution of Komori's revelation about the liver's source demonstrates another ex post facto adjustment to Tsurumaru's original text. According to the initial account, Komori proudly boasts that the liver belonged to a human being. However, he never divulges the liver's source. The very next interrogation addresses that discrepancy. Kishi's statement adds to Tsurumaru's by having Komori state that the liver was not just from a human being but from a prisoner of war. Ito corroborated Kishi's recollection. After the Ito interrogation, Matake conveniently adjusted the story. In his version, Komori informed the group that the meat was an American POW's liver. It would take one final testimony to finalize the key revelation. During the July 17 interrogation of Oda Toyura, he stated for the first time that Komori specifically declared that the liver being served had been taken from a POW who had been operated on at Kyushu Imperial University. All of the disparate pieces—human liver, taken from a POW, taken during operations at Kyushu Imperial University—finally came together after five interrogations that saw a little bit more ambiguity being squeezed out at each step.

Like the emergence of Shiokawa at the lunch, the revelation that the liver came from an American POW who had been operated on at Kyushu Imperial University significantly bolstered the prosecution's case. It established without a doubt that cannibalism occurred. The constant allusions to human liver proved this beyond a reasonable doubt. The revelation's final form proved incredibly useful for both phases of the trial. In the most immediate sense, it showed that the Kaikosha doctors knew where the special meat came from and willingly ate it. Even more significantly, it indirectly corroborated the facts in the experimental operations phase. It solved the mystery of what Komori did with the liver that he removed and walked around the university showing everyone. He didn't make bedbug poison with it; he ate it.

The slipshod creation of the liver-eating story stemmed from the a priori assumptions and expectations of an entire section's worth of Westerners. Granting Team 420 the benefit of the doubt, they saw what they wanted to see. The way in which facts were obtained and later synthesized reflected the desire to support what they believed to be the truth rather than inquiring into what was the actual truth. They knew that the Japanese were animals before coming into contact with them. Centuries of Western culture, decades of American isolationism, and years of War Department propaganda told them as much. What they believed they discovered simply added to the catalog supporting a racist misconception. From an investigative point of view, Team 420 followed a false lead to its completion—a situation exacerbated by the Kaikosha Hospital doctors' willing though no-less-false self-implications.

While the final versions of the liver-eating testimonies resembled conclusive admissions of guilt and appeared to chronicle an incident of extraordinary depravity, the consistencies and inconsistencies virtually canceled each other out. None of the testimonies matched to any impressive degree. In fact, each statement appeared to have at least one unique fact. In many instances, it came at the expense of a previously stated fact. While far from a perfect scenario, as a cumulative whole, testimonies served their purposes. It was not essential that they express the same thing. It mattered more that some of them express certain key points. As long as a working narrative took shape, that was all that mattered. The onus of a final synthesis belonged to the prosecution and would be made during the course of the trial.

• • •

In August, the Legal Section turned their attention back to the people directly involved in the Kyushu Imperial University atrocities. Their brief but surprisingly fruitful foray into the dark side of human nature left them with a clearer understanding of the people they dealt with on a daily basis. Savages. The doctors locked in Sugamo Prison, the academics at Kyushu Imperial University, Komori, Ishiyama, Sato, Yokoyama, the tattered-dress woman shuffling through the local market, the demobilized Jap soldier, the hunch-backed daikon-faced old man, and the dirty sun-scarred child dancing for GI chocolate—all savages. It all made perfect sense in occupied Japan.

15

Closure: September 1947–March 1948

In the year that had passed since Marvin last heard from the Legal Section, his life continued on its oft-interrupted push toward normalcy. The sharp-ice vestiges of his lost crew and time in captivity thawed and dripped into memory's drain. Without a doubt, time healed whatever emotional fissures his experiences created. It gently molded First Lieutenant Marvin S. Watkins, lead pilot of a B-29 Superfortress and former POW, into Mr. Marvin S. Watkins, Colonial Heights resident and Virginia State Highway employee. Mercy and providence finally descended on a man who had given so much to his country, his family, and people he knew only through association.

Marvin's relationship with Beatrice played a major role in his quest for postwar absolution. She reinvigorated him, and, in turn, he brought out the best in her. He took a somewhat sheltered young woman and groomed her into the consummate Southern belle—appreciative of the finer things in life yet comfortable moving through the mundane cups of coffee and electric irons required by daily life. During their first years together prior to marriage, they set down the blueprints for a partnership that would span half a century.

For the first time since his return to Church Road, everything seemed to be in place for Marvin. On September 10, 1947, a telecom from Colonel Alva Carpenter was transmitted to the Civil Affairs Division:

Request you contact former First Lieutenant Marvin S. Watkins, 0801224, last known address Church Road, Va., and secure his services as a witness. He is the sole survivor of a B-29 crew shot down over Japan in which six of those survived the wreck of the aircraft were subjected to fatal experimental operations by medical personnel of the Kyushu Imperial University. He can testify as to their condition after the crash and as to the fate of some 39 or 41 prisoners who were killed at the University or at Western Army Headquarters, Fukuoka. This case will involve some 30-odd Japanese accused.[1]

Two weeks after the initial correspondence with Marvin, September 14, the Legal Section received a reply from CAD. Watkins was available whenever they desired his presence.[2]

In an attempt to account for the remains of whatever members of the Watkins crew had been unaccounted for, Team 420 dove into yet another investigation to supplement the multitude of in-progress phases. The fates of the four fliers who died prior to the experiments needed to be determined conclusively. It was an indirect way of declaring which members of the crew had died during the experiments, since it would narrow the possibilities from eleven to seven. Robert Miller assumed complete responsibility for ascertaining the facts.

Fortunately for Miller, a major portion of the work had already been completed by the Quartermaster Graves Registration, whose responsibility it was to find American soldiers' remains and grant them proper burial. They filed detailed reports documenting everything from the original location of burial to complete autopsy information for each corpse.

Yet another puzzle faced Miller. He needed to decipher the identity of each flier, then determine how each one died. In order to do this, he would have to interrogate every person who had come into contact with the fliers before and after their deaths. This entailed questioning the local police in each prefecture in which POWs had been captured as well as the numerous villagers who had formed impromptu search parties immediately after the B-29's descent.

Four unidentified American corpses were buried in Yokohama Cemetery, which was designated by the United States as an American cemetery on foreign soil. Theirs was a tortured and drawn-out journey from life in Guam to death in Kyushu and finally to rest in Honshu. Yet, their plight remained far from complete. Without identities, the steadily decomposing bodies—unclaimed by friends, family, or government—belonged solely to the earth. It wasn't that nobody wanted them; it was simply impossible to determine a loved one from a stranger.

Two bodies were disinterred from a public cemetery in Miyiji-mura, nearby the crash site. Local police positively identified the remains—known respectively as X-1 (X-549) and X-2 (X-550)—as those belonging to B-29 fliers whose plane crashed on May 5, 1945.[3] Members of the Graves Registration filed formal disinterment reports that eventually found their way to Robert Miller's possession.

Exhumation of the bodies revealed that X-1, while in a state of decay, had not progressed to late-stage decay. His nose looked like a nose, and his cheek, a cheek.[4] X-2, however, exhibited heavy late-stage decomposition. Tender flesh failed and fared less favorably in this instance.[5] X-1 had been stripped naked postmortem. A deformed bullet slug nestled deep in his skull. It shattered white bone and shredded his gray matter. Because of the torn skin at the bullet's point of entry, it was more prone to decay than other parts of his body left intact. Patches of flesh had been eaten away from his head, leaving the jagged wound exposed.[6]

Unlike X-1, X-2 remained partially clothed. His government-issued khaki shirt and woolen undershirt still clung to his body as tight in death as in life. But his flesh did not exhibit a similar loyalty. It had already embarked on its journey back to the elemental world. Very little remained of the man he had been. Only clues of his death remained. His body suffered from extensive physical abuse. His skull was fractured—shattered like a glass orb in a soft velvet sack; there must have been severe internal bleeding from injuries. Whatever had killed him possessed great strength.[7]

The other two crew members' bodies, X-3 and X-4, lay in separate shallow, makeshift graves in the Japanese countryside—most likely in the vicinity of their deaths. X-3's grave sat a mile up the side of one of Kyushu's terraced mountains surrounded by waving trees, blankets of grass, and Milky Way clouds. His badly decomposed body, however, continued suffering. In life and death, the violence never ended. The bones in his body indicated severe trauma, particularly to the head. His skull appeared as if it had cracked in half, disjoining top and bottom along an equator of destruction. The area under his eyes—cheek and nose bones—no longer held any form. Nothing remained—only a disturbing bullet hole in the young soldier's temple.[8]

X-4, the final body that the Graves Registration exhumed, rested two miles from the mountainside grave of X-3. As with most of the corpses, decay had already set in and advanced considerably. His right hand and foot had been completely severed from his body. There seemed to be some indication of abdominal trauma perhaps inflicted during a struggle and stab wound. Beyond that, there was very little hard information.[9]

Between December 1 and December 5, 1947, Miller conducted an on-the-spot investigation of the facts surrounding the deaths of the four crew members. He organized an efficient task force consisting of local police officials from Kumamoto and Oita who tended to the more tedious, preparatory aspects of the investigation. They made preliminary surveys of both background facts and witnesses. They questioned scores of villagers regarding the plane crash and capture of the American fliers. In carrying out these tasks, they helped free Miller from the laborious but necessary steps that would only have distracted him from synthesizing the bigger picture. They acted as filters and screeners siphoning out the excess fat—waste matter that sucked hours away—and saved Miller from wasting time on unnecessary interrogations. And even with the entire process in place, Miller managed to interrogate over eighty local villagers who possessed credible information pertaining to the fate of the Watkins crew.[10]

The screening and questioning process entailed several steps. Investigators first asked witnesses to outline the details of their knowledge of the events surrounding the crash. Similar outlines were produced regarding the capture and murder of the Watkins crew. Without the aid of photographs, each witness was asked to describe the American crew member from memory, paying particular attention to height, weight, clothing, personal effects, and any other features that might differentiate one crew member from another. Immediately after being provided with a description, the investigator showed pictures of each flier to the witnesses and asked whether they could match any of the pictures with the flier they previously described. If the witnesses showed promise, the investigator performed a more deliberate and detailed inquiry in order to establish how much credence should be placed on their testimony.[11]

From the dozens of interrogations conducted, only eight witnesses possessed the necessary mixture of credibility, information, and coherence. They were the only witnesses from whom sworn written statements were taken.[12] And while the questioning and fact-finding efforts of Miller and his Japanese assistants seemed to shed considerable light on the fate of each flier, there was something lacking. Miller's attempts never hit the target dead-on. Somehow, they veered to the left or right, missed a little too high or low, or lacked the force to make any impact. The mostly contradictory recollections, muddied by the mixture of time and unfamiliarity with Western faces, often complicated the process and confused investigators. While the facts surrounding the murders fell into place, a common consensus could never be reached when it came to picking out photographs to identify the fliers. Miller managed to ascertain everything except what he came to the area expecting to find: the identities of the four fliers.

Prior to his initial arrival, the task at Miller's feet appeared deceptively simple: obtain positive identification for each of the bodies. Even the process seemed like it would be straightforward, especially compared to the increasingly frustrating labyrinth that Case 420 had become. In reality, this phase of the investigation would bear fruit but only when the final cog in the investigative engine joined him. Miller waited for the last American man who had seen the entire Watkins crew alive.

Marvin Watkins returned to Fukuoka in November 1947 for the first time since his liberation,[13] but it wasn't until February of the following year that he visited the site where his plane crashed.[14] For twenty-one days—February 9 to March 2—Marvin traveled with Robert Miller and a Legal Section translator. During the course of the month, they flew all over Japan, from Tokyo and Kyoto to Fukuoka and Karatsu. The overwhelming majority of their time, however, was spent in Fukuoka speaking with the same witnesses Miller had questioned two months earlier.[15] This time around, with Marvin Watkins's personal knowledge of his crew, the process of identifying the fliers went smoother.

Miller's main strategy revolved around utilizing features particular to each flier. If they wore rings—whether marriage, graduation, or for decoration—it could narrow the field considerably. The same held true for something as simple as a necklace. Hair length, skin color, physical build, moles, bruises—they could all help. In addition, Miller had in his possession a group photograph of the Watkins crew taken a month before their descent into Kyushu. It represented a far better likeness of the fliers than the individual photos that had been taken years before.[16] Ideally, it would help the witnesses in their identifications. But in the end, all Miller could do was hope for the best. He had already established the facts surrounding their captures.

Marvin spent nearly two weeks in Fukuoka, from February 17 to the February 29.[17] Together with Miller and Nakahara, he ventured into the Kyushu countryside. The land that had been blurred by his descent from the sky lacked the urgent sense of misery and danger it once held. While it might not have seemed like nirvana, it must have carried an odd tranquility. The rotten mushroom plume of smoke creeping from the metal ash heap of a broken B-29 gave way to the green puffs of tree leaves and grass growing in the horizon. The columns of mountains stretching to the clouds, almost supporting them, represented majesty rather than menace. The bushes and ravines that once signified possible hiding places from a wicked enemy became what they always were—bushes and ravines. Even the people who chased after Marvin with swords, spears, and venom that only the devil could understand must have seemed simple and human.

And then there were the murderers, softened by years and peacetime. A cocktail of fear, hatred, and vengeance made monsters out of common peasants. Their destructive and cruel wartime actions screamed out in defiance to nature, society, and the world. Killing made them the ultimate upstarts, taking what was not theirs to take and doing so with bold authority. But now, when summoned by an American investigator, they obeyed like children awaiting punishment.

Marvin accompanied Robert Miller during the investigation and aided in the interrogations.[18] He met with the men who killed his

The Watkins crew.
Top, left to right: First Lieutenant Marvin S. Watkins, Second Lieutenant William Fredericks, Second Lieutenant Charles Shingledecker, Second Lieutenant Charles Kearns, Second Lieutenant Dale Plambeck.
Bottom, left to right: Corporal Robert Johnson, Staff Sergeant Teddy Ponczka, Corporal Robert Williams, Corporal Leon Czarnecki, Corporal Leo Oeinck, Corporal John Colehower.

crew, sitting close enough to spit on them and stab at their eyes, throats, and hearts with his pen. The satisfaction of clamping his hands down on their necks would have been immeasurably satisfying, yet Marvin tempered his need for vengeance in order to give his crew and their families the closure they deserved. More than revenging their deaths, it was the greatest thing Marvin could do to honor them. And that was what he did.

All the while Marvin revisited his past, he maintained a constant link to his present and future. He and Beatrice wrote each other daily.[19] No matter where he stayed the night, he taped a picture of her on the wall.[20] It was important to remember that someone waited for him at home. A good girl missed him. It meant the world and gave strength and comfort during a time when he flirted with a past that could wrap and swallow him at any moment. If he remained afloat and didn't plunge into the swamp of depression, self-doubt, and guilt, Beatrice's presence in his life undoubtedly played an instrumental role. And if closure—sweet peace—ever emerged from Marvin's return to Japan, her hand helped guide him to it.

On February 26, 1948, with the investigation in its final stages, Marvin Watkins took another step closer to being freed from the past. He and Robert Miller sat down together, as friends and partners, and conducted a final interrogation regarding his crew, the circumstances around the crash, and their fates. This time, however, a significant portion of the questions related to the four crew members they had been investigating.[21]

After running through the facts behind his capture one last time, Miller queried Marvin about his crew.

"I want you to describe in detail the physical characteristics and give any other information that might help in the identification of the four men from your crew who were killed before being captured. I'm referring to Shingledecker, Kearns, Oeinck, and Johnson."[22]

Marvin's chest expanded and his shoulders rose slightly as he readied his answers in his head. He looked down at the photo that he and his crew had taken at North Field Airfield.

"I have in my possession a crew picture which was taken on Guam in April 1945. This is approximately one month before our crew was shot down. The men wore clothing, similar to that shown in the picture, on the flight. This photograph indicates very closely the way these men looked at the time we were shot down, and it also gives an opportunity to compare the various men."

Marvin named and identified each member of his crew. Half stood while the other half kneeled. Johnson, Ponczka, Williams, Czarnecki, Oeinck, and Colehower in the front row. Marvin, Fredericks, Shingledecker, Kearns, and Plambeck stood up. Behind the crew, their B-29 was serenely waiting to take to the sky.

"Can you describe Robert Johnson for me?" Miller asked.

"Corporal Johnson was about five feet eight or nine inches tall. He weighed approximately 145 to 150 pounds. He was well filled out and his face was quite round and full. He had a decided squint. He had very blond hair and was light in complexion. He was definitely the fairest man in the crew. He was unmarried. I am not certain of his religion, but I do not think he was Catholic."

"Did he have any accessories, like a watch?"

"Only officers were issued watches, and he had to wear his personal watch."

"Other accessories?"

"I do not remember rings, medals, or other similar items which might serve to identify him. I know of no other characteristics which might describe him."

"Let's move on now," Miller said. "Tell me about Kearns."

"Lieutenant Kearns was about five feet ten inches tall. He had a husky build with a large body and a deep, wide chest. He weighed approximately 180 pounds. His stomach was quite large. His hair was light brown and quite wavy. I would say that it was about three inches or less in length. In contrast, Johnson's hair was cut much shorter, was very straight, and had a tendency to grow forward."

"Was Kearns married?"

"Yes. Kearns was married and wore a wedding ring," Marvin replied. "He was the only member of the crew that smoked cigars, and he was the only one of these four who smoked a pipe. I do not think Johnson smoked."

"What was his religion?"

"Kearns was a Catholic and wore a small medal around his neck. I believe he wore an issue watch which was round, black-faced, and quite large. It had a sweep second hand."

"Are there any other characteristics that you can remember that might help differentiate him from the others?"

Marvin thought for a moment, then replied, "His ears were close-set to his head. I know of no wounds, scars, or other distinguishing marks."

The conversation then shifted to Shingledecker. As with the rest, Marvin started with a brief description of him.

"Shingledecker was about the same height as Kearns but of a more slight build. He weighed about 150 pounds. He had black wavy hair which was slightly longer than a crew cut. It curled to his head slightly, so I do not know just how long it was."

"Did he wear any rings or other accessories?"

"He was married but did not wear a wedding ring. He also wore an officer's watch."

"Is there anything else you'd like to add?"

"On the day of our flight, I had a leather jacket with a zipper. It was waist length. I loaned it to him while we were still in the plane. Later, when I was captured and held in a stockade, I saw my jacket in a pile of clothing being thrown off the truck in which we were brought to the stockade. I am not certain that it was taken from this truck, but it was on the ground next to the truck when we got off. I recognized this jacket as mine because of the color and the fact that it had first lieutenant bars sewed on it. As far as I know, the only other crew member who had a leather jacket was Fredericks."

Marvin stopped but immediately started again. "Of the four men who were killed immediately after jumping from the plane, Shingledecker's hair was the darkest. I do not know what his religion was."

"Did he smoke?"

"Yes, cigarettes."

"And did he have any features that might distinguish him?"

"I do not know of any distinguishing marks or characteristics. Of the four, he had the darkest and heaviest beard. I would estimate that he had not shaved for at least eighteen hours before crashing and his beard would have been noticeable by that time."

Oeinck was the last crew member to be discussed.

"Oeinck was about five feet eight inches and of build similar to Johnson's. He had dark brown hair, straight, and with a crew cut about one and a half to two inches long. His hair was fine and fluffed up. It did not lay close to his head the way Shingledecker's did."

"Was he married?"

"Yes. He was married and I believe he wore a gold wedding band. I don't know what his religion was."

"Any distinguishing features?"

"I know of no distinguishing marks or characteristics other than those listed."

Miller asked one final question.

"Did any of these men have an injury before the crash?"

"Oeinck had athlete's foot and was receiving medical treatment for it. He had a bad case of it, but I do not know if he had any bandages."

Marvin's recollection that Oeinck had athlete's foot severe enough to receive medical treatment was the one fact necessary to cement the other identifications. Everything fell into place. The mystery had been solved.

Okubo Koretsugo, an old farmer, stood in his rice paddy in Aso-gun at 9:30 A.M. The spring sun sang across the Kyushu countryside and a whisper tickled the back of his neck. He surveyed his plot. It was good because it was his. Rice was his country's staple, its most important crop. Rice and life blended into a single symbol that Westerners could never understand. A gentle overhead rumble pulled his attention from his crop, and when it raged into a roar, Okubo ran for cover.[23] He heard about the bombings. He knew about Tokyo and Nagoya and Nagasaki.

A squadron of American B-29s ploughed through the clear skies. They were not alone, however. Japanese fighter planes swooped in and out of the bombers' firing range, pumping bullets through the flying fortresses' steel skin. A dog fight, Okubo thought. He watched in fearful amazement as a Japanese fighter, one of his country's own, pounded a bomber into flames and submission. Soon, another fighter swooped right into the nose of the crippled plane.

As American fliers bailed out, Iwashita Kiyoni, another farmer, focused on a soldier. It was Second Lieutenant Howard T. Shingledecker. He just sat in the sky. And as the hungry fighter planes circled through the air, it almost seemed cruel that he could not come down quicker. The Zeroes locked in on him and fired with their armor-piercing guns. A shot from any one of those bullets would shatter a hole in him. They missed. But as they dove toward him, the pilots made sure to come as close to their target as possible. One of the planes came close enough to shred the floss-like suspension lines that connected him to his parachute.

Takanami Koretoshi saw the same thing, and when Shingledecker plunged from the sky, the rice farmer rushed from his paddy to where the body came down. A crowd had gathered around Shingledecker's twisted body and Takanami pushed them back. He roped off the area and waited for the authorities to arrive. Four farmers carried Shingledecker's body to Yamaga Town Hall, where it stayed until its burial.

Second Lieutenant Kearns landed safely and hid in the woods. Fear must have dominated his judgment, because without being spotted, he fired two shots at Uchiyanagi Chikara. Armed with a shotgun, the Japanese hunter reacted the way he did when any target drew his attention. He turned, aimed, and shot in one motion. It was reaction without thought, and by the time he realized what had happened, Kearns lay on the ground and clutched his buckshot-pierced face. He writhed in agony. He could not be saved. Uchiyanagi then grabbed a scythe from a nearby scarecrow and stabbed Kearns until the agony disappeared. His body was carried to Yamaga Town Hall and placed with Shingledecker.

Staff Sergeant Teddy Ponczka did not get far from the crash site and was apprehended almost immediately. Okuchi Takeichi found him squatting in a rice paddy surrounded by screaming townsfolk. He pushed them away. "Don't hurt him," Okuchi screamed. The crowd backed away. Okuchi helped Ponczka out of the paddy and took his gun. He saw that the American was wounded and arranged for a stretcher to be made. For thirty minutes, Okuchi chased away angry countrymen using a stick. Keishi Shoida eventually helped place Ponczka on the stretcher and carried him to the Takeda police station where a doctor treated his wounds.

Shiga Mitsuma was the mayor of Miyahi village, the town where Second Lieutenant William Fredericks landed. A cacophony of voices drew him to the spot where the pilot stood, leaning against a rock and surrounded by people. He ordered the crowd not to hurt Fredericks, who greeted the mayor by handing over his pistol. Shiga took the American to the town office, allowed him to rest, and fed him. Although Fredericks appeared to be wounded, he was not in pain.

Corporal Robert Williams evaded capture the longest. For the entire evening of May 5, he wandered through mountain and forest. By daybreak, fatigue and hunger conquered the radio operator's will, and as Watanabe Kosakuma walked his cow down a road, the American flier jumped in front of him. Williams gestured that he was hungry by rubbing his stomach. Nonaka Hidori met Watanabe and took the prisoner to his house. He fed Williams, then helped him look for his parachute. Williams was taken to Miyaji village and turned over to the Kempei Tai.

Corporal Leo Oeinck descended in the outskirts of a small village named Hoshiwa. He wandered toward town, making it about two thousand meters before being confronted by a number of locals. A struggle ensued and Oeinck was shot by farmers Iwashita Tsunshiko and Sato Tokihiro. However, he did not die immediately and lay on the ground moaning in pain. Otsuka Asashi approached him and stabbed him repeatedly—whether it was out of mercy or vengeance, only he knew the truth. Unlike the other deaths, this one proved very bloody. Utsonomiya Kameguma and Kai Yoshihiko volunteered to help bury Oeinck. They stripped him naked and gave him a proper Japanese burial.

Witnesses from Hoshiwa village in Minami Oguni-mura recalled seeing Corporal Leon Czarnecki descend from a hill near a forest. The Civilian National Defense Corps searched for him but could not locate him. Finally, he was captured in Oita-ken and brought to the Kempei Tai.

Ito Sadao saw a blond-haired American in the woods at Minami Oguni-mura but could not prevent him from running away. A little later, it was Sato Tokihiro, aided by Ishibashi Yohito, who captured Corporal John C. Colehower. Before Colehower was brought to the Kempei Tai in Miyaji, the town's assistant mayor talked to him and fed him. Soon afterward, Colehower was handed over to the proper authorities.

Goto Shigetoshi and Ino Sakima apprehended Second Lieutenant Dale Plambeck. Sakamoto Isamu lived near Oginokusa village, where Plambeck was captured. When he arrived at the scene, he saw Plambeck being beaten by a crowd. He stepped between the assailants and the American, saving his life for the time being. Ino Yoshima fed Plambeck, then accompanied him to the Kempei Tai in Miyagi.

When Corporal Robert Johnson drifted to the earth, he may as well have fallen to hell. He knew about Japan; it was not like home. He knew about the Japs; they were aliens and animals and killed children. They lived on rice and were proud of it. They mastered the art of the double cross and ate raw food. He knew about them because the army warned him about the Japs. When the crowd around him grew and all but one of the bullets in his gun had been fired fruitlessly, he lay down his gun. But then he picked it up and gripped it tight, and before the Japs could take another step toward him, Johnson turned the barrel of the gun to his temple. It was over. That was war.

The revelation that Oeinck suffered from a severe case of athlete's foot proved to be the key fact. Everything fell into place once Miller made a definite identification of one crew member. Oeinck represented the key. Eyewitness testimony created a degree of confusion between Oeinck and Kearns. Both had been shot, but there had been conflicting reports as to who had died and in what manner. Most witnesses, in fact, picked Kearns as the man shot and stabbed. However, during the interrogation of Sato Tsutsumi, he stated that the American he had killed had a bandage on one of his toes. That fact outweighed all the other facial identifications. There was no way to confuse a bandage. There was nothing culturally different, not like a foreigner's face. With Oeinck's ID and fate established, Kearns's was as well.

The two remaining deaths fell into place as well. In fact, they had been the most conclusive prior to the Oeinck revelation. Eyewitness accounts of the suicide indicated that the man who killed himself had light hair and a heavy build. Some even described the man as having a double chin. Johnson's remains—heavier than the others, light hair, and a gunshot wound in the head—corroborated their statements.

All that remained was Shingledecker. By elimination, he was the final one. However, like Johnson, Shingledecker's identity had been tentatively established before Oeinck's and Kearns's. The several witnesses who saw his body and those who carried it to be buried picked out his picture consistently. Each witness recalled that one of his legs had been broken so badly that it twisted in the opposite direction and hung awkwardly when he was being carried. The only corpse without a gunshot wound had a severely fractured left leg. It was Shingledecker.

The crew members who had not made it to Western Army Headquarters had been accounted for, consequently solidifying the identities of the men who died at Kyushu Imperial University.

For Marvin, the experience provided further closure. Though he had one more stop left on his trip, it was merely a formality. The Yokohama District Courthouse would only be a detour on his way home. He had nothing but the future now.

16

The Trial: 1948

Case 420—the Kyushu Imperial University atrocities—went to trial on March 11, 1948, in Yokohama, a city just outside the limits of Tokyo proper.[1] Each superficially disparate piece of the puzzle that started with a chance revelation by the Kurume Counter Intelligence Corps was gathered in one place. The time had come to organize and assemble the portrait for the entire world's viewing and judgment. When it was finished, history would decide the ultimate fates of all of the participants, American and Japanese.

For the first time, the entire surviving cast of characters—the accused, Legal Section investigators, the prosecution, the defense—directly involved with Case 420 sat in the same room. The key players investigated by Team 420 during the last two years listened in helpless submission while their names—Sato, Fukushima, Yokoyama, Aihara, Mori, Morimoto, Senba, Hirako, Tsutsui, to name a few—and charges against them rang through the courtroom like a church bell. From the investigative team, only Tait was present. Most of the other investigators had either returned to headquarters in Tokyo or could not be in the courtroom since they would be testifying as prosecution witnesses at some point during the trial.

Watching over the entire proceeding was General MacArthur's man, Colonel Alva Carpenter. He would keep a close eye on the facts being brought into the public forum. Because of the proximity of this case to matters that Washington currently struggled to keep from world attention, it became priority that certain lines of questioning be stymied, regardless of their pertinence, probative value, and effectiveness. The trial could not be about the wider, systemic biological experimentation program; the trial had to put on legal blinders and focus solely on the direct facts—local and university clinic specific—and not on the circumstances that made the murders possible. More importantly, Carpenter was there to make sure that the international press presented the Kyushu Imperial University vivisection trial to the world in its most sanitized version—as the cannibalism trial. If a successful diversion of emphasis—not lying but a classic propaganda technique—could be effectively employed, the chances of the trial and the murders being associated with Ishii and others became negligible.

It had the makings of a genuine courtroom battle, not an overdramatized, quick-cut, eye-line, match-laden Hollywood production. There would be no key witness to provide crippling testimony, no surprise declarations by domestic servants, and no bush-league guerrilla-warfare ambushes with hidden evidence. The Kyushu Imperial University atrocities trial moved in the real world and under the restrictions of real laws. The prosecution's task involved laying out a step-by-step, detailed, logical, and conclusive case supported less by emotion and more by analytical rigor.

Before the prosecution could even attempt to address the facts surrounding the operations, they had to set up several key events that led up to the actual murders. First, they had to identify the victims, the majority being the Watkins crew. The next step entailed establishing the role of Western Army officials in setting the precedent for the murders. This entailed showing the military situation at Western Army during the late stages of the war, staff policy, the position of responsibility within the command, and the acts committed by Western Army members. Only after establishing those facts could the prosecution deal with the heart of the case. The defense, in turn, needed to take every facet of the prosecution's case—evidence, testimony, and argument—and treat it like a projectile in a skeet shoot: follow the target, take aim, wait until the right moment, and shoot it into oblivion. Destroy the argument and win the case.

SCAP conducted the trial in the Yokohama District Court Building. Unlike many other B and C trials that sprung up in ill-equipped East Asian cities, the Kyushu trial unfolded in an actual courtroom. Everyone realized that the sensational potential of the case promised extended international media coverage, and under General MacArthur's watch, only the proper theater would do him proud. When the curtain rose for the trial and the world's gaze turned to MacArthur's dominion yet again, it had to scream of high drama. And it did.

The trial turned out to be less of a hearing and more of an event. A buzz electrified the air. Spectator seating filled up like seats at a prizefight. The interest in the atrocities case often surpassed the space allotted to the public. It was not uncommon to see people three or four deep lining the walls or peering into the room through the numerous windows leading into the courthouse's halls. Americans and Japanese stood side-by-side huddled tightly under the dark varnished wooden panels just under the courtroom's warehouse-like ceiling. But surrounding them, U.S. Army military policemen stood guard, surveying civilians and defendants alike—a constant reminder of who held the authority in the trial. It represented yet another unnatural situation; former combatants and current unequal compatriots fostered the familiar illusion of coexistence.

As in most courtrooms, the bench faced the attorneys and the public. Six men sat behind a wooden perch as foreboding as the sullen paneling. The presiding members of the commission consisted of Colonel Thomas F. Joyce (8th Army), who acted as the president of the multinational commission; Lieutenant Colonel Alfred D. Yates (Royal Army Educational Corps); Lieutenant Colonel Harold E. Opsahl (Medical General Dispensary); Lieutenant Colonel Willard F. Moore (8th Army); Major Charles C. Ringwalt (8th Army); and Captain Lucian D. Bogan Jr. (11th A/B Division). Together, they shared the responsibility of hearing the case, determining guilt, and ultimately dispensing the proper punishment. Behind the commission members, the American and Japanese flags stood opposite one another like sentinels at a military post.

At 0930, March 11, 1948, the trial of *United States of America* versus *Kajuro Aihara et al.* (Case Docket 290) convened. Under the yellowing artificial light pouring down from the pendulum-like ceiling lights and the swirl of giant fans, the prosecution and defense dug into their corners and prepared for a legal prizefight. A team of three lawyers comprised the IPS delegation in charge of presenting the case against the accused. Paul K. Von Bergen acted as chief prosecutor; George T. Hagen and Richard O. Baird acted as assistant prosecutors. Together, they shared the responsibility of arguing and conducting direct and redirect examinations. And while an amalgam of different and autonomous Japanese lawyers acted as the theoretical defense council for the various accused, the attorneys responsible for actually arguing the case hailed from the United States. A five-man team, led by Frank Seydel, acted as defense council to the defendants as well as spokesmen for the Japanese lawyers.

Colonel Sato watched the trial alone in his thoughts but physically surrounded by twenty-nine other people. Some he knew personally, like Fukushima, Yokoyama, Hirako, and Torisu. Others must have been unfamiliar. Yet, somehow, providence placed them in similar predicaments and force-fed them similar fates. In the end, they would face judgment as a group. So the defendants sat together, sequestered in what must have functioned as jurors' boxes during normal proceedings. Sturdy wooden borders caged them in place.

George Hagen opened for the prosecution. He charged thirty Japanese nationals associated with Western Army Headquarters, Kyushu Imperial University, and Kaikosha Hospital with a variety of crimes ranging from murder to desecration of the dead POWs' bodies. Even before opening statements were made, the two legal opponents jockeyed for the upper hand and the commission's favor, but from the outset it was apparent that the defense would be waging a lonely battle in the courtroom. While the commission may not have been blatantly biased toward the prosecution, they seemed to make a point of flatly denying any objections made by the defense. However, after the charges against the defendants—including cannibalism—had been read, the defense assumed the offensive. What should have been a mere formality turned into the first confrontation of the trial and a clear indication that the case would test the boundaries of international jurisprudence and the notions of what constituted a prosecutable war crime.

Frank Seydel stood up and sternly addressed the commission. "The motion that the defense desires to make at this time is to strike Specification Number 2 against Kishi Tatsuro, and the whole specifications against each of the following: Ito Akira, Matake Shinchiro, Oda Tayuru, and Tsurumaru Hironaga.[2]

"The reason for the motion is that the specification does not state a crime or offense. For information to the members of the commission, the substance of the specification in each case is as follows: that the accused did 'willingfully and unlawfully eat part of the liver of an unknown American prisoner of war.' "

Seydel took exception to the notion that cannibalism fell under the auspice of a war crime. While he never challenged the heinousness of the act, he reserved his moral judgment; instead, he analyzed it in terms of the existing code of laws that defined war crimes. He cited the SCAP directive granting that the commission "shall have jurisdiction over all offenses, including but not limited to . . ." and went on to define certain offenses. Ultimately, he concluded, "A crime is a violation of something that is a rule and is published beforehand by some sovereign power. A crime is a violation of a rule and that rule is so published that everybody may understand and guide his conduct accordingly. It isn't something that is a brainchild out of the prosecution's mind; neither is it something that any one or all of the commission may think is the wrong thing. Mind you, gentlemen, this must be a violation of a rule and custom of war."

Colonel Joyce thanked the defense, then turned to the prosecution. "Does the prosecution have a remark to make on the motion of the defense counsel?"

"Yes, sir," Hagen replied. "We have."

"Do you have a copy of the motion to strike?"

The prosecution offered their rebuttal, essentially arguing that cannibalism did indeed constitute a war crime.

"These men are not charged with desecrating the bodies," Hagen stated. "We are not charging them with that at all, with the exception of one man who is charged with the specifications. The others are charged purely and simply with cannibalism, that they did eat a human liver. We don't charge that those other men or any of the men were even there when the man was killed, when the liver was taken out of the body. They are charged with eating the liver, or, as we say, cannibalism. This is so new, so novel, it isn't in the book. As far as American warfare is concerned, we have never run into it, even from the time of the Indians, so probably it wasn't necessary to pass a federal law or pass a law or enter into a treaty or agreement or pass a convention to decide that cannibalism was wrong.

"To uphold the contention of the defense would be this: it would say that whenever a man or a nation could conceive some new deviltry, it would go unpunished because civilized nations had not thought to agree to make it a crime. Certainly, that is not the way international law has been construed in Nuremberg or here in Tokyo."

Then Hagen's argument turned sarcastic. It would not be the last time. "To follow the defense a little further, I'd like to call the attention of the court to other possibilities of that type of argument. Let us say that you took the skull of a man and made ashtrays or drinking cups out of the top half—I am sure you wouldn't find any law to apply to that, but would you say that was not a crime? Take this case in Germany where they took a tattooed piece of skin off a man and made a lampshade—would you say that should go unpunished?"

Cannibalism, the prosecution maintained, was a war crime, and the defense's motion was without foundation.

Seydel responded to Hagen and the commission: "We stand on the proposition that everyone of us recognizes, I don't care what part of the country or the world he comes from: there shall be no punishment without a law; there must be a law before there is a punishment. The prosecution has not shown where it says that cannibalism is a crime or a violation of the rules and customs of war."

"Does the defense attorney argue that cannibalism is a custom of war?" the commission asked.

"The burden is on the prosecution, sir, to show that cannibalism is a violation of the laws and customs of war."

Ultimately, the commission ruled in favor of the prosecution. The defense would have to contend with the cannibalism charges after all.

The last thing Marvin wanted as he waited to testify was to be seen as a hero. Admiring stares, laudatory nods, pity-ridden whispers—none of them mattered. He did not want anyone's sympathy or coddling or praise. Yet, it was all too easy to twist the Kyushu Imperial University atrocities trial into the Watkins trial. It was, after all, his crew, and a conviction of the accused seemed like justice in Marvin's name.

The Legal Section brought Marvin into the courtroom for one reason, and he knew it. The scope of his knowledge that was admissible in court was limited to his capture and time in captivity. And while it might have seemed minor, Marvin's experiences would lay the groundwork for the prosecution's entire argument. The first step was always the most important; it set the case in motion and would decide the case's direction. Marvin's testimony had to show without a doubt that he and his crew had been denied the official status of prisoner of war. As official soldiers, it was their right, and denying it was tantamount to being sentenced to death without a trial.

There was no denying the importance of Marvin's appearance. His words would be the first from a witness and would set the tone for the trial to come. And as soon as the court accepted the mounds of evidence presented by the prosecution, his journey would draw to a close and he would be allowed to return home. The burden that had shifted around his consciousness for so long would disappear and he would return to the normalcy he left back in Beatrice's care.

Marvin wore his full military gear as an active U.S. Army Air Force officer for the last time. He stood tall. Head held high. Chest pressed against his beige button-down shirt. Marvin's army uniform stretched where it had once sagged, held steady where at one time it had shifted. His arms filled his sleeves, and when he bent his arm or reached for a piece of paper, muscle—not bone—pushed through the fabric. He resembled the all-American soldier proud to serve his country. His fleshy cheeks burst with color. His smooth, lightly tanned skin shined with vitality.

In a matter of minutes, this imposing, impressive, and immutable man—Marvin S. Watkins from Church Road, Virginia—would march into the courtroom and face the enemy; only this time, he wore the rank of captain and would not be the one in captivity.

A shackled Colonel Sato—aged, wrinkled, and stoic—listened to the prosecution's opening statement from behind a wooden barrier. If the world took the gaijin's word as true, he would hang, no doubt about it. The confusion, rage, and indignation that once set his mind aflame did not even register a smoky ash-heap smolder. Passion gave way to apprehension because no man wants to die.

Sato's accomplices—superiors and subordinates—surrounded him. General, colonel, captain, doctor, and nurse all wore similar Sugamo Prison–issued jumpsuits, erasing the vestiges of privilege, rank, status, and gender.

Each statement made by the prosecutor filtered through an interpreter. Meanings and subtleties were undoubtedly lost. Sato and company's incarceration was not only physical. They were also language's prisoners, and as such, always hovered at a distance, never fully participating. It was almost like not being present during your own trial. There were some things they could pick up, however, such as the prosecution's contemptuous tone, the defense's exasperation, and the commission members' calculating coolness from their judiciary perch. It must have been a small consolation for such a major event.

Hagen outlined the case against the accused, starting first with an introduction to Western Army Headquarters and their handling of downed airmen. Once the context of the crimes had been established, he began introducing each of the accused and the roles they played in the atrocities.

Sometimes, Sato heard something familiar, usually a name. Tokyo. Kyoto. Hiroshima. Fukuoka. Kyushu. Ito. Then Sato heard something too familiar.

"If there is a fall man in this case," Hagen stated bluntly, "it probably is Colonel Sato; Colonel Sato was a staff officer in charge of the Air Intelligence Section, and as such, of the fliers."

What was being said?

"What I meant by fall man was this. Not that he wasn't directly involved, but after the war he called upon Lieutenant General Yokoyama at his house, and Lieutenant General Yokoyama said to Sato, 'As a commanding general and as having established the policy, I am responsible for these acts. However, as the commanding general is responsible only to the emperor, and since that will reflect upon the emperor, you, Sato, with Fukushima, will volunteer to take the responsibility for these acts.' "

Name again.

"But Sato is certainly not without blemish. He was a principal organizer and agitator to kill the particular fliers involved. He was present at three of the four operations. The fliers were killed. He arranged with the officers under him to get them from the Western Army Headquarters to the hospital, and he also gave a party for some of the surgeons after the third series of operations at which he thanked them. We find Colonel Sato present too at the 16th and 17th of November meetings."

The long-headed man with white hair and spectacles—Colonel Joyce—sitting behind the bench spoke. What was he saying? No matter. When the prosecutor continued speaking, he now referred to Colonel Akita. For now the danger was over.

Hagen methodically identified each of the accused, then detailed the roles they played in the murders. He started with the staff of Western Army Headquarters and finished with the alleged cannibals from Kaikosha Hospital.

Hagen summarized their offenses. "These operations were of an experimental nature and were performed on live, healthy human beings—American fliers who were captives of the Japanese Empire. They were not for the health or welfare of any of the said fliers. There were various reasons. One, they were used for practice. . . . Secondly, they were used for research. Thirdly, they were just plain puttering with human beings. And in the fourth place, it was just a plain, ordinary crime of killing in its most vicious and professionally advanced form. . . . Gentlemen, this is a very brief estimate of the situation. It constitutes a murder case involving joint participation of many Japanese in very responsible positions in Japan and a series of murders in the most sadistic and vicious form. Thank you."

The opening statement spanned two days in court, March 11 and 13. The presentation of evidence consumed six days. In the meantime, Marvin waited and prepared for the questions he assumed he'd be asked. He ran through the images and his capture and captivity like a college basketball coach brooding over films of his team's last game. He needed to be sure the defense—something of a temporary enemy—could not trick or confuse a contradiction from him. A small slip-up could damage his testimony. He had let his crew down once; there would not be another time.

On March 17, Marvin Watkins heard his name called. The prosecution summoned him into the courtroom. They needed his testimony. Marvin's moment had come.

Marvin marched into the courtroom. Steady steps carried him through the crowd past gawking onlookers, stern but baby-faced military policemen, and a throng of reporters. The entire courtroom watched him. Not only was he the first witness to take the stand, he was also the only surviving member of the crew in question. He knew them. Those men who were murdered. Or were they boys? He had heard their voices, lived with their expressions, understood their shortcomings. Marvin knew them like nobody in the entire room, including their murderers, could ever know them. He represented the final, tangible link to their last moments, and everyone recognized that fact. And when all eyes descended on Marvin, he probably felt each and every glare, because the human stare can be as heavy as the person from which it emanates.

One of those stares, perhaps the heaviest, belonged to Colonel Sato. Perhaps he watched with scorn or anger or humiliation or indifference. Perhaps it had been so long since he interrogated Marvin that had it not been for the court's formal introduction of the witness,

Sato would never have recognized him. Context, circumstance, and memory made everything foreign and at the same time familiar, including Sato and other WAHQ staff who knew him.

And when Marvin pushed his way to the witness box, looked around, and saw the Japanese standing trial all dressed like members of the same ill-fated council of the damned, did he recognize any of them? Perhaps relief filled Marvin's body. In not recognizing, a distance builds between two parties. But considering the fate of Marvin's crew, lack of recognition could have proved frustrating. He might have immediately known Tsutsui, being the sole woman on trial, but as for the remainder, they could have been anyone. In a cruel twist, the men responsible for the actual murder of the Watkins crew stood as the least recognizable. Marvin could not have known any of the Kyushu Imperial University doctors; the same with the Kaikosha doctors. He was already in Tokyo when they committed their crimes.

Hagen indicated for Marvin to be sworn in. When the formality of an oath finished, the witness took his seat on the stand, but before Hagen could begin, Seydel addressed the commission. He did not see how Marvin's testimony related to the case being tried, nor did he see what proof Marvin could provide.

Hagen offered a straightforward response. "If the commission wishes, we will make an offer of proof in every case. However, I think it is quite obvious from most witnesses called what the nature of the proof is going to be, and objection can be made at the right time. How, if we make an offer of proof in every case, it merely means that we spend extra minutes with every single witness. Mr. Watkins was the pilot of the plane from which six of the twelve named as victims in this case came. He was with the plane when it crashed in Kyushu. He was captured when the crew crashed. He is here now. I think it's obvious to what he is going to testify."

"Sir," Seydel responded. "That is not a response to the request for an offer of proof."

"I think an offer is sufficient to advise you." Hagen smirked. "I do not think it is necessary to give you a detailed explanation of every information he is going to give. If the commission so requests, of course I will do it."

Seydel turned to Colonel Joyce. "Mr. President, if this witness is offered for the purpose of proving identity, then any testimony that he has or may offer will be of no probative value, because the identity of the twelve fliers has already been admitted into the record, and that is why the defense desires to know what the prosecution desires to prove by this witness; not for the purpose of prolonging but for the purpose of expediting this case. And the prosecution has smiled and laughed and indicated a manner of disapproval by ridicule. I hope that the president will take note of that."

"Neither counsel," Colonel Joyce said, addressing both parties, "defense nor prosecution, need to give this commission any instructions as to the conduct of this court. However, the action of the prosecution is offensive, and an apology will be rendered at this time."

"Sir, if the smiles of the prosecution members is so offensive to the court, we are very sorry that that took place."

Before proceeding with his direct examination, Hagen reminded Marvin that he was still under oath, then proceeded to introduce him to the commission through a number of personal background questions. After establishing Marvin's credentials, Hagen moved on to the crew. In deliberate fashion, Marvin called out the names of the men he lost in Japan as if paying them tribute. He said their names loud and clear so that the entire room could hear.

"My copilot was Lieutenant Fredericks. My navigator was Lieutenant Kearns. My bomber was Lieutenant Shingledecker. My radar observer was Lieutenant Plambeck. My flight engineer was Sergeant Ponczka. My radio operator was Corporal Robert B. Williams. My gunners were Corporal Oeinck, Corporal Johnson, Corporal Colehower, Corporal Czarnecki."

Hagen then introduced the picture of Marvin and his crew as evidence, after which Marvin testified that it was a picture of him and his crew taken around April 1945 on Guam.

After a brief recess for lunch, the direct examination shifted to the incidents of May 5, 1945, specifically the Watkins crew's bailout and subsequent capture. Once again, Marvin recounted the events he had rehashed in his mind back in Church Road and at each family's house from Virginia to New York and with Robert Miller in Japan.

"Had you been injured in any way at the time of the crash?" Hagen asked.

"I was not injured from the crash at all," Marvin replied. "I was only injured by beatings from the Japanese civilians when I hit the ground—when I was captured."

"Had you been—at the time of your arrival at Western Army Headquarters—did you have any visible signs of injury?"

"At my arrival at Western Army Headquarters, I had only a head injury. I was struck twice on the back of my head by a civilian before I arrived at Western Army Headquarters."

"Did you receive any medical attention when at Western Army Headquarters?"

He hadn't.

Seydel cut in. "I move the question and answer be stricken as having no relevancy in this case."

"If the commission please," Hagen replied. "The charge—one of the charges is that the status of the honorable status of prisoners of wars was denied. Obviously this witness—the type of treatment he received would not be identical treatment accorded other crew members. It most certainly does have some bearing as to the facts. It isn't conclusive, but it does have some probative value as to whether the others received treatment."

"Well, I don't believe I need to answer that," Seydel shot back. "It seems to me if that is true, then the kind of treatment accorded any captured fliers at any time might have some probative value. This witness is not named in any specification, and the kind of treatment he might have received is no indication of what kind of treatement others might have received. But, gentlemen, even if it were, there is no allegation there was mistreatment or abuse of these persons. Identity has already been admitted."

The commission denied the defense's objection. They wanted to hear the facts of the case. It was a simple request but would be made increasingly difficult because of Seydel's constant objections.

"What was the condition of Ponczka when you were placed in the same cell with him?" Hagen asked as he resumed his examination.

Marvin thought for a moment, then answered carefully. "Ponczka was on a stretcher. He had been stabbed in the back between the shoulder blades with a bamboo spear. He had also been hit in the left groin by a stick, which paralyzed his left leg. He was unable to walk."

Seydel rose in protest. "Objection to the question, and I move it be stricken as having no probative value in this case."

"If the commission please," Hagen replied. "Failure to give medical attention or denial of medical attention is certainly of probative value as to whether the prisoners received treatment as prisoners of war."

"Under what specification?" Seydel snapped. "Would the prosecution point that out?"

Hagen argued that Ponczka was mentioned in the specifications of the case, and that because of this fact, the line of questioning was of probative value. Despite continued objections from the defense, the commission ruled in favor of the prosecution and denied the objection.

Marvin continued where he had left off. "When I arrived at Western Army Headquarters, Sergeant Ponczka was on the truck with me, but I did not know because I was blindfolded. When I was taken from the truck at Western Army Headquarters, I noticed Sergeant Ponczka was there."

"At the time of his arrival, was he on a stretcher?"

Marvin indicated that Ponczka was on a stretcher for the entire time the two shared a cell but never received any medical attention.

Hagen asked Marvin to describe the cell in which he and Ponczka spent their time. According to Marvin, their cell measured ten square feet and had a bench. Ponczka's stretcher was placed on the bench. The only other thing in the room was a small box nestled in a corner that served as their toilet. They were even denied water with which to wash.

• • •

After another objection by the defense, Hagen asked, "What accommodations were there for sleeping?"

Seydel rose. "Objection to the question as being immaterial."

This time, the commission agreed with the defense. "Objection is sustained. The prosecution was admonished that the court is not interested in that sort of testimony."

Hagen started to address the court. "If the commission please, the denial—"

"The court will take judicial notice of the kind of sleeping quarters he had. He slept on tatamis."

Hagen corrected the law member. "He didn't sleep on tatamis."

"On the floor."

"If the commission please," Hagen continued. "Here we have a man who was on a stretcher, and I think it goes to aggregation. I admit most everything—"

"Did you ask where the witness slept?" the law member asked.

Hagen argued that while nobody expected each prisoner of war to receive "what we normally expected them to get," forcing an injured prisoner to share his stretcher represented something more than a case of lack of attention.

The commission accepted Hagen's argument and asked Marvin to answer the question.

"Sergeant Ponczka was more or less paralyzed in his legs and couldn't walk. Therefore, he remained on the stretcher the entire day. There was no outlet for me to sleep except on the concrete floor or on the stretcher with Ponczka. There was no cover. So we slept together to keep warm. We pulled straw from underneath the mat. That was the only way to keep warm. That was our only means of keeping warm—rotating—turning back and forth. I had to sleep with him and he had to sleep with me."

"Did he need blankets?"

"Yes," Marvin answered.

"During the time you were with him, what food did Ponczka receive?"

"We both received the same food, which was a rice ball and a few pieces of daikon each meal."

"Were you able to move about the cell?"

At this point, Seydel objected to the question as immaterial. He knew where the prosecution's argument was headed and wanted to cut it off. He did not want the denial of POW status to come from Marvin's mouth. It made a difference from whom it came. Seydel tried to seize the initiative by arguing that nobody in the courtroom was denying that the Americans held at Western Army Headquarters had been denied prisoner-of-war status. However, the defense qualified his statement by reminding the commission that Western Army officials might have viewed their prisoners as "suspected war criminals, suspected of indiscriminate bombings." The prosecution, Seydel argued, hadn't presented any proof that the Americans *deserved* to be treated as prisoners of war.

The court denied the defense's objection. Taking his cue from the commission, Hagen continued his direct examination regarding Ponczka and his condition while in captivity. Marvin would be heard. The defense, in a sudden panic, continued to object to every question posed by the prosecution until the commission saw no other course but to address Seydel. In responding to yet another of the defense's objections, the commission replied, "Well, if the defense wouldn't persist in its objections, it is . . ."

"Do you think the defense has been obstructing the progress of this trial so far?" Seydel cut in adamantly.

"You are registering 100 percent objections . . . 100 percent." The law member chastised the defense. "We would have been through with this witness and on to the next subject . . ."

Once again, Hagen resumed his direct examination. He was determined to establish the denial of POW status through Marvin's words. He had set up his argument like a chess master positioning his pieces for an inevitable victory. The time had come to solve for mate.

"Was Ponczka interrogated when you were with him—was Ponczka taken out for interrogation when you were with him?"

"Ponczka was not taken out at any time while I was with him," Marvin replied.

"Were you interrogated when you were held at Western Army?" Hagen's questions brought Marvin within inches of atonement.

"Yes," Marvin replied sternly. "Several times."

"During the interrogation, was the subject of your classification as a prisoner of war discussed or not brought up by the interrogators?" Hagen had cleared the path for both himself and Marvin.

"Yes, it was."

"What were you informed?"

Marvin paused and chose his words carefully. He had been asked to take the stand as a witness in order to establish one thing. The time had come for him to deliver the first blow to the Western Army officers responsible for his crew's deaths.

"I was informed that I was not a prisoner of war; I was a captive of the Japanese."

Marvin's testimony made it clear that the Japanese chose to disregard the convention of protecting captured combatants of both sides with the status of prisoner of war. It would have protected them under the Geneva Convention, allotting them basic rights to food, shelter, and safety until the end of hostilities.

After Marvin's declaration, Hagen asked a few more questions, then presented the witness to the defense for cross-examination. Seydel declined, and after hours of testimony, Marvin's time on the stand drew to an abrupt end. He had, however, achieved his objective.

Marvin S. Watkins completed his final task the way he embarked on his first mission and his return to Japan—with dignified courage. His debt to his crew was as even as it would ever be. Little remained for Marvin in Japan except his past. There was nothing to gain or lose; fix or break; hang on to or give up. All that lay ahead of him awaited his return to Virginia. An extended stay in Japan would have been pointless. His presence would not influence the outcome of the trial one way or another. The result would be the same with him watching or with him reading the verdict in the paper. Most important, he wanted to return home to Beatrice. He could not start a family in earnest while he knew he had a final tour of duty to perform in Japan. Now he could. Things would be as they should be.

17

Prosecution: 1948

While Colonel Sato watched the parade of former Western Army Headquarters officers march from outside obscurity to courtroom prominence, Lieutenant General Yokoyama suffered the fiercest blows to his credibility, innocence, and future. His postwar plans for escaping prosecution failed miserably. In an attempt to create immediate distance between himself and the atrocities that occurred under his command, Yokoyama ordered Sato and Fukushima to construct a concealment plan on their own, rather than playing an active part. As a result, he sank or swam with their competency. The two proved dreadfully incompetent. Yokoyama's choices exposed him to be equally inadequate. And as a reward, he received front-row seats at the trial that would decide whether he spent the remainder of his life locked in a glorified box or swinging in the gallows.

With the fliers' identities tentatively established, the prosecution moved on to the next point in their argument: establishing the role of Western Army Headquarters in the atrocities.[1] Without the luxury of being able to call any of the accused to the stand for direct examination—SCAP directives forbade defendants from testifying against each other—the prosecution relied on the testimony of people not directly involved in the case. This presented two problems. First, a good deal of the drawn-out material ended up being more hearsay than firsthand knowledge, further weakening a case being built on circumstantial evidence. Second, because of the fact that the planning and execution of the atrocities involved an overwhelming majority of high-ranking Western Army senior officers—the people most qualified to describe the inner workings and policies of high-level offices—the prosecution found themselves backed into a corner with only the testimony of lower-ranking officials speculating on the procedures, directives, and responsibilities of the accused. In the best cases, the prosecution presented witnesses who held the same position—for example, adjutant—but at a different time. But even in those cases, their testimony was weakened by the fact that wartime policies, particularly at the local levels, were often fluid entities that changed with the shifting currents of war.

Fortunately for the prosecution and much to the chagrin of the defense, the commission granted them generous leeway in what was "immaterial," "irrelevant," and "of probative value." Most of the defense's objections received immediate and decisive rebuffs, something not altogether surprising. If any line of questioning, no matter how distantly related, received ample explanation from the prosecution as to its pertinence, it sufficed for the commission.

Hagen called a wide range of witnesses belonging to various Western Army sections, including Wako, Kusumoto, and Murata. He carefully guided their testimony from one key issue to another. He pressed the Legal Section witnesses on issues regarding the proper treatment of POWs according to international law and the jurisdiction of the detention barracks at Western Army Headquarters. Members of the Medical Section testified to the care given to the American prisoners, or the lack thereof, and the unlikelihood of their being sent to a civilian hospital rather than a military one. Hagen questioned members of the Adjutant Section more meticulously. He delineated for the commission each step the Adjutant Section took while responsible for the prisoners, which was for the majority of their time in captivity. He showed the commission how they maintained detailed records of each prisoner and how they played the primary role in overseeing the POWs' well-being. With the commanding general's blessing, the Adjutant Section had the final say regarding the release or transfer of prisoners from the detention barracks, regardless of their final destination.

By laying out the responsibilities and proper procedure of each Western Army section, the prosecution implied that the defendants belonging to each section bore responsibility for allowing the murdered prisoners to pass through their prospective commands.

Time and again, witness testimony indicated that any decision to release the American POWs passed through Yokoyama's office and needed his seal (han) of approval. It corroborated everything the Legal Section investigators learned during their extensive interrogations of Western Army Headquarters officers a year before. Both the Adjutant Section and Legal Section needed his office's approval. In addition, it was Yokoyama who established the policy within his own command regarding the treatment and disposal of enemy POWs. In the prosecution's words, "It was his intention that the prisoners should not survive the Kyushu invasion." Yokoyama's fate grew bleaker with each word muttered by witness and lawyer.

Establishing Komori's role fell on the testimony of one key witness: Maekawa Tozo. Prior to his transfer to the Western Army Medical Section, Maekawa served for a little over a year (January 1944–April 1945) in the main prisoner-of-war camp in Fukuoka. After completing his transfer to Western Army Headquarters, Maekawa handled the Medical Section's general affairs and supplies, supervised the hired personnel, and oversaw the sanitary conditions for soldiers and prisoners alike.

After going over the procedure for processing prisoners of war at legitimate POW camps and at Western Army Headquarters, Hagen addressed the main reason he had Maekawa on the stand.

"Did you know a medical probation officer named Komori?"

"Yes."

"Did you know him well?"

"Yes, I knew him well."

"Had you been classmates at medical college?"

"We went to different medical schools. However, it was the same high school."

"Did Medical Probationary Officer Komori visit Major General Horiuchi during the time that you were at Western Army?"

"Yes."

"During April and May 1945, as far as you know, about how many times a week did Probationary Officer Komori visit Major General Horiuchi?"

"During some weeks, he would not come to see Major General Horiuchi at all. However, during some weeks, he would come about two or three times."

"Do you know whether or not Probationary Officer Komori and Major General Horiuchi were friends . . . were personal friends?"

"As the Japanese would say, they were personal friends."

"When Komori came to see Major General Horiuchi, did he go directly into his office, or did he first stop in your office at the reception desk?"

"Most of the time, Komori went directly to Horiuchi's office. However, at times he would stop over at my office."

"What was Komori's connection with Western Army Headquarters, if any?"

"Komori was really assigned to the Kokura Army Hospital. However, he had been sent on dispatch duty from Kokura Army Hospital to the Western Army Headquarters."

"At Western Army Headquarters, what was his assignment or duty?"

"He had received orders to give medical treatment at the Kaikosha Hospital."

"Was Komori a doctor of surgery?"

"Yes."

"What was Komori's reputation as a doctor—good? Was he reputed to be a good surgeon or not?"

"He was known to be a very efficient surgeon."

Hagen asked his witness to describe Komori's responsibilities. According to Maekawa, Komori belonged with the Western Army

Headquarters Medical Section and Kaikosha Hospital. He had no official association with Kyushu Imperial University, however.

The prosecution began the complex and delicate task of tying the seemingly isolated vivisections in with the Japanese military and government. It was a bridge that would have to be constructed one metal beam at a time.

"During 1945, were any of the doctors at Kyushu Imperial University connected with the Medical Section of Western Army Headquarters in any manner, in any official manner?"

"Among the university, the professors there were, or was, a person or persons, who had nonofficial connection with the Medical Section of the army."

"What kind of work were they doing?"

"Since I did not have any connection with this, I do not know the exact details. However, it is my belief that these professors who had nonofficial connection with the army were aided by the army whenever research that the army could use was carried on, or when a certain problem was brought by the army to them, and also that they helped and gave instructions concerning treatment in the various army hospitals, which were under the army."

"Did you know a Dr. Ishiyama from Kyushu Imperial University?"

"I knew of his name, but I did not see him during the months of April or May."

"Do you know whether or not in April and May 1945 any of these doctors from Kyushu Imperial University were engaged in research for a blood substitute?"

"Yes, it was Professor Tomoda. He was a surgeon."

"Do you know if any doctor at Kyushu Imperial University during that same period was engaged in research as to the possibility of using seawater as a substitute for blood volume?"

Joseph Greene of the defense stood up. "Object to the question as leading and suggestive."

"Objection denied," the commission responded.

Maekawa answered. "About the end of May, there was a meeting of those who were nonofficially connected with the army. At that time,

I heard that there was research in using seawater as a blood substitute. Other than that, I did not hear."

"After your arrival at Western Army Headquarters, did you hear that captured airmen were to be used for experimental purposes?"

"Yes, I have heard."

"Did you hear of such before or after any airmen were so used?"

"I firmly believe that it was before. I heard this before the actual operations were performed."

"About what date did you first hear of such?"

"Sometime between the 10th and 12th of May 1945, within these two days."

"And from whom did you first hear of such?"

"Probationary Medical Officer Komori."

Maekawa related how he first learned about the operations from Komori. Unlike other witnesses, he admitted to hearing about the procedures before they occurred. According to his testimony, Maekawa learned about the planned experiments upon paying a visit to Komori at Kaikosha Hospital around the 10th or 12th of May 1945. While discussing various unrelated topics, Komori mentioned in passing that it was decided that American B-29 prisoners would be used for medical experimental operations. When Maekawa asked how it came about, Komori replied that Ishiyama issued his request to Colonel Sato and that the higher officials of the army had decided that the use of POWs was acceptable. He added that he informed Komori that before any action was taken with the POWs, the chief of the Medical Section of the Western Army, Major General Horiuchi, should be consulted and permission granted. Komori insisted that since the higher officers gave permission, Horiuchi must have been informed as well.

Roughly four days later, Maekawa ran into Komori in the staircase of the Medical Section. The meeting occurred late in the afternoon. "I asked him where he had been, and he said he was on his way home from Kyushu Imperial University," Maekawa recalled. "I asked him, 'What did you go there for?' and after a while he said that the operation on the fliers had been performed at the university." Komori boasted that the operations involved the lung, heart, and liver. In addition, he carried at his side a container filled with blood. When asked about its contents, Komori replied that it was the prisoners' blood.

When the defense took over the witness, they wasted little time picking away at Maekawa's credibility like a pigeon pecking at a piece of bread. Stanley Blumenfeld assumed responsibility for the task. Drawing from statements made by Captain Wako and Captain Murata, the defense quizzed Maekawa about his propensity to boast and exaggerate. Apparently, the truth depended on the day, time, and Maekawa's mood. Both officers stated that Maekawa bragged about being present for the operations. However, when asked directly about observing, Maekawa denied it vehemently. Blumenfeld's efforts were for naught, unfortunately. When he submitted a motion to strike a large chunk of Maekawa's testimony from the record, the commission swiftly denied his motion. The picture of Komori and the operations would be allowed to stand.

Robert Tait sat beside the team of lawyers who depended on him during the two years of intense and often frustrating investigation. It was an honor, and nobody doubted that he belonged. Looking around the courtroom must have felt satisfying. None of it—the commission, the witnesses, the evidence, the theories—happened without his efforts, supervision, and ingenuity. He and his team of investigators—Team 420—made it. Even though the entire cast could not join him at the prosecutor's table, he represented them proudly. They had come a long way since the brutal July morning when Ishiyama hung suspended from his cell wall and the case seemed doomed to languish in perpetual mystery. Even before going to trial, Team 420 had laid out the case fact by fact for the prosecution's benefit.

The following phase of the trial reflected the scope of Team 420's investigation. It reached beyond Fukuoka, Kyushu, and the entire Western Army. The Legal Section and prosecution's crosshairs focused without question and without apology on the Imperial Palace. Inadvertently, it offered a slight psychological respite for the thirty suspects actually standing trial. For the Western Army officers, the most damaging part of the trial—facing charges that they conspired to have the members of the Watkins crew murdered—had passed. Though more charges awaited them, they did not consist of capital offenses. The same could not be said about the Kyushu Imperial University surgeons who had yet to even hear their names mentioned. For them, the worst was yet to come. And they'd have to wait.

Having attempted to establish Komori's role, the time came to expand the scope of the trial. The prosecution was ready to tie the seemingly local atrocities that were perpetrated in Fukuoka with Tokyo's concerted, calculated, and fatally misconceived push toward victory or at least survival. It proved larger and more important than anyone sitting in the stuffy wood-and-metal–encased courtroom could ever imagine.

On one level, it entailed the mischief of the Manchurian incident, the arrogance of the Greater East Asian Coprosperity Sphere, and the desperation of Pearl Harbor. The Eastern philosophies and kokutai ideologies that granted the Japanese a transcendental hall pass to cruelty and savagery against fragile-skinned gaijin underlings influenced their treatment of patient and prisoner alike, clearing them of moral culpability.

At the same time, the Japanese intelligentsia's scientific inquiry at all costs mixed with notions of ethnic superiority, ultimately producing the corroded thread that ran directly from Ishii's biological death mills in Harbin, to Wakamatsu's quarantine stables in Mukden, to Naito's Densenbyo Kenkyusho in Tokyo, to the hollowed and vacuous hallways of Imperial universities across the country, finally ending in a dusty, ill-lit, wooden-hut-cum-dissection room in bombed, burned, and broken Fukuoka.

The first witness of note to take the stand for the prosecution was Nakashima Yoshisada, a former professor and director of radiology at Kyushu Imperial University. In addition to his responsibilities as a teaching professor, he served as superintendent of the Medical School, a position on par with the dean and subordinate only to the president of the school.

Hagen questioned Nakashima for two days on a variety of topics. He described the inner workings of the university from an administrative viewpoint. Hagen guided him through the different topics, each of which served as a background for the prosecution's argument. The questioning regarding hospital procedure set up the juxtaposition of how the system worked under normal circumstances and how the American POWs disappeared through the cracks. Inquiries into Ishiyama's nature showed him to be a dictatorial figure within his clinic and a political hawk outside it. The picture painted of the First Surgery chief showed him to have a personality consistent with the crimes he allegedly committed. This helped prove that the incidents could have and did take place. However, since it undercut the prosecution's case against Ishiyama's subordinates, Hagen made a point to establish the feudalistic nature of the Japanese university system but ultimately displayed that the final decision of whether to obey murderous orders fell on the individual. They could not find shelter from culpability under the guise of "following orders."

Interestingly, the questioning of individuals holding higher decision-making positions often resulted in moments of candor, especially regarding committing atrocities during times of war. When questioned on whether Ishiyama's subordinates could have gone to the Medical School dean or to Nakashima when they received orders to do something they did not wish to do, Nakashima replied with honesty.

"They could have consulted one of us. However, as a practice, this was not done. For example, during peacetime, if they were told to kill someone, I believe that they would not have followed his orders. However, depending upon the circumstances, there may have been exceptions. I cannot give any such exceptions. But, for example, although it is considered wrong from the standpoint of humanity to kill other human beings, during wartime this is done and this is considered a meritorious deed, and the person who killed is not accused of any wrong deed. Therefore, when you mention things which they did not wish to do, there are different degrees to that."

The moral and ethical ambiguities of war still managed to seep into the courtroom no matter how diligent the occupation forces tried to portray them as distant memories. The illusory reality of the prosecution, defense, and commission did not hold among the Japanese contingent in the courtroom who knew all too well that wartime atrocities often came down to perspective. Not only did the victors get to write the history books, they also held trials, defined the crimes, and made up the rules as they went along. Punishment and retribution—right or wrong, nobody besides the vanquished much cared—belonged to the spoils of war.

By the time Admiral Hyakutake Gengo took the stand, the trial had already stretched into its twenty-ninth day. To date, he was the most prominent and influential figure to appear before the commission, including Lieutenant General Yokoyama—the man who ran all of Kyushu during the war. From a purely military standpoint, in terms of rank and respect, Admiral Hyakutake belonged with the likes of MacArthur, Patton, Eisenhower, Nimitz, Ingersoll, and Halsey. During the months leading up to Japan's attack on Pearl Harbor, Hyakutake held a seat in the emperor's War Cabinet. On paper, Hyakutake was the navy's third in command; in reality, he was second.

Regardless of Hyakutake's influence and ability as a military administrator, it made little sense to have him running an educational institution, at least had it been peacetime when rationality holds firm. Yet, inexplicably, with the Ministry of War's blessing, the Ministry of Education somehow managed to appoint a man who hadn't had a day of experience in the field of education as head of the third most respected university in all of Japan. Even more miraculously, the various deans and superintendents elected him president of the university. The only means of explaining the university-wide brain freeze lay in the reality that Imperial University—Tokyo, Kyoto, Kyushu, and Osaka—represented a de facto extension of the Imperial Japanese Army. Taking it one step further, much of what went on within university walls could be considered army operations. Ultimately, this included research of all kinds. This is where Hyakutake meant the most to the prosecution. He embodied the very link that needed to be shown; Hyakutake Gengo made an abstract assertion into a tangible reality.

Von Bergen led the questioning. "Did all reports on special research projects conducted by medical professors in the university that were being sent to the Medical Section of the university pass through you for approval?"

"The ordinary reports should have passed through me because there is an office channel that it had to pass through. However, since it was wartime, military secrets, I believe, did not pass through me." Hyakutake's attempts at deflecting responsibility did not fool anyone.

"Do you know this for fact, or is it merely your belief?"

Seydel rose. "The question has been answered; object to it."

"Objection denied."

Hyakutake answered the question with his own. "Which part do you refer to?"

"That as to information on secret projects going on without passing through you?"

A member from the commission interrupted, "Military secrets is the term he used."

Von Bergen added, "Referring to military secrets."

The question was repeated for Admiral Hyakutake.

"If your previous question refers only to the medical department," he replied, "then I wish to withdraw my last answer. I gave the last answer considering the university as a whole because such a thing was true in the engineering department. As far as the medical department is concerned, there may have been such a ting, but I do not know."

Von Bergen was satisfied with Hyakutake's admission that secret research was conducted with the army's blessing. He passed the witness to the defense.

Blumenfeld's initial attempts at discrediting Hyakutake as a witness proved disappointing. He focused on the obvious, and his efforts suffered because of it. Because of the admiral's prominent position in the War Cabinet that attacked Pearl Harbor, Blumenfeld tried to use that to the defense's advantage. It backfired, and the commission chastised them for it. Pearl Harbor was an issue for Tokyo and the IMTFE, not the Yokohama courtroom. When Blumenfeld shifted the focus of his cross-examination, he set his sight on the connection between the Imperial universities and the Imperial Japanese Army. Whether it was intended or not, the defense inadvertently proved the existence of clandestine, cooperative research projects between Japan's academic and military sectors.

"Mr. Hyakutake, were there any military secrets between the military and the engineering department in Kyushu Imperial University?" Blumenfeld asked.

Colonel Joyce admonished the defense. "The defense counsel will refer to the witness as admiral."

Hyakutake replied, "There should have been some secrets." Then he described examples in the engineering department in which secret rocket fuel additives had been worked on in the engineering department. Such matters, he testified, would not pass through his office.

"What do you mean by 'it should have been'?" After asking, Blumenfeld retracted the question and withdrew it from the record. There was another way to ask.

"Now, Admiral," he said, choosing his words carefully. "You said there should have been such military secrets. Don't you know as a matter of fact whether there were, or there were not, as president of Kyushu Imperial University?"

Hyakutake's response was evasive. "Even if I knew in general, if I could not state definitely what it was, there is no other way than expressing it the way I did."

"Well, if the army had contacted anyone in the engineering department to perform some experiment, wouldn't you know about it, as president of Kyushu Imperial University?"

"Naturally such things would be reported to me. However, since I was in a position where I should try to keep secrets a secret, it was not necessary for me to go out and ask as to the detail of such a thing."

"I am not asking you for details, Admiral," Blumenfeld shot back. "I am asking you now to state as a fact as to whether or not the engineering department was performing any experiments for the military during the tenure of your office."

Von Bergen rose from his seat. "May it please the commission, this matter has already been testified to. As a matter of fact, it's been gone into in three or four questions. The question is repetitious and intimidating, and I am asking that it be withdrawn."

Blumenfeld took exception to Von Bergen's accusation. "I don't think I am intimidating anybody."

"Well, it's immaterial. The objection of the prosecution is denied," Colonel Joyce ruled. But he added, "It's a waste of time, however."

Hyakutake answered Blumenfeld's question. "Yes, there was such a thing. For example, I heard that they were working on chemicals for rockets."

"Was that unusual, for a department of the university to work on a project in cooperation with the military, unusual to Kyushu Imperial University, or was that the situation throughout Japan?"

Von Bergen objected to the question as immaterial.

"I think it is material," the defense responded. "I want to show by this question that it was not an unusual thing during this period of the war for various universities to be engaged in experiments and projects."

Then the commission made a telling remark: "The commission knows all of that and admits it."

The comment put an end to the defense's line of questioning and ended any possibility of unearthing more details about the extent of the Japanese biological experimentation program. But with the commission's muted declaration—coming from an officially sanctioned body representing SCAP and Washington—they publicly acknowledged the existence of something that the U.S. government would continue to deny for over a half century. It was there for the entire world to see in 1948: the existence of an extensive and intricate Japanese biological experimentation program that used live human beings as guinea pigs.

Hyakutake's assessment of the achieve-your-objective-at-all-costs pressures of war and its unavoidable madness reminded the courtroom of the depravity that spawned indiscriminate bombings, atomic massacres, and calculated scientific executions: "In wartime, I believe the same happened in the United States. All the effort was toward the winning of the war, and all efforts were turned towards that aim; and in the contact between the army and the university, there may be some things which must be kept secret. In the relationship between the university and the army, this relation must be strengthened in order to fulfill the objective; and therefore, I as a military man was a more suitable man than the ordinary professor who did not know anything about the military setup. This is my opinion."

Tomoda represented the prosecution's final significant link between the Japanese military and university-level research. More important, he was the one person who could link Ishiyama's seawater research with the Japanese military, albeit indirectly. As such, his testimony played the most important part in this phase of the prosecution's testimony.

Tomoda acted as chief of the rival Kyushu Imperial University surgical clinic, the Second Surgery Clinic. He engaged in blood substitute research similar to Ishiyama's only using his own theories and materials. Rather than using seawater as a substitute, Tomoda extracted alginic acid from the abundant farms of seaweed surrounding Japan. In the event that human blood plasma was unavailable, the substitute, theoretically, would be injected into the patient as a temporary solution to maintain or raise blood pressure. According to Tomoda, it significantly lowered the damage in injured patients losing excessive amounts of blood.

Because of the obvious similarities between Ishiyama's research and Tomoda's research, the prosecution attempted to parallel the two professors, their clinics, and their research. It was as close to resurrecting Ishiyama from the dead as the Yokohama courtroom would come. If the comparison went over successfully, it meant that the dynamics of gaining approval, funding, military aid, secrecy, and reporting of data could be established—something that was feared impossible with Ishiyama's suicide.

"Did or do you know whether the Japanese National Research Council had any connection with your research as to a blood substitute?" Hagen asked.

"I have received the money for the expenses from the Research Council of the Education Ministry," Tomoda replied.

"Was there anyone else in Kyushu who also got such a subsidy?"

"I believe that the following had subsidy from the Ministry of Education: Professor Hojo of the Forensic Medicine Clinic and Professor Ishiyama of the First Surgery Clinic and Professor Toda of the Bacteriological Clinic and Professor Sawada, Third Internal Medicine Clinic."

"What did Ishiyama receive his subsidy for?"

"I believe that he had the subsidy to carry on research on seawater."

"Did you work with Ishiyama in the common goal to devise a substitute for blood?"

"We did not cooperate with each other. There were two clinics, as I mentioned before, and these two clinics carried on their researches independently, and all the finances or the assistance and the rooms were different. We carried on researches independently."

"Did Ishiyama ever invite you to witness any experiments on humans in which seawater was used?"

"There was no such time."

In fact, further examination showed that the two surgery clinics and their chief surgeons butted heads publicly on the issue of blood substitutes. Blood substitute efficacy emerged as a major point of conflict between Ishiyama and Tomoda. During a meeting of Fukuoka doctors, Tomoda presented his data and theories to the attendees. When he finished his presentation, Tomoda found his research, data, and theories under attack from Ishiyama, who had been listening attentively. Ishiyama's main objection to Tomoda's idea of extracting alginic acid from seaweed lay in the notion that during wartime the extraction process simply took too long and lacked practicality. Instead of alginic acid, Ishiyama argued, the use of seawater proved both economically and medically feasible, more so than Tomoda's suggested substitute. Moreover, research had been conducted in his laboratory using seawater in various animals and proved effective.

Von Bergen asked Tomoda his opinion on seawater as a blood substitute. "Doctor, do you have an opinion on the efficacy of seawater as a blood substitute or as a substitute for blood volume?"

"I have not carried out systematic research or chemical research on seawater. However, since I had carried on experiments with alginic acid, I can give my critical opinion. Although the seawater does not raise the blood pressure very much, and even if it does, the pressure cannot be maintained for a long period of time, since human blood and plasma could not be obtained in large quantities during wartime, in the absence of such superior materials seawater could be a substitute in such cases because it can be obtained simply and in large quantities. So as a substitute in wartime, this would be a good substitute."

"Haven't you stated that both you and Rin—a Formosan doctor—resented Ishiyama's suggestion that seawater was as adequate as alginic acid?"

"I believe Rin misunderstood him, since he was working on alginic acid, and he misunderstood Ishiyama's statement to mean that alginic acid is inferior to seawater, so I believe that Rin resented Ishiyama's statement because of his misunderstanding."

"At that time, wasn't it much more simple to obtain seawater than it was alginic acid?"

"Yes."

"Then why did you, the National Research Council of the Ministry of Education, and the War Ministry, feel it was necessary to utilize army personnel and to spend more money in developing alginic acid?"

"From my personal interest, I made a request to the War Ministry to obtain supplies for carrying on this experiment, and I also made a request to the Ministry of Education Scientific Medical Research Council and stated that alginic acid was a superior chemical in raising the blood pressure, and this was recognized by this research council."

The direct examination ended on questions regarding Ishiyama's dictatorial nature and whether the members of his staff could have refused to operate on the American prisoners. Like the other witnesses preceding him, Tomoda acknowledged that they could have refused but added that with the feudalistic nature of the Japanese university—not just Ishiyama's clinic—it would have been unlikely, difficult, and professionally damaging to disobey.

Tomoda represented the last key witness for this phase of the prosecution's argument. Not only would he provide direct proof of the Japanese government's interest in blood substitute research, it also served as a link to the most important phase of the trial: the vivisections.

After almost three years worth of toil, a finalized picture of the eight men's last tortured moments would emerge.

The doors leading to the autopsy room slid open.[2] The procession of doctors marched in silence. Ishiyama, Komori, Mori, Hirao, Torisu. They were the celebrants in a grim ritual. Their gowns flowed behind them, shifting with the movement of their legs and hips.

They cleansed their hands with water and soap. The hot liquid streamed out of the faucets—steam rising from their fingers, the sink, and the drain—scalding the dirt from their skin. They rubbed their hands together, washing away their impurities because people were imperfect beings.

While the doctors scrubbed, the Western Army soldiers carried the first prisoner—probably Fredericks—into the autopsy room. The American lay unconscious, still blindfolded and bound. The two guards placed him on the flat surface of the dissecting table.

The guards who carried Fredericks into the room untied his hands and straightened out his prone body. His limbs offered no resistance. He had already been through so many rounds of sedation that he posed little threat to anyone in the room, even after the soldiers left. The soldiers removed his shirt, revealing a wound consisting of several pierced holes that on first inspection appeared to be bullet holes. There was not one exit wound, however, making the scenario unlikely. According to Komori, the flier had received the wound during his descent from the B-29.

Ishiyama pointed to the flier's shoulder and announced that the lung had been punctured and would need to be removed. The claim, however, made little sense, since Ishiyama had not even X-rayed.

Ishiyama moved to the right of the prisoner's chest and cleaned the wound, sterilizing it with iodine. He smeared it and watched the brown liquid glimmer, then grow dull as it dried. He washed the area with alcohol, then draped a sterile operating sheet over the body, the final step in preparing for the operation.

The members of the First Surgery Clinic surrounded the American. Miki directly assisted in the operation by passing instruments. On Ishiyama's left side, Torisu would be responsible for holding one of the clamps in place. Hirao stood directly opposite Ishiyama, and Komori to his right and Mori to his left. Senba assumed a position at the head of the flier in order to watch the flier's pulse. Most important, from that spot, he would be able to administer the seawater blood substitute that Ishiyama wanted to test. Tashiro and Nogawa stood to his rear and took turns keeping the electric lamp directed toward the procedure.

Once the skin on the patient's chest was cut, Ishiyama pulled it back. A resilient layer of muscle needed to be cut through in order to reach the lungs. Ishiyama separated the ribs from the breastbone by disconnecting the patch of cartilage that acts as a bridge between the two. With this achieved, the ribs were then laid out in the same manner as the skin and flesh—peeled back and away from the breastbone. Four inches of the American's third and fourth ribs were removed in order to clear a path to the lungs.

In a telling omission, Ishiyama skipped the one step that would have ensured that Fredericks' lung survived the procedure. Had he simply inserted a tube to pump air into the mouth and down the air pipe, lung collapse could have been completely prevented. Ishiyama, however, had no plans of allowing the prisoner to survive.

"As soon as the pleura was opened, the prisoner seemed to have a hard time breathing and he rocked on his shoulders. That action lasted for about two or three minutes. All the doctors waited until he stopped rocking," Tashiro recalled.

A profuse stream of blood poured out of the wound with each violent cough Undeterred, Ishiyama ordered the doctors to close the wound.

As one of the Anatomy Section members—Makino Reichiro—decided to take temporary leave of the room, Ishiyama made a bizarre but telling request. He asked for a coffin to be sent to the room.

Ishiyama approached the barely breathing body strapped to the dissecting table. He inspected the wound, considered how to best accommodate Komori's request for blood, then did the unthinkable. He untied the sutures and dug his hand into the flier's chest. Within minutes, the patient died.

"Ishiyama then took out the clotted blood with his hand, and with

Interior view of the Kyushu Imperial University autopsy room

a dish, dipped out the fluid blood. He put this in the same flask. The flask contained about 3,000 cc of blood," Senba recalled.

Ishiyama prepped Ponczka in a manner similar to Fredericks. The initial steps of the second lung operation proceeded similar to the first. As Ponczka's life slipped from the world, Komori again requested some blood, and just like he did in the prior experiment, Ishiyama complied without a thought. When asked what he would do with the blood, the Kaikosha doctor replied glibly that he would make bedbug poison out of it.

For the length of the two operations, Anatomy Section doctors hovered around the autopsy room. They had been granted permission by Hirako, the Anatomy Section chief, to gather samples from the deceased. Tanaka Katsumi removed sections of the abdomen—slices of stomach, pieces of liver, chunks of kidney and bladder, inch-long tubes of intestine. Makino helped himself to whatever remained of the chest region. Goshima removed sections of the deceased's wrist. While they worked, Miki Ryu began injecting Mueller solution into the American's neck, ruining the rest of the body for the other Anatomy Section members. Miki apologized and explained that he wanted to take out the American's brain. Goshima, Tanaka, and Makino left their comrade to complete his task. Nothing remained for them.

During the second set of operations, Mori received instructions from Ishiyama to perform a stomach resection. That would be the first operation of the day. Hirao was to assist and Komori would eventually take over the procedure. The three doctors moved to the stone wash basin and scrubbed. When they finished, Komori administered the ether while Mori waited for the prisoner to completely go under.

Mori began by making an incision from the base of the sternum to the umbilicus. Komori then cleaned up the remaining fatty tissue. He clamped the artery in two places, then tied it. Once he was satisfied that the artery was shut, he dug his scalpel into the arterial walls and severed them. With the blood supply cut off from the stomach, Komori separated the lower portion of the stomach, called the pylorus, from the upper end of the small intestine, called the jejunum. With one end loose, he sliced the esophageal end of the stomach free and pulled the organ out of the stomach.

When Ishiyama moved to the stomach operation to observe for a moment, he saw an operation on the decline. Immediately, he ordered the surgeons to the side and told them that he would perform a heart massage on the patient. In the meantime, he also ordered Senba to administer seawater in order to maintain a safe blood pressure. An incision similar to the one he made for the lung operations was made, then retracted.

Ishiyama took the heart in the palm of his left hand, and with a scalpel he cut about a one-inch incision in the heart. He then inserted a pointed instrument into the incision and started to poke around. When he finished, Ishiyama sewed up the incision with thread. About twenty or thirty minutes after the heart operation was completed, the prisoner died.

Undeterred, Ishiyama shrugged off the death and returned to the table he originally attended and the operation that most interested him—a liver resection. As the patient lay unconscious on the dissecting table, Ishiyama applied a local anesthetic to the abdominal area. He then proceeded to make a vertical incision from the lower sternum to the umbilicus. Ishiyama ordered Senba to administer seawater in order to raise the patient's plunging blood pressure. In the meantime, he continued to hack away at the liver, regardless of the blood gushing into the abdominal cavity. The seawater treatment was futile. The prisoner's vein collapsed and he died soon afterward.

The third set of operations appeared to have as much a chance of succeeding as the previous two. The prisoner was brought in on a stretcher while the doctors scrubbed. The guards placed him face down on the dissecting table. The nurses nestled his head into a metal head support and clamped it into place in order to keep it from moving during the operation.

Ishiyama gripped the steel scalpel in his hand and pierced the skin by the second vertebra around the junction of the neck and head. He eased the scalpel up and around the POW's head, then back down to the second vertebra, but on the opposite side. The final incision resembled a tennis racquet. Blood gushed from every inch of the incision. Streams of crimson slid down the prisoner's neck. With every attempt to clear away the blood, a new puddle formed in the wound until it overflowed and coursed down his skin.

Ishiyama inserted his hand into the skull and pushed the cerebellum to the left. Unfortunately, it refused to allow Ishiyama clear entrance into the deeper regions of the skull.

At that point, Hirako Goichi entered the room and walked directly to the operating table. Ishiyama asked Hirako where the root of the trigeminus nerve could be found and how to locate the substantia nigra. Hirako struggled to describe their positions in the brain relative to the current point of entrance. In order to better aid Ishiyama, Hirako went to his office and returned with a preserved human brain.

With a brain in his hand, Hirako explained to the First Surgery chief that neither the substantia nigra nor the root of the trigeminus nerve could be reached from the point of incision in the occiput.

Ishiyama refused to give up completely. But he and Komori did not try to save the prisoner's life. They tried to salvage what remained of a botched experiment. Without an aspirator to suck up the blood, however, they stood no chance. When the prisoner's bleeding drained his ability to breathe and his heart stopped beating, Ishiyama and

Komori stepped away from the dissecting table, walked to the scrubbing basin, and washed the blood from their hands.

The final set of operations took place on June 2, 1945. Ishyama turned to Senba and instructed him to use one of the prisoners solely for the purpose of testing the efficacy of the seawater blood substitute. While Senba and Hirao prepped their patient, Ishiyama, Komori, and Morimoto did the same for the other prisoner. They lacked, however, the willingness to do the job correctly. Instead, they cut corners. With the flier's fate already determined, Ishiyama opted to forego the shaving and sterilization of the incision area. He simply laid the chest bare and made an incision. He performed a lung operation in the exact same manner as his previous experiments. The result, unfortunately, mirrored them as well.

Senba and Hirao worked diligently on their patient. Because Senba was more of a researcher than a surgeon, the task of drawing blood from the prisoner fell on Hirao. As the blood drained from the body, Senba began administering the seawater. This process went on for nearly an hour and a half before the patient's condition deteriorated enough that emergency resuscitation measures were taken. But by that point the American's blood pressure plummeted so low that nothing could be done to save his life. When he died, Senba and Hirao cleaned up, packed their instruments, and left.

Ishiyama hastily prepared for the final procedure. In all likelihood, Robert Williams was the victim. Again, Ishiyama chose not to shave or sterilize the incision area. He dug his scalpel into the area just below the rib cage and dragged it down the abdomen and around the belly button. Morimoto retracted the incision, exposing Williams's abdominal cavity. Ishiyama decided to perform another liver resection; again, he would be removing the left lobe.

Ishiyama continued the operation for as long as possible. Eventually, his efforts fell victim to the same obstacle that thwarted his previous experiments—an accumulation of blood that made operating impossible. As Williams's blood pooled inside his abdominal cavity, he died.

18

Closing and Clemency: 1948–1950

The defense opened their case to the commission on July 7, 1948. As if following the prosecution's lead, they divided their argument into three similar phases: military, university, and the liver eaters.

Alpert addressed the charges against the Kaikosha doctors first and made it clear that he would assume an aggressive stance. He made a motion to dismiss all the charges leveled against Matake, Kishi, Ito Akira, Ito Tsurumaru, and Oda and argued that on a very basic level the prosecution failed to make a case against them. The circumstantial evidence presented by the prosecution lacked even a single piece of independent testimony to support their case.

"I will tell you why," Alpert declared as he explained the shortcoming. "Because that incident never took place. It is a figment of the imagination."

The brazenness of the defense's statement reflected the confidence they held in their conclusion. But Alpert was not finished; he took it one step further. He insisted that if such a heinous incident had occurred, it would be impossible to keep secret. Wouldn't someone at the hospital—participant or gossip monger—discuss it at some point? According to Alpert, "Not only did the liver-eating incident never take place but there was no plan to conceal it because it never took place."

Thorpe presented the case for the members of the Kyushu Imperial University staff. The defense claimed that the evidence presented by the prosecution failed to show that the accused had done anything other than cower under Ishiyama's dictatorial tactics. While they might have been guilty of a lack of fortitude, they were not murderers. Ishiyama and Komori—the two dead men—deserved the blame and responsibility. It was a very convenient strategy for the defense and not entirely original, since the Kyushu doctors had planned on blaming Komori to begin with.

Greene argued the case for the Western Army Headquarters officers. His argument was simple: the onus lay in the hands of the prosecution to prove guilt beyond a reasonable doubt and they had fallen well short of their required goal. Circumstantial evidence, testimonies of accused used against one another, and charges of conspiracy amounted to a weak and desperate case. Moreover, you could not use an inference drawn from circumstantial evidence as a fact to argue another point. Proving guilt by way of a chain of inference was illegal. In addition, none of the accused—besides Yokoyama and Sato—had direct and authoritative responsibility for assuring the well-being of the prisoners. They could not, therefore, be found guilty. They were following orders. Yokoyama, on the other hand, could not be held accountable for everything his subordinates did, especially when committed in secrecy, which the defense claimed the vivisections were.

One aspect of Greene's address stood out. Throughout the course of his speech, he made motions for dismissal of charges for every member of Western Army Headquarters with the exception of Colonel Sato. According to Greene, the prosecution had presented evidence that would need to be addressed by the defense. In the eyes of both the prosecution and the commission, this was a telling action. The defense's strategy became apparent. Sato would shoulder the blame for the military phase of the trial.

In no way trying to aid Sato, the prosecution pretended to be concerned about fair justice. In reality, it was just another way of attacking the defense's case. The commission, however, had the responsibility of presiding over a just trial and demanded to know whether the defense had informed Sato of their decision. They hadn't told Sato, claiming that it was their own decision to make. The colonel's situation did not look good and would only get worse when the time came for him to be heard.

Colonel Sato took the stand as the defense's first witness. He served as their primary source of information for the Western Army Headquarters phase of the case. Nobody else would take the stand. Only Sato's voice would be heard. Whatever his testimony established would be representative of each officer on trial.

For a team representing a man with his life to lose, the defense denied Sato the right to be heard with the benefit of their guidance. The truth, however, turned out to be grimmer. They submitted a statement made and sworn to by Sato that unequivocally declared his guilt. The only thing the defense's token direct examination of Sato revealed was that there was a single sentence that he wanted to correct for the record. Coincidentally, the correction Sato made further removed the responsibility from his Western Army superiors' shoulders. If there existed a foil to Marvin's position in the case, it was Sato. Where Marvin achieved redemption, Sato became a sacrificial lamb.

The prosecution was livid. Hagen expressed his exasperation at seeing his case destroyed by an unofficial guilty plea. "This appears to be a narrative drummed up by someone other than Sato. It was read twice to him and he adopted it. Maybe they did talk him into signing it . . . there is no certificate that anyone ever took this statement in Japanese from the accused. It is a Charlie McCarthy statement which may appear to be Sato's, but the language, the wording, is not.

"I read for the benefit of the law member: 'I alone am responsible . . . ' Responsible for what? Everything he is accused of? Does he understand that? Does his lawyer, who has never read the statement, understand that? 'I alone am responsible . . . ' He is assuming responsibility for every charge and spec against him. Does he understand that? I don't think so. Does his personal counsel understand it?"

The commission ignored Hagen's plea and denied the objection. The statement entered the trial record as evidence, and the defense's strategy remained intact for the time being. The prosecution, however, would do their best to muster a counteroffensive.

Hagen's cross-examination of Sato focused on discrediting Sato's statement. Ironically, what should have been a dream—a guilty plea—was actually a nightmare.

"Were you told that if you signed this statement that it would help some of the accused go free?" Hagen asked.

Seydel jumped to his feet and interjected, "Object to that question as an attempt to prejudice the mind of the commission and nothing further; it isn't that the answer is important to the commission; it's the question and the thought that he is transmitting to the question."

The commission denied the objection and wanted to hear Sato's answer.

"I was not told," he replied. "However, I know about that."

"How do you know about that?"

"I could judge that for myself."

"Were you told that if you didn't sign a statement to that effect that they would not defend you?"

Seydel objected once more. The commission responded as they had done with most of the defense's objections—with a denial.

Sato indicated that at the time he signed the document, he had not been told anything by the members of the defense. However, an interpreter had suggested it.

"Colonel Sato, since these Kyushu operations occurred, have you at any time been offered money if you would assume the responsibility for what happened at the university?"

"Object to that question as immaterial," Seydel said. The prosecution's line of questioning threatened to do irreparable damage to the defense's case that hinged on Sato's acceptance of responsibility. If he had taken a bribe or been coerced into his decision, it would be impossible to protect his superiors and subordinates. Unfortunately for them, the commission denied their objection.

"I was not told any such thing," Sato replied.

Hagen corrected Sato. "I am not asking you if you were told any such thing. I am asking you if you were offered a sum of money if you would assume the responsibility."

"Strike the last question," Hagen continued, turning his attention back to Sato. "After the termination of the war, did Lieutenant General Yokoyama offer you a sum of money if you would assume the sole responsibility for the Kyushu case?"

Seydel objected to the question, claiming that it was prejudicial. The commission responded with an assurance that they are not easily misled and a denial of the defense's objection.

Sato was finally allowed to respond to Hagen's answer. "General Yokoyama did not."

"Who did, if anyone, offer you money?"

"Object to the question as immaterial," Seydel seethed.

"The objection is denied."

This time, Sato's response lacked the conviction his previous response carried. "I cannot give his name. However, I believe that it was not any such thing as compensation. However, he thought of our family future as we would be tried as war criminals."

"By that you mean that the money was to go to your family?"

"I believe so," Sato conceded.

"When was that offer made?"

"It was either in January or February 1946."

Sato stated that the offer was made about a month after Colonel Oki arrived at Western Army Headquarters. He stressed that the money was not compensation but was offered "in order to help our families."

"Was this offer of money to be to your family?"

"I believe so," Sato admitted.

Seydel needed to stop the questioning however he could. Again, he addressed the commission, only this time he focused on the most influential member of the tribunal.

"Mr. President, I move to strike the last question and answer on the grounds that we are not here concerned with what inducement may be offered to a man to stop concealing and to tell the truth; and according to the statements of the witness, that is just exactly what the offer was: stop concealing, stop conspiring to conceal, and tell the truth, and your families will be taken care of. Now, that is not material to this inquiry. What the motives were, inducing the man to tell the truth as it appeared on the sworn statement, we are not concerned with. Let him tell the truth, and let the prosecution attack those statements or any other statements that he desires to make."

Hagen had had enough of Seydel's interruptions and turned his attention to the defense. "If it please the commission, I am wondering sometimes whether counsel is *defending* this accused or not." The prosecution went one step further and insisted that from that point forward all arguments from both sides be translated for Sato. Hagen's claim: "So that the personal counsel of the accused may know exactly the proceedings that are going on."

Seydel shot back immediately and mockingly: "We don't think, sir, that until the commission is convinced that the prosecution is *defending* the witness that such remarks are in order."

After listening to the exchange, the commission denied the defense's objection and allowed Hagen to repeat his previous question, prompting yet another objection and denial.

Sato had nowhere to go. He had to answer the question: was the money intended for his family?

"Naturally, that is so," he admitted.

Hagen got what he wanted from Sato—an admission that he had been offered money in exchange for a statement admitting his guilt.

The next major step in Hagen's strategy entailed dispelling the defense's assertion that none of Sato's superiors—Yokoyama, Fukushima, Inada, Jin, and Horiuchi—had been aware of the operations and that he alone bore responsibility for the atrocities. More than discrediting Sato's testimony, having positive testimony from Sato implicating them would seal the military phase of the case in one blow.

Hagen tried to establish that the Adjutant Section had to be aware of the operations. Since they were responsible for keeping records at the headquarters, it was natural to try to establish their knowledge.

Sato admitted that he was aware that he would have had to account for the fliers but did not have any discussion with Goiyama regarding their release. In fact, Sato claimed that he did not speak with anyone at Western Army Headquarters at the time the first operation took place, all the while knowing that headquarters procedures necessitated that he file a receipt any time a flier was transferred anywhere. No plans had been made to account for the sudden dip in prisoner number.

Hagen shifted tactics and used food as a way to prove that others besides Sato's subordinates had knowledge of the executions. Sato admitted that Goiyama decreased the amount of rations in proportion to the decreasing number of prisoners. That change would have to be filed in a report that ended up with the senior ranking adjutant—in this case, Jin.

"What explanation was made after the first operation to account for the decrease by two in the number of fliers held?" Hagen asked.

"As far as I know, there was no written report," Sato claimed. "However, when the report was made orally according to Goiyama, the explanation was made that they had been sent to Kyushu Imperial University."

Hagen had essentially established that Lieutenant Colonel Jin knew about the operations. Someone knew. Yet, Hagen wanted more and continued pressing Sato about the concealment plans. He did not get as much from Sato as he had hoped and refocused his examination on Yokoyama. Hagen wanted to establish that Yokoyama's policies led to Sato's actions. If possible, he wanted the colonel to admit that the commanding general knew about the Kyushu Imperial University vivisections.

"In accordance with the policy at Western Army Headquarters in May and June 1945, if you had not sent these fliers to Kyushu Imperial University where they were killed, what would have happened to them?"

"I believe that everyone would have been executed in June," Sato replied.

"Wasn't it the policy of Western Army Headquarters from and after the first of May 1945 to execute every flier received at headquarters and who wasn't forwarded to Tokyo?"

Sato claimed that he could not explain the matter simply. Hagen asked for an explanation, regardless of length. Sato explained that prior to May 10, 1945, Western Army Headquarters policy dictated that captured fliers be tried before a military tribunal. However, after May 10, it was his belief that Yokoyama changed the policy and that fliers would be executed without a trial.

"After the fliers," Hagen stopped and corrected himself. "After Watkins's crew had been killed at Kyushu Imperial University, what efforts were made to advise Tokyo that Watkins's crew had been killed?"

Sato responded that no effort had been made.

"Colonel Sato," Hagen said sternly. "After the operations, did you write a letter to the Sixth Intelligence Section of the Tokyo headquarters advising them that Watkins's crew had been killed and asking for the disposal of Watkins?"

Sato admitted writing the letter but denied that he sought Watkins's execution. Rather, he claimed to have been seeking to establish that Marvin was still alive. If he was, Sato reasoned, concealment plans would need to be worked out. Hagen did not believe Sato and pressed him for more answers.

"Why did you write that particular letter to Major Kikkawa rather than to some other official at the headquarters?"

"I thought that Kikkawa knew where the fliers were and heard that Kikkawa carried on investigations and handled other matters regarding the fliers, so I thought he knew where the fliers were." Sato added, "Besides, I did not know any other person in Tokyo."

"Did you have any communications with anyone in Tokyo after the operations in which you advised that the balance of the Watkins crew be killed?"

He didn't. Neither did he know of any member of the intelligence section of Western Army Headquarters communicating with Tokyo on the subject.

"When you were in Tokyo in July 1945, did you contact the Kempei Tai as to whether or not they had in their possession a flier by the name of Watkins?"

"I did not." Sato shook his head.

Hagen changed the subject unexpectedly. "In your statement, I find the following sentence which I would like to have you explain further: 'Nothing was considered forbidden if it was directed against the enemy.' "

"It was the determination of the commanding general at that time," Sato explained. "I thought that it meant that if the purpose was clear any method would be permissible."

"By the use of the word 'enemy,' do you mean that to be construed to be 'captured enemy'?"

"According to the intention of the commanding general, they naturally would be included."

"From the time of the operations up until your demobilization on 30 November 1945, were you ever reprimanded by any of your superiors for your actions in connection with Kyushu Imperial University?"

"No."

"Were you ever commended for the same actions?" Colonel Joyce asked.

Before Sato could respond, Sedyel interjected. "Mr. President, will you also ask if his superiors knew of it?"

"They couldn't have commended him if they didn't know of it," Joyce replied.

Sato replied that he had never been commended.

Joyce continued the questioning. He would be the one to complete the prosecution's task.

"Did your superiors know of your actions at Kyushu Imperial University?"

Sato's answer was simple: "Yes."

Seeing the defense's case crumbling before his eyes, Seydel jumped in and insisted that Sato be allowed to clarify when his superiors knew. It allowed Sato to backtrack and claim that they had only been informed about the vivisections after the fact. It was the closest anyone would come to establishing that the high command of Western Army Headquarters knew about the vivisections. The best they would get out of Sato was an admission that Yokoyama's policies set the stage for the vivisections.

While Sato was not the defense's final witness, he was without a doubt the most significant. With his testimony intact, their argument that he was responsible for releasing the Watkins crew to their deaths held. By bearing the burden of his superiors and subordinates, he would secure their release.

Four members of the Kyushu Imperial University accused—Senba, Hirao, Torisu, and Hirako—took the stand, and the defense's direct examination consisted of their swearing that testimonies submitted by the defense were true. The evidence did not deny their involvement; it only stated that they felt forced into the situation. That was all.

Unfortunately, the prosecution's tactics were not much better or groundbreaking. They fell back on trying to rebut each written testimony submitted by rehashing the circumstances behind the operations—facts they had established months earlier. Nothing new was established. While each doctor admitted to participating in the operations in a limited role, the doctors claimed that they felt unable to refuse Ishiyama's requests because of his dictatorial manner and because the Japanese military appeared to have ordered the experiments. They feared punishment if they refused.

The final phase of the defense's case—the liver eaters—followed suit. Seydel followed up the bold assertion that the cannibalism incident was an unfortunate fabrication by supporting it with testimonies from the accused. Each written and sworn statement recounted Legal Section interrogations filled with physical and verbal intimidation that often spilled over into actual violence. It painted a picture of coercion on the part of Tait, Resendes, McKnight, and Miller. The defense relied solely on the written testimonies of the accused.

The prosecution, in turn, focused their efforts on disproving the defense's claim and attacked the documents. They tried to establish the fact that their initial confessions represented the valid events and that given the time it was natural that the Kaikosha doctors should make an attempt at escaping punishment by retracting their incriminating statements.

The defense rested on August 11, 1948, a little over a month since making their opening statement.

Closing arguments commenced on August 16, 1948. Seydel represented the defense team and addressed the commission. He would assume the responsibility for both the American and Japanese attorneys. The prosecution, on the other hand, opted to platoon their staff and allow Baird, Hagen, and Von Bergen to triple-team the final argument.

For the defense, it stood as their final opportunity to convince the commission that Sato held sole responsibility for the Western Army phase of the atrocities. If the commission accepted the defense's version and Sato assumed the blame, the other members of Western Army Headquarters standing trial would be acquitted of the most serious charges. While they stood a good chance of being found guilty of concealment, they would still escape with their lives and short sentences.

The same held true for the Kyushu Imperial University accused. If the defense could sway the commission into accepting that Komori and Ishiyama planned and executed the operations while the accused were simply following orders, the members of Ishiyama's First Surgery and Hirako's Anatomy Section would likewise be acquitted of the most serious charges—namely murder.

The defense team's final task involved the Kaikosha doctors accused of cannibalism. The logic of their arguments had to convince the commission that the incidents never happened and that Team 420 had engaged in questionable techniques in order to solicit confessions of guilt.

The prosecution found themselves with the same clear-cut goals they had pursued throughout the trial. They needed to establish that since the Kaikosha doctors confessed to their crimes, they had to be guilty; in addition, they had to show that in both the Kyushu Imperial University and Western Army Headquarters phases, all of the accused could have declined to participate. The most important thing that needed to be established was that while Sato might have played a central role in the events, he could only do so with the approval of his superiors and willing cooperation of his subordinates. If the prosecution convinced the commission of that single fact, the pieces of the entire case fell into place.

Seydel stood before the commission and laid out the final

conclusions for the defense's arguments. He started with the Kaikosha doctors.

"Mr. President, perhaps the subject that is most recent in your mind in this trial is that of the alleged liver eaters, so I will discuss that first," he opened. "The evidence of the prosecution depends on conviction upon the alleged confessions."

Those confessions, Seydel argued, came about as a result of a constant state of duress and intimidation on the part of the SCAP Legal Section. While confessions bore a significant amount of weight in courtrooms, coerced statements were inadmissible. Moreover, they were illegal, even when viewed in terms of current American jurisprudence. In addition to resulting from coercion, the Kaikosha doctors' confessions suffered from another shortcoming. Confessions that implicated coaccused held no weight in the courtroom. Time had proven that a person confessing to a crime tended to shift the blame on other people in order to lessen his own punishment. They represented half-truths.

"Now, that is the case of the prosecution," Seydel concluded. "They are depending entirely upon these confessions."

The prosecution offered no proof to corroborate the statements. Not one of the confessions was written in the handwriting of the accused and even more suspect was the fact that not a single independent witness emerged in favor of the prosecution's assertions. In other words, Seydel argued, the prosecution failed to present the commission with sufficient evidence to convict the doctors.

A more daunting challenge faced Seydel in the Western Army Headquarters phase of his argument. There were more players involved and the prosecution had managed to call a number of independent witnesses to the stand. Moreover, the defense's entire case hinged on one person, one testimony, and with any luck, one guilty ruling—that of Colonel Sato. As bizarre as it was, his credibility had to be protected so that the commission had no choice but to find him guilty. A guilty verdict had to happen according to the defense's reasoning, however. The entire responsibility had to fall on Sato in order for the others to go free.

Seydel laid the groundwork by introducing Kyushu as one of the most feudalistic societies in modern Japan. In addition to its medieval atmosphere, Japan's southernmost island had been the prime candidate for an American invasion target. As a result, the military maintained a tight grip on Kyushu and its population. Ishiyama essentially played the dictatorial role of an old-time warlord in relation to his university underlings, and Western Army Headquarters ruled supreme. The notion of dissent simply did not exist. The university staff could refuse Ishiyama, much less the army, which they felt ordered the operations. When considering the case, Seydel argued, it had to be kept in mind that though they participated in the operations, they did so against their wills and fearing for their lives. Moreover, they were not involved in planning the operations. That responsibility fell on Ishiyama and Komori.

According to Seydel, the situation at Western Army Headquarters was even more stifling than at the university. It was a military operation in the most feudalistic area of Japan. Their ultimate accountability, however, was to Tokyo. They reported to Tokyo and received orders from the capital. The concealment plans emanated from Tokyo's halls and therefore they bore responsibility, not the Western Army Headquarters officers.

"Those are the persons," Seydel declared, "that should be punished for waging aggressive warfare. Those are the persons who on the 15th of August said, 'Destroy everything'; and in order to follow up on the thing, they had meetings thereafter. Those are the real conspirators."

The defense blamed Komori for initiating the series of events that would culminate in the vivisections. Seydel portrayed him as a man "whose shadow, whose figure, and whose infamy lies after him." Komori advanced the idea of experimental operations; he spoke to Sato in order to gain access to the POWs; he received clearance from the superintendent of the hospital; he approached Ishiyama about operating and served as the first assistant during the operations. Komori, it was argued, deserved a third of the blame.

Yokoyama, however, could not be held responsible for the vivisections. Sato kept the operations secret and only divulged the truth to Yokoyama after they had already taken place. There were no official reports filed; had Yokoyama authorized the operations, there would have been a written record. Seydel added that had Yokoyama given the go-ahead for the operations, they would have taken place at a military hospital and not at the university hospital. No, a man could not be held criminally liable for something that he knew nothing about. Moreover, he could not be held responsible for the actions of his subordinates—in this case, Colonel Sato—particularly when those actions occurred in secret. Yokoyama was innocent; Sato was guilty.

Seydel's argument for Sato's superiors and subordinates was essentially the same. Proof of their innocence rested with Sato's guilt. Inada, Ito, and Fukushima knew nothing about Sato's secretive plot, and Aihara, Goiyama, and the remainder of Sato's subordinate officers were following orders that they were not at liberty to disobey. Therefore, they bore no responsibility. They were innocent; Sato was guilty.

By the time the defense's closing argument addressed Sato's role, it was clear that the word "innocent" would not be mentioned in conjunction with his name. And it wasn't. The best Seydel had to offer on behalf of his client was a plea to be nice to him. While Sato might have been guilty of orchestrating the operations, he did not actually hold the knife. Seydel claimed that he was not responsible for the criminal act, only for the acts he committed. "And whether they are criminal or not is for the commission to decide" was the defense's simple and obvious assessment of the situation. As one final slap in the face, Seydel concluded his argument not by professing Sato's innocence but by declaring that he did not deserve to be hung.

"Now, gentlemen," Seydel said, "if you were trying Sato, Ishiyama, and Komori only before this commission, Ishiyama being alive, Komori being alive, you would consider who played the major role in this affair, who were those who were just followers; and you would resolve that Ishiyama was the man, Komori was the man; that Sato was merely a minor operator; and you would therefore resolve that the punishment for Sato would be less than you would give to either Ishiyama or Komori. Thank you."

The prosecution's closing argument, while longer, was essentially less elaborate than the defense's effort. They fell back on stating the obvious and reciting point by point everything they had argued during the prosecutorial phase of the trial.

Baird spoke first and addressed the issue of the Kaikosha doctors. His argument was straight to the point if not reductive. The accused were guilty of their crimes because they admitted them. People did not admit to crimes they did not commit. And only after confessing to their wrongdoings did the liver eaters understand the implications of their admissions and recant their statements. In order to shift blame, they concocted the story of being intimidated. Again, Baird resorted to elementary school reasoning in order to prove his point.

"This commission has heard the testimony of Mr. McKnight and of Captains Tracy and Miller," he stated. "There is no doubt in the minds of the prosecution who should be believed, and we believe the commission will take the testimony of these investigators to be the truth."

Hagen took up the argument where Baird left off—the military phase. He argued that concealment and conspiracy to conceal were serious charges. Both represented crimes committed and planned with a "cool head," not in the heat of the moment. They were premeditated acts and heinous. Everyone from the top down deserved to share equal responsibility.

"We do not claim that each and every accused did everything that is alleged in the concealment. That is not necessary. If one enters into a conspiracy for a certain purpose, he is bound by the acts of each and every person in that conspiracy."

Moreover, the desire to conceal proved another point.

"Concealment efforts usually indicate a consciousness of guilt—and throw a guilt-revealing light upon acts that might otherwise seem innocent."

Hagen, however, knew where the heart of his argument and the Prosecution's case lay. Like Seydel, Hagen knew that the case depended on proving Colonel Sato guilty on his own terms. Sato could not be convicted as the sole conspirator. He had to be seen as the main participant in a headquarters-wide drive to kill.

Hagen addressed the defense's case bluntly. "To contend that Colonel Sato acted on his own and contrary to headquarters policy is preposterous."

A career officer would not jeopardize his life's work in order to embark on some misguided and doomed mission to execute POWs without the support of his superiors. It was foolish to believe he would ruin his career because he hated his enemy. He had nothing to gain, so why take the chance? Hagen posed another question. Supposing Sato did act in defiance of the Western Army high command, how could he get the entire headquarters—from generals to corporals—to follow his lead and follow his orders? And if he acted in defiance, why wasn't he reprimanded when the war was over? Finally, Hagen addressed the defense's contention that Sato might have misunderstood Yokoyama's orders. A misunderstanding happens once, the prosecutor argued, not over the span of a month. Yes, Sato was guilty, but not in the way the defense contended.

The remainder of Hagen's argument centered around points that had been reiterated time and again during the course of the trial: Yokoyama set the tone and policy for the operations to take place; the high command cooperated with Sato while subordinates could have willingly disobeyed the colonel; moreover, it made no sense to think that generals in the Imperial Japanese Army would bend over backward, risking their lives, to cover up the misdeeds of a colonel—unless they had something to lose.

Hagen concluded, "This case has been a long one and an important one. Now the decision is up to the commission. We ask that the commission in carrying out their duty as we have done and as all of us have done, prosecution and defense, carry it out in mind and in line with the Potsdam Declaration, which was the solemn agreement of the four Allied powers that those who were guilty of war crimes would receive stern justice."

Von Bergen was the last attorney to be heard, and aside from repeated derogatory remarks about the Japanese, his argument mirrored those set forth by his partners. While admitting that Ishiyama played the key role in Kyushu Imperial University's involvement in the crimes, he denied the defense's contention that it was impossible for the members of his clinic to disobey his orders. Von Bergen pointed to the numerous people who took the stand and testified that had they been in similar positions, they would not have participated. Then, one fact at a time, the chief prosecutor catalogued the offenses of each of the university members standing trial and the circumstances behind their actions. The strategy of his closing argument relied more on bludgeoning than persuasion.

Von Bergen concluded his argument with a final plea for stern justice and a final dig at the Japanese people. "It would have been better for the fliers to have been killed in honorable combat than to have endured what they endured here in Japan. The situation was different in those days. The Japanese held the upper hand. Now, they are all good Japanese. They only murdered eight Americans. There is no punishment that is commensurate with the heinous aspects of the crime perpetrated by each of these accused, singly and brutally, and history will never forget it."

The commission handed down verdicts for the Kyushu Imperial University atrocities trial on August 27, 1948. Of the university staff, Hirao, Mori, and Torisu were found guilty of willfully and unlawfully killing approximately eight American prisoners by vivisecting them; maltreating and desecrating the American prisoners by mutilation, dissection, and removal of body parts; and preventing honorable burial for the deceased. In addition, the commission found Torisu guilty of conspiring with Sato and Yokoyama to conceal the atrocities from occupation forces. As a result, the three doctors were sentenced "to be hanged by the neck until dead."[1]

Sato and Yokoyama received similar sentences. They were "to be hanged by the neck until dead" for all of the same charges as the university doctors. In addition, the Western Army officers were found guilty for denying the American prisoners human treatment, safe custody, and protection; prisoner-of-war status, which international law entitled them to; concealment of facts from the Japanese Prisoner-of-War Information Board and occupation forces; and conspiracy to conceal the atrocities.

While the commission found Morimoto, Senba, and Yakumaru guilty of the same charges as those sentenced to death, they got off easier. They escaped death but would spend the remainder of their days imprisoned and engaged in hard labor.

The remaining suspects—except the Kaikosha doctors—received sentences of hard labor of varying degrees. Aihara received twenty years for his part in the release of the prisoners; Fukushima got fifteen years for playing a role in the concealment; Goshima received six years for taking samples from the deceased prisoners' bodies. The Kaikosha doctors accused of cannibalism had the charges dismissed completely.

With the increasing overt hostility between the West and Communist East, battle lines emerged all across the globe. In particular, America and the Soviet Union jockeyed for strategic advantages. The political climate in Asia changed drastically as a result. The first conflict of the Cold War brewed in a divided Korean peninsula. The Soviet Union's 1947 U.N. Security Council opposition to general elections throughout the north and south further entrenched the two sides.

With America's new antagonist situated in northern Asia and the first probable area of conflict in Korea, Washington's priorities in Asia shifted. Prior to the war, the Philippines were considered ideally situated with respect to the Asian continent. MacArthur often referred to the archipelago as the "doorway to Asia." This proved particularly true during the Pacific War when Japan lay just north of the country. But after the war, the Philippines were too far south to play a major role in the Cold War. Now, Japan, with its proximity to Korea and the Soviet Union, rose in its significance. Unlike the Philippines, which held a quasi-autonomy, Japan "belonged" to the United States, at least for the time being. If Washington built a nation and government with amicable ties, it would prove priceless. American airbases could be built; troops could be massed during times of conflict; air and water space would be accessible—Japan, Korea, and the Soviet Union shared much of the same waters; the advantages were enormous. The American doorway to Asia had been relocated.

The time had come to put an official end to the Pacific War. In 1950, American Ambassador-at-large Philip Jessup held a series of meetings with MacArthur in which they unofficially discussed what the course of action in Japan should be. According to Jessup, MacArthur felt that signing a peace treaty with Japan was a priority. The Japanese had held up their end of the Potsdam Agreement and it was in America's best interests to follow suit. Moreover, the treaty and its conditions should be negotiated in Tokyo. It made America look better. But there MacArthur had an ulterior motive, as well.

In a letter from Jessup to the State Department, Jessup offered a recollection and opinion: "As you know, he [MacArthur] feels very strongly that we should go ahead with the negotiation of the Treaty. I fully agree with him. In this connection, he stressed a point which the Consultants also had in mind; namely, that the negotiation of the Peace Treaty would be one of the dramatic steps by which we could recapture from the Russians the initiative in terms of general Asiatic thinking."[2]

Assistant Secretary of State for Far Eastern Affairs W. Walton Butterworth further reiterated concerns about losing Asia to the Soviet Union and China to Secretary of State Dean Acheson. In a memo with the subject heading "Japanese Peace Settlement," Butterworth wrote: "The present situation is viewed as one in which the occupation in its present form has passed its peak, the Japanese and most, if not all, of the friendly Allied Powers favor the conclusion of an early peace treaty if security can be maintained, the Soviet Union and Communist China together have substantial capabilities of influencing Japan's future behavior, and it is of primary political importance that the United States be in a position of favoring and attempting to obtain a satisfactory peace treaty."

A National Security Council directive outlined the steps necessary for establishing a lasting peace and friendship with Japan. It stated that a peace treaty could not be negotiated while Japanese soldiers still stood trial for war crimes. It was implied that an overwhelming majority of convicted Japanese war criminals would have to be granted clemency. After a peace treaty was signed and Japan was a completely sovereign nation, they could decide what to do with the remainder of the prisoners.

On March 25, 1950, two years and thirteen days after the Kyushu Imperial University atrocities case went to trial, the Office of the Judge Advocate General (JAG) ruled that due to severe judicial errors on the part of the presiding commission members, the rulings were deemed questionable. According to the review panel, the accused were denied access to their lawyers by the president-law member. During numerous recesses, Colonel Joyce refused to allow the defense to speak to their clients but allowed prosecution witnesses to confer with the prosecution under similar circumstances.

In addition, JAG found that the commission conducted the proceedings improperly and that the president-law member "unduly harassed counsel for the defense and at times disparaged defense's efforts." Thirteen exchanges between the law member and defense in which the commission berated the defense were cited as "some" examples. Making matters worse, the reviewer found that the commission unfairly prevented the defense from mounting an effective case because of an inordinate number of objections issued by law members on their own initiative. By continuously interrupting the defense, the commission members essentially denied him the opportunity to present his case. In short, the president-law member "exhibited a decided lack of judicial temperament and control."

The judge advocate general offered a critique of Colonel Joyce: "In all fairness to the president-law member, however, it should be stated that the board is convinced that the errors noted were not occasioned by improper motives but arose from misguided zeal and a basic misunderstanding of correct legal procedures." In other words, he was simply incompetent.

The review panel concluded: "In view of the foregoing, the Board of Review has no hesitancy in concluding that the infirmities noted combined to deprive each of these accused of the fair trial guaranteed him by the supreme commander for the Allied powers, and that therefore the proceedings properly should be remanded for a new trial. . . . Nevertheless, any reluctance to recommend a rehearing must be subordinated to the interests of substantial justice. Accordingly, we hold that to sustain this case would indeed make a hollow mockery of the rules intended to provide accused war criminals with certain basic rights and would establish the precedent that accused war criminals have little or no actual rights where the evidence introduced against them tends to establish their guilt of the offenses charged. Such action is repugnant to our sense of justice and inconsistent with the basic principles contained in the trial regulations."

The findings and sentences against Hirao Kenichi, Mori Yoshio,

Torisu Taro, Yokoyama Isamu, and Sato Yoshinao were subsequently disapproved. Rehearings for the other defendants were also ordered.

After years of legal and political wrangling, the sentences that had been reduced to slaps on the wrists were completely nullified in 1958 when responsibility for Japan's war criminals reverted to the Japanese government. Quietly, the men convicted by American tribunals rejoined Japanese society. Presiding over the agreement was Secretary of State John Foster Dulles and U.S. Ambassador to Japan Douglas MacArthur.

That the Kyushu Imperial University atrocities case made it to trial represents something of an enigma, especially when considering the proximity of its subject matter to the dark, microbial secret that SCAP and Washington needed desperately to keep hidden. Yet the fact that this case did go to trial tells us something. It tells us that it had something that the others didn't.

First off, make no mistake, the Kyushu Imperial University atrocities trial was a biological warfare trial. It was, however, the "lite" version—something like a prepackaged, made-to-order, already censored, ready-for-public consumption trial—devoid of key names, specific subject matter, logical questioning, and competent lawyers. But the links were there had anyone in the courtroom—prosecutor, defense, law member, stenographer, or audience member—bothered or been allowed to follow certain lines of questioning to their logical ends. In particular, questions referring to government funding for army-approved research; the implementation of a military man with no education experience in the presidency of the third most prestigious school in all of Japan; the link between Ishiyama and Tomoda's blood research and the army. In fact, had the lines of questioning been taken one simple and obvious step further regarding the blood research—establishing to whom the doctors reported and what institution organized the blood substitute research—they would have led straight to Ishii's door. The link between Kyushu Imperial University and the Densenbyo Kenkyusho was waiting to be brought out. From there, the DK would lead to Naito, Abe, and Ishii—all of whom essentially ran the research center. But whenever it appeared as if someone would open that door, no one bothered to pull it open. Eventually, however, the commission offered a veiled acknowledgment of the clandestine biological research program, though the comment was designed to put a stop to any lines of questioning that would have led to the revelation of more sensitive facts.

Considering its timing, Washington could not have asked for more. It came at a juncture when the Soviet Union threatened to expose the American push for biological weapons and the compromises they made to achieve a strategic advantage. Had the truth come out, it would not have been pretty—whether a matter of national security or not. What was at stake was more than just biological warfare secrets. Public opinion and America's newfound standing as one of two world powers was at stake. And while public opinion by itself seems innocent enough, considering the fact that both Washington and Moscow were actively recruiting countries to their sides made the world's opinion that much more important. What country would side with a nation that harbored criminals guilty of some of the most heinous atrocities known to man? There was a moral high ground to be lost.

So what were Washington's options with the Russians ready to continue the public pressure? Washington could have continued to deny the Russian charges, but such stubbornness would probably only have resulted in some commando journalist's front-page exposé in one of the world's major papers. Someone was bound to dig if constant reminders of the topic continued surfacing. Divulging select facts left too much to chance. Reveal the wrong fact and it could lead to another, then an information snowball effect would ruin everything. Coming clean was an obvious "nonstarter."

A final option was to accept the situation, then figure out how to make the most of it. Enter Case 420. Most likely, it had to go to trial. It was too closely tied to the Western Army Headquarters beheadings trial to be swept under the carpet. This turned out to work in Washington's favor. The Kyushu case was about biological experimentation, but it was not about microbial warfare; the Kyushu case belonged to the same umbrella program as Ishii et al., but it belonged to a different branch with different aims. At every point, the Kyushu case seemed just off-center enough to be about something but not be about it at the same time. It was an intelligence community's dream.

By taking the Kyushu trial to the press and refocusing the public's attention where it wanted, Washington engaged in a classic example of what intelligence circles refer to as white propaganda. It is the dissemination of misinformation through conventional mass communication like newspapers, radio, and television.

Making the Kyushu case a faux biowarfare case gave Washington breathing room. If it could be pulled off successfully, they would gain a number of advantages. It would strengthen their image as a firm but just nation that tried criminals. It would also seize the propaganda initiative from the Russians and blunt their newspaper offensive. Most importantly, it supplied Washington with a chance to deny charges of harboring Japanese criminals. It granted them the gift of plausible denial.

Of course, there is always the chance that the Kyushu case was what it was—a trial of criminals, no more, no less. And when considered in terms of the commission's initial ruling, it makes sense. But when seen in light of commuted sentences and eventual clemency, things take on a different look. How was it that such a celebrated and high-profile trial—as Carpenter boasted—was staffed by a panel of six incompetent men, the most bumbling being the president of the commission? For a theater run with an iron fist where even newspaper stories had to be cleared by MacArthur's people, it seems highly unlikely that such an attention-grabbing trial would have anything but top-notch personnel. Anything else would have been an embarrassment to MacArthur. Yet there they were, a commission whose inability to understand and carry out the rule of law "forced" the judge advocate general to reverse their ruling.

But what of the case itself? Again, it was a matter of what aspect was stressed. Case 420's investigators, the prosecution, defense, and law members, all viewed the case as if they were using a microscope. They focused and magnified one aspect—the murders in Fukuoka—while blocking out the bigger contextual picture—the biological experimentation program. Theoretically, they did nothing wrong and unearthed the facts they sought successfully, but in a sense they looked for and discovered the bare minimum that would be necessary to take the case to trial. Time and again, Legal Section reports implied a connection between the Kyushu Imperial University case and other biowarfare cases under investigation. Again, the link was there. Legal Section investigators simply chose to ignore it.

Other aspects of the case seem shaky. The notion that Sato and Komori—a midlevel officer and a lowly probationary officer—could circumvent Japanese army protocol so easily, then have prisoners released and murdered, makes little sense. And even with Ishiyama's conviction, the case still does not stand up. The authority to order the execution of POWs by way of scientific experimentation needed to come from Tokyo. Even Ishii needed Tokyo's blessing. To say that Sato, Komori, and Yokoyama didn't need it is absurd.

The question then arises as to whether the accused acted on their own accord. Ishiyama is the perfect example. He is essentially portrayed as the renegade professor, much the way Ishii was characterized by his cohorts when they actively tried to distance themselves and their superiors from him. Yet it makes no sense. Granted that personalities differ, but the Japanese military and academic worlds were both highly codified and rigid institutions. The wiggle room needed to be a loose-cannon scientist would not exist. Even in cultures less feudalistic—for example, American or European—a pattern of atrocities like those committed by Ishiyama and Ishii would never happen. One incident, maybe. Twice, unlikely. Three times? They could only occur with some higher-up's blessing.

So what can be taken from the Kyushu Imperial University trial? It brings current notions of the Japanese biological warfare program into new perspective. It expands the view and opens a couple of new window shades. Popular notions tend to revolve around the "glamour" of weapons of mass destruction, but in truth the Japanese biological experimentation program entailed more mundane but often no less destructive, aspects. Chinese and Russian prisoners were frozen alive, then thawed out, then allowed to die. Innocent civilians were forcibly filled with air until they died. Americans were vivisected and filled with seawater. A murder by way of anthrax and a murder by way of surgical scalpel amounts to the same thing, only one is less exotic than the other. But tell that to the victims.

It also destroys the American government's assertion that no American POWs suffered or died at the hands of the Japanese biological experimentation program. Clearly eight American B-29 fliers did. The public record states this unequivocally. And if they died, it opens the possibility that captured Americans held at POW camps like the ones in Mukden were subject to experimentation—a claim made by former POWs but denied vehemently by Washington politicians. By allowing the Kyushu case to go to trial, Washington inadvertently supplied future generations of investigators with the gift of plausible possibility. The 2,192-page transcript of Docket 290—the *United States v. Kajuro Aihara et al.*—stands as a validation of every allegation—past, present, and future—of the notion that American prisoners of war suffered under the Japanese biological experimentation program. The POWs in Mukden, Harbin, and Kyushu all belonged to the same tragedy.

Epilogue

The runway on North Field, Guam, was an unforgiving strip of cement. If a pilot's takeoff wasn't perfect, the outcome wasn't complicated: he and his crew died. The airstrip measured roughly 8,000 feet long but felt shorter once the bomber hit speeds upward of 100 miles per hour. The overrun area—the extra space after the runway ended—measured roughly 200 feet; beyond it lay a dense thicket of trees that ended with a cliff plunging hundreds of feet straight to the pristine Pacific Ocean waters.

Accelerating down the runway had to be executed with the utmost care. Stopping a 31,000-pound piece of machinery wasn't like hitting the brakes on a Ford; it took time and distance. Aborting was far from ideal but loomed as a definite possibility. It didn't take much to destroy a plane's ascent. If a B-29 hadn't hit 115 miles per hour by the time it reached the 6,000-foot mark on the runway, it would not make the takeoff. Once the plane passed that mark, the only option was to continue up toward the clouds, or through the trees and down into the ocean.

A little before 0600 hours on May 5, 1945, First Lieutenant Marvin S. Watkins and his crew waited patiently for their turn to taxi into position at the front of the runway. From there, it would be a matter of seconds until they were airborne. Fortunately, General LeMay scheduled takeoff for early morning; the weather teetered in the mid-70s. Had takeoff been scheduled later in the day—most missions left at 1500 hours—the temperature might have reached the 100s, and after sitting in the sun for the entire day, the shimmering metal shell of the bomber became impossible to touch. The inside of a sun-soaked bomber made you think of hell and fire and things you never wanted to think about before taking off on a mission.

Marvin Watkins, the bomber's chief pilot, shouldered the responsibility of his crew's well-being, particularly when they were on the plane. The soft-spoken but self-assured Virginian watched over the crew and over the course of time developed into a big brother of sorts. He was not much older than his crew mates—at least not old enough to be considered a father figure—but his position dictated that he maintain a degree of authority over them. With it came the burden of culpability. If anything ever happened to his men, Marvin would never forgive himself.

The key crew members involved with the takeoff all sat in the front fuselage. Marvin, the ranking officer and bomber's pilot, sat in front of the plane's extensive controls and indicators that told him everything about the bomber—from the RPMs to the mixture of air and fuel in the engines.

Second Lieutenant William Fredericks, the copilot from a small northern New Jersey town, sat across the narrow aisle from Marvin, facing a similar set of controls. He would watch the controls for Marvin during takeoff and inform him when they hit the 6,000-foot mark on the runway.

Sergeant Teddy Ponczka, the engineer from Philadelphia, made up the third key member of the crew involved in the takeoff: he would monitor the plane's oil pressure and fuel-to-air ratio in the engine.

There wasn't much to say while waiting to take off for a mission. After all, what could you say to a man whose wife and child waited for him back home in America? Or whose parents counted the missions until his tour was completed at twenty-five? Nothing. Words meant little if anything. It was simply one of those times when silence became part of the proper, unspoken protocol. And they all knew instinctively what they wished to communicate: the hope that the mission went smoothly. It meant a safe return and one more completed mission in the bank. Of course, everyone sitting in the B-29—the Watkins crew—understood and accepted the fact that a return to North Field was far from guaranteed. They weren't fools. That was war.

In reality, the Watkins crew did not have to wait long to take off. Planes flying missions left in thirty-second intervals. No sooner had one plane left the island when another taxied into position and readied itself to make its own run down the airstrip. So even if Marvin and his men had been the final crew—the twelfth—to take off, they would only wait six minutes.

Marvin made a final preflight check of his instruments. At the same time, Fredericks conducted a similar inspection. He would relieve Marvin during the course of the flight and served as a second set of eyes for the pilot as the plane entered enemy airspace. Their indicators had to work perfectly.

North Field served as the XX Air Force's major airbase in the Pacific Theater during the latter stages of World War II. The major aerial assaults against Japanese targets—Tokyo, Kyoto, and Hiroshima—emanated from Guam. The base had two runways, both of which led into a wall of trees, then to the cliff at the end of the island. A taxi strip ran parallel to each runway; a "parking lot" of bombers on hard stops fed the strip. Beyond the airstrips lay the XX Air Force's barracks. For the time being, North Field, Guam, was home for hundreds of men like Marvin and his crew.

The bomber directly in front of Marvin started its dash down the runway. An inconspicuous crawl evolved into an engine-blasting, black rubber–burning, all-out 120-mile-per-hour sprint toward the sky. The crew and pilot in that bomber knew about the wall of trees and cliff, and as the B-29 neared the end of the strip, ground crews and fellow airmen held their breaths. Slowly, like an old man pushing out of bed, the plane lifted into the air and over the trees. The takeoff ordeal was not finished, though.

No sooner had the plane become airborne than its nose dipped; the monstrous bomber plunged toward the water. Onlookers choked a collective gasp as it disappeared from the horizon, blocked by land and beyond people's visions. Unlike potential takeoff disasters, this was a planned maneuver that allowed pilots to use the plane's weight and momentum to pick up speed without sucking much-valued fuel. It was risky and not a necessity; the maneuver could easily result in disaster. A few millimeters of excessive yoke movement could send the plane into a downward tailspin. With the bomber flying at speeds over 150 miles per hour, the ocean surface may as well have been cement and the plane a crystal figurine.

But in this case, there was no disaster—only the majesty of a sleek bomber coursing toward the sun like Apollo's chariot. Everyone exhaled.

Now it was Marvin's turn, and he guided his B-29 onto the runway. He centered the plane. Began counting the seconds. Thirty, twenty-nine, twenty-eight, twenty-seven. It would be his turn to test the laws of physics.

So many things could go wrong during the course of a mission that it felt as if the crews had two enemies: the Japanese and fate. For a stretch of three long missions, the Watkins crew struggled to make it back to North Field, each time having to conduct emergency landings on Iwo Jima because of engine failure, lack of fuel, or structural damage to the plane. In eight missions since their arrival on Guam in March 1945, they appeared destined for death. Adversity followed them like the smoke trailing from their engines.

Marvin and his men were warned time and again: "If you are shot down over enemy territory, do not get taken by civilians. Go to the military." Local villagers—the logic went—killed American soldiers immediately. And if the Watkins crew ever forgot the advice, the side arms slung over their shoulders served as ominous reminders that if things went badly, they could go very badly. If you were shot down over enemy territory, there was nothing a pistol could do to aid you. Everyone understood why it was given to them: suicide.

Nobody could blame the Watkins crew if uncertainty clouded their eyes. Nobody would hold it against them if their mouths dried up and their stomachs tangled into knots and their neck muscles suddenly made it impossible to look anywhere but forward. Clammy palms, puddle brows, springboard knees, marble fingers, empty breaths—they were all understandable. Only fools felt no fear in the face of danger and death; it fell to the brave to overcome their insecurities.

Marvin rested his hand on the four throttles that formed a single lever, pressing his palm against the cold metal. He waited for the signal from the ground crew, but in his head he continued his countdown—ten, nine, eight, seven, six, five. His fingers curled, locking the throttle beneath his grip. Everything had to be perfect. Four. Perfect. Three. Perfect. Two. Perfect. One.

Push.

Marvin eased the throttle forward, and an amorphous groan gushed from the engine. The bomber rolled forward like a baby crawling for the first time. Its movement bordered on unnoticeable from the inside of the plane unless you glanced out of the window.

The bomber's gunners sat in the middle fuselage, an area where the central fire control gunner, Corporal John Colehower, and the left and right gunners, Corporal Robert Johnson and Corporal Leo Oeinck, were stationed during the mission. During takeoff, the tail gunner, Corporal Leo Czarnecki, joined them in the seats. He would return to his station immediately before the cabins were pressurized at 500 feet. Like the bombardier, navigator, radar and radio operators, there was nothing for the gunners to do during takeoff—except think.

"10 miles per hour," Fredericks called out.

Thousands of pounds of metal and explosives drifted down the airstrip. The inside of the bomber remained steady. The blurry hint of a rumble leaked through the plane's chambers and the metal structure's weak guttural groan continued.

The Boeing B-29 represented the state of the art in long-distance bombers. It was majestic. Next to it, the B-17—its predecessor—looked like a sparrow. The wingspan of the B-29 Superfortress stretched 141 feet tip to tip; from nose to tail, it measured 99 feet; and from top to bottom, it stood 28 feet high. Four 18-cylinder engines carried it from the ground to the air. Six guns were positioned throughout the plane: two over and under the front fuselage, two side and one top gun over the bomber's midsection, and one tail gun. The plane's long, narrow, streamlined design added a sleek elegance to the

B-29 as it coursed through the air. It looked as if it were a boat floating along a soft, steady, unseen current. There was no other plane like it.

Yet for all of the B-29's technological and aeronautical advances, it possessed one devastating drawback: the U.S. military had approved it for combat without thoroughly testing it. Early B-29 crews discovered the bomber's limitations firsthand, and many times it cost lives. Planes crashed on takeoff; engines exploded from faulty maintenance—a learning curve often accompanied the introduction of new technology. The necessary fuel load proved so variable and dependent on different factors that bombers often ran out of gas on the way back to North Field from a mission.

"20 miles per hour."

The edge of the airstrip and the thin layer of trees melted into the horizon. Marvin guided the plane forward, paying careful attention to the nose. He made sure that it remained centered on the strip as he babied the plane forward like a parent urging a child into his first steps. As its wheels spun faster, an occasional bump interrupted the smooth ride; as the engines churned, the soft rumble grew harder and the plane groaned louder.

From Colehower's vantage point, he could see straight out of the central bubble and into the clouds. Heaven and God and paradise were all up there, hidden and waiting to reveal themselves. At least that's what people said in church. He knew better, though. He knew his truth. In a few hours, the sky's tranquility would crumble like a ball of ash. It would be filled with black anti-aircraft explosions, white-hot shards of shrapnel, Japanese fighter planes, and swarms of enemy gunfire. Rather than discovering heaven, nothing but hell existed between the clouds.

"30 miles per hour."

The loneliest part of the mission arose when the rumble of the engine grew loud enough that speaking actually became pointless. The bumps in the ride got harder and more frequent. Alone with your thoughts, your mind drifted to the past—a child on a farm in Pennsylvania, a teenager walking home from a Philadelphia high school, an uncertain worker on his first day in a factory. Suddenly, the reality of war and death crystallized—"40 miles per hour"—stacking doubt on doubt. You shuddered because the plane no longer slid down the airstrip—it bobbed and shook and groaned and a weary hum painted your ears.

"50 miles per hour."

And you saw faces, distant smiles, and eyes frozen against time. Memories rushed back, but distance tempered whatever solace they once offered: the wind playing with loose strands of your wife's hair, pushed back in a ponytail, drifting against the milky arch of her neck; the way her brows smiled with her eyes when she laughed; the cotton touch of her hand—they all faded with the runway.

There was nothing to say and you sat alone—"60 miles per hour"—stiff jointed, clutching onto your prayers. Isolated from the world by sound—four earthquake rumbles from the engines—the crushing hum of the plane piercing through the air—the desperate groan of the plane's body bending back against the air—"65 miles per hour"—the soldiers toiled alone in sound.

"70 miles per hour."

Marvin watched the runway and guided the bomber. Fredericks monitored the RPMs and called out the speed. Ponczka focused on the oil gauge. Eveyone else waited.

"75 miles per hour."

Marvin's feet held the rudders steady; his hands gripped the yoke. Straight. The plane had to be straight and pointing to the trees, which suddenly seemed to concretize and leap closer—too close. If Marvin wasn't careful, the bomber wouldn't have enough speed to hit the takeoff. At 6,000 feet on the runway, he had to be at 115 miles per hour. If he wasn't—and Fredericks would inform him immediately—there was still a few seconds to abort the takeoff before plunging into trees and possibly off the cliff.

"80 miles per hour."

And the runway was shrinking. The plane shook. A violent rumble and hum cloaked the crew. Out of the side blisters in the middle of the plane, the wings flapped up and down like a bird's wings—"85 miles per hour"—though they were supposed to have a degree of flex so that they did not snap like twigs. But did they have to bend like cheap plastic boards?

"90 miles per hour."

Disgustingly little runway left and at least 25 more miles per hour to break ground. Only Marvin, Fredericks, and Ponczka could see how the plane faired—"93 miles per hour." The yoke danced in Marvin's hand—"95 miles per hour"—and the seats seemed ready to tear the bolts from the floor—"97 miles per hour"—and the edge of the island was no longer a blur—"99 miles per hour"—and they could discern individual trees.

"100 miles per hour."

Fifteen MPH more and the 6,000-foot mark lay too close. Nobody wanted to abort.

"105 miles per hour."

The plane could tear through the trees but in the form of a fireball. The bomber's engines screeched from stress.

"110 miles per hour, almost there."

The pressure from the plane's velocity tightened the crew's chests.

"115 miles per hour . . . 117 miles per hour . . . 6,000 feet . . ."

Marvin felt the plane lighten. It was beginning to break ground and the downforce on the tires lessened.

"119 miles per hour."

Marvin eased the yoke back. No response. The leaves on the trees were visible.

"120 miles per hour."

The rumble and shaking and hum and screech dissipated quickly as the plane freed itself from the ground. They cleared the trees and the cliff and floated 700 feet above water. Marvin pushed the yoke forward, easing the plane downward. The bomber plunged toward the water. It pushed faster and faster until Marvin pulled back on the yoke one last time. The plane climbed toward the sky and Japan. There was no turning back.

Notes

Prologue

1. Author interview with Glendon Watkins. June 2002.
2. Author interview with Robert Michelson. November 2001.
3. Deacon, Richard. *Kempei Tai: A History of the Japanese Secret Service.* New York: Beaufort Books, 1983.
4. Ibid.
5. Testimony of Marvin S. Watkins. March 20, 1947. SCAP Files. Record Group 331. National Archives at College Park, College Park, Md. (hereafter referred to as NACP).
6. Ibid.

1. October 1945: CIC Headquarters

1. Trial transcript. *U.S. v. Kajuro Aihara et al.* Case Docket 290. Record Group 153. NACP.
2. *The History of the Counter Intelligence Corps.* New York: Garland, 1989.
3. Ibid.
4. Ibid.
5. Memorandum to the officer in charge. November 24, 1945. Subject: War Atrocity. Re Progress Report. SCAP Legal Section Case Files. RG 331. NACP.
6. Although the term SCAP technically referred to General Douglas MacArthur's position as head of the occupation in Japan, it came to refer to the entire occupation force.
7. Memorandum to the officer in charge. November 24, 1945.

8. Ibid.
9. Ibid.
10. Memorandum to the officer in charge regarding War Atrocity Progress Report. November 24, 1945. 496th Counter Intelligence Corps Detachment Headquarters, 5th Marine Division. SCAP Legal Section Case Files. RG 331. NACP.
11. Ibid.
12. Memorandum to the officer in charge regarding War Atrocity Progress Report. December 15, 1945. CIC Metropolitan Unit 94, Oita Detachment. SCAP Legal Section Case Files. RG 331. NACP.
13. Memorandum to the officer in charge regarding War Atrocity Progress Report. November 24, 1945.
14. Ibid.
15. Ibid.
16. SCAP Legal Section Case Files. RG 331. Section 290. Box 1775.
17. Statement of Masaru Mizota. Memorandum to the officer in Charge. November 24, 1945. Subject: Certified true copy of Confession of Killing on July 28, 1945, an American crashed B-29 crewman. SCAP Legal Section Case Files. RG 331. NACP.
18. Memorandum to the officer in charge regarding War Atrocity Progress Report. December 15, 1945.
19. Approximation of interrogation based on the summary report filed by Cheles.

2. October 1945: Western Army Headquarters

1. Dialogue based on testimonies of Fukushima Kyusaku, Sato Yoshinao. SCAP Legal Section Case Files. RG 331. NACP.
2. Interrogation of Fukushima Kyusaku. August 18, 1947. SCAP Legal Section Case Files. RG 331. NACP.
3. Ibid.
4. Ibid.
5. Interrogation of Sato Yoshinao. February 13, 1947. SCAP Legal Section Case Files. RG 331. NACP.
6. Interrogation of Fukushima Kyusaku. August 18, 1947.

3. October–November 1945

1. Yokoyama Isamu Military History. SCAP Legal Section Case Files. RG 331. NACP.

2. Interrogation of Yokoyama Isamu. August 18, 1947. SCAP Legal Section Case Files. NACP.
3. Interrogation of Sato Yoshinao. February 13, 1947.
4. Dialogue based on interrogation of Sato Yoshinao. February 13, 1947.
5. Interrogation of Yokoyama Isamu. August 18, 1947.
6. Yokoyama Isamu Military History.
7. Interrogation of Yokoyama Isamu. August 18, 1947.
8. Yokoyama Isamu Military History.
9. Jones, F. C. *Manchuria since 1931*. London: Oxford University Press, 1949.
10. Interrogation of Sato Yoshinao. February 13, 1947.
11. Interrogation of Fukushima Kyusaku. August 18, 1947.
12. Memorandum to the officer in charge regarding War Atrocity Progress Report. December 15, 1945.
13. Dialogue based on summary of the CIC interrogation of Sato Yoshinao as reported in the Decemer 15, 1945, CIC report.
14. Ibid.
15. Interrogation of Fukushima Kyusaku. August 18, 1947.
16. Ibid.
17. Ibid.
18. Ibid.
19. Memorandum to the officer in charge regarding War Atrocity Progress Report. December 15, 1945.
20. Ibid.
21. Ibid.
22. Ibid.
23. CIC memorandum for the officer in charge. March 28, 1946. Subject: Copy of list of American airmen beheaded in Southern Military District H.Q., Fukuoka-shi, written by confidential informant in Fukuoka. SCAP Legal Section Case Files. RG 331. NACP. Dialogue based on summary of interrogation cited in report.

4. December 1945–February 1946

1. Interrogation of Fukushima Kyusaku. August 18, 1947.
2. Ibid.
3. Ibid.
4. Ibid.
5. Ibid.
6. Ibid.
7. Dialogue based on interrogation of Fukushima Kyusaku. August 18, 1947.
8. Interrogation of Sato Yoshinao. February 13, 1947.

9. Testimony of Inada Masazumi. August 18, 1947. SCAP Legal Section Case Files. RG 331. NACP.
10. Ibid.
11. Testimony of Ito Shoshin. October 18, 1946. SCAP Legal Section Case Files. RG 331. NACP.
12. Report of Investigation. July 2, 1949. SCAP Legal Section Case Files. RG 331. NACP.
13. Interrogation of Sato Yoshinao. February 13, 1947.
14. CIC memorandum to the officer in charge. December 12, 1945. Subject: War Atrocity. SCAP Legal Section Case Files. RG 331. NACP.
15. Ibid.
16. CIC memorandum for the officer in charge. March 29, 1946. Subject: The beheading of thirty-one (31) prisoners of war by Fukuoka Garrison and subsequent conspiracy to conceal this atrocity. SCAP Legal Section Case Files. RG 331. NACP. Dialogue based on summary of interrogation cited in report.
17. Ibid.
18. Esposito notes in his report: "Note also that there are several rather important discrepancies to be noted between the evidence set down in Exhibit 2 and the evidence set down in Exhibits 3 and 5. All of these three exhibits, (2, 3, and 5) are reports by Sato Yoshinao."

5. April 1946

1. Testimony of Kusumoto Tominosuka. August 20, 1947. SCAP Legal Section Case Files. RG 331. NACP.
2. Ibid.
3. CIC interrogation of Kusumoto Tominosuka. No date. SCAP Legal Section Case Files. RG 331. NACP.
4. Ibid.
5. CIC interrogation of Nishihara Kanji. No date. SCAP Legal Section Case Files. RG 331. NACP.
6. Testimony of Akita Hiroshi. May 6, 1947. SCAP Legal Section Case Files. RG 331. NACP.
7. CIC interrogation of Akita Hiroshi. No date. SCAP Legal Section Case Files. RG 331. NACP.
8. CIC interrogation of Fukushima Kyusaku. No date. SCAP Legal Section Case Files. RG 331. NACP.
9. CIC interrogation of Inada Akamine. No date. SCAP Legal Section Case Files. RG 331. NACP.
10. Second CIC Interrogation of Oki Genzaburo. No date. SCAP Legal Section Case Files. RG 331. NACP.

6. The Families: January–March 1946

1. *New York Times.* January 1, 1946.
2. *New York Times.* January 2, 1946.
3. McCullough, David. "The Buck Stops Here." *Truman.* New York: Simon & Schuster, 1992.
4. *New York Times.* January 4, 1946.
5. Missing Air Crew Report. No date. SCAP Legal Section Case Files. RG 331. NACP.
6. Interrogation of Marvin S. Watkins. March 20, 1947.
7. Dialogue based on recollections of Marvin Watkins during questioning.
8. Interrogation of Marvin S. Watkins. March 20, 1947.

7. Sato and Aihara: June 1946

1. Interrogation of Kajuro Aihara. April 1, 1947. SCAP Legal Section Case Files. RG 153. NACP.
2. Interrogation of Kajuro Aihara. June 30, 1946. SCAP Legal Section Case Files. RG 153. NACP.
3. Ibid.
4. Testimony of Wako Yusei. August 25, 1947. Legal Section Case Files. RG 153. NACP.
5. Ibid.
6. Ibid.
7. Ibid.
8. Testimony of Yukino Koshi. June 18, 1946. Legal Section Case Files. RG 153. NACP.
9. Testimony of Murata Sadayoshi. December 12, 1946. Legal Section Case Files. RG 153. NACP.
10. Ibid.
11. Ibid.
12. Ibid.
13. Testimony of Wako Yusei. August 25, 1947.
14. Testimony of Onishi Tamotsu. November 6, 1947. Legal Section Case Files. RG 153. NACP.
15. Ibid.
16. Ibid.
17. Ibid.
18. Ibid.
19. Testimony of Toji Kentaro. December 29, 1947. Legal Section Case Files. RG 153. NACP.

20. Testimony of Onishi Tamotsu. November 6, 1947.
21. Testimony of Murata Sadayoshi. December 12, 1946.
22. Ibid.
23. Ibid.
24. Ibid.
25. Testimony of Onishi Tamotsu. November 6, 1947.
26. Testimony of Toji Kentaro. December 29, 1947.
27. Testimony of Murata Sadayoshi. December 12, 1946.
28. Ibid.
29. Testimony of Sato Yoshinao. June 30, 1946. RG 153. NACP.

8. University Suspects: July 13–17, 1946

1. SCAP Files. RG 331. NACP.
2. Testimony of Hirao Kenichi. July 13, 1946. RG 153. NACP.
3. Testimony of Tsutsui Shizuko. July 14, 1946. RG 153. NACP.
4. Testimony of Torisu Taro. July 14, 1946. RG 153. NACP.
5. Testimony of Hirako Goichi. July 15, 1946. RG 153. NACP.
6. Testimony of Morimoto Kenji. July 10, 1947. RG 153. NACP.
7. Testimony of Mori Yoshio. September 3, 1947. RG 153. NACP.
8. Testimony of Senba Yoshitaka. September 2, 1947. RG 153. NACP.
9. Based on testimonies gathered between July 13 and July 19, 1946.

9. Ishiyama: July 15–17, 1946

1. Interrogation of Ishiyama Fukujiro. July 15, 1946. SCAP Legal Section Case Files. RG 153. NACP.
2. Ibid.
3. Ibid.
4. Ibid.
5. Gold, Hal. *Unit 731: Testimony.* Yen Books, 1996.
6. Interrogation of Ishiyama Fukujiro. July 15, 1946.
7. Harris, Sheldon H. *Factories of Death.* London: Routledge, 1994.
8. Interrogation of Ishiyama Fukujiro. July 15, 1946.
9. Interrogation of Ishiyama Fukujiro. July 17, 1946. SCAP Legal Section Case Files. RG 153. NACP.
10. Report of Investigation Division, Legal Section, GHQ SCAP. July 18, 1946. Inv. Div. No. 604. R. N. Tait. "Suicide of Fukujiro Ishiyama at Dotemachi Prison, Fukuoka City." SCAP Legal Section Case Files. RG 153. NACP.
11. Ibid.

12. Ibid.
13. Ibid.
14. Ibid.

10. Marvin: Spring–Fall 1946

1. Author interview with Beatrice Watkins. August 2002.
2. SCAP Files. RG 331. NACP.

11. One Step at a Time: August–December 1946

1. Report of Investigation Division, Legal Section, GHQ SCAP. August 19, 1946. R. N. Tait. "Japanese Western Army Atrocities." SCAP Legal Section Case Files. RG 331. NACP.
2. Tait comments: "It was obvious during the review of these reports that many of the persons arrested were exerting their utmost effort to vindicate themselves, through lies, and concealment of information. By making general counteraccusations of minor importance, they were successfully attempting to confuse the investigating agents." Report of Investigation Division. August 19, 1946.
3. Ibid.
4. Ibid.
5. Ibid.
6. Ibid.
7. Report of Investigation Division, Legal Section, GHQ, SCAP. October 15, 1946. R. N. Tait. "Kajuro Aihara et al. (Japanese Western Army Atrocities)." Inv. Div. No. 420. SCAP Legal Section Case Files. RG 331. NACP.
8. Ibid.
9. Ibid.
10. Memorandum. September 21, 1946. Subject: Casualty Information No. 6751; To: The Adjutant General of the Army. Marvin Watkins. SCAP Legal Section Case Files. RG 331. NACP.
11. SCAP Files. RG 331. NACP.
12. Legal Section Memorandum. October 19, 1946. L. H. Barnard. SCAP Legal Section Case Files. RG 331. NACP.
13. Report of Investigation Division, Legal Section, GHQ, SCAP. October 8, 1946. L. H. Barnard. "Fukujiro Ishiyama et al." SCAP Legal Section Case Files. RG 331. NACP.
14. Ibid.
15. Ibid.
16. Ibid.

17. Ibid.
18. Ibid.
19. Ibid.
20. Report of the Investigation Division, Legal Section, GHQ, SCAP. November 18, 1946. L. H. Barnard. "Fukujiro Ishiyama et al." SCAP Legal Section Case Files. RG 331. NACP.
21. Ibid.
22. Ibid.
23. Ibid.
24. Report of the Investigation Division, Legal Section, GHQ, SCAP. November 28, 1946. Joseph Sartiano. "Fukujiro Ishiyama et al." SCAP Legal Section Case Files. RG 331. NACP.
25. Ibid.
26. Ibid.
27. Letter from Hirako Goichi. December 3, 1946. SCAP Legal Section. RG 153. NACP.

12. Synthesis to Schism: January–April 1947

1. Memorandum. January 17, 1947. Subject: Bacteriological Warfare Experiments by Japanese. To: Assistant Chief of Staff, G-2 FEC. Military Intelligence Section, General Staff, GHQ, FEC.
2. Ibid.
3. Inv. Div. No. 330. "Motoji Yamaguchi; Yujiro Wakamatsu; Yasuzaka (fnu); Yasautaro Hosaka, alias Yasutaro Hozaka; Shiro Matsushita, alias Shiro Yamashita; Lt. Gen. Shiro Ishii." SCAP Legal Section Case Files. RG 331. NACP.
4. Inv. Div. No. 330. "Lt. Gen. Shiro Ishii." SCAP Legal Section Case Files. RG 331. NACP.
5. Inv. Div. No. 1117. "Infectious Disease Research Laboratory." SCAP Legal Section Case Files. RG 331. NACP.
6. Inv. Div. No. 997. "Noboru Ariyama and Atsushi Sato." SCAP Legal Section Case Files. RG 331. NACP.
7. Report of Investigation Division, Legal Section, GHQ, SCAP. January 28, 1947. Neal R. Smith. "Motoji Yamaguchi et al." Inv. Div. No. 330. SCAP Legal Section Case Files. RG 331. NACP.
8. Ibid.
9. Ibid.
10. Report of Investigation Division, Legal Section, GHQ, SCAP. January 23, 1947. L. H. Barnard. "Kajuro Aihara et al." Inv. Div. No. 420. SCAP Legal Section Case Files. RG 331. NACP.

11. Report of Investigation Division, Legal Section, GHQ, SCAP. January 28, 1947. Norman Tracy. "Kajuro Aihara et al." Inv. Div. No. 420. SCAP Legal Section Case Files. RG 331. NACP.
12. Ibid.
13. Ibid.
14. Mori went so far as to declare that Fredericks resembled his brother-in-law.
15. Report of Investigation Division, Legal Section, GHQ, SCAP. January 28, 1947. Neal R. Smith. "Motoji Yamaguchi et al."
16. Memorandum for Record. February 7, 1947. Subject: Russian Request to Interrogate Japanese on Bacteriological Warfare. To: Chief of Staff. Military Intelligence Section, General Staff, GHQ, FEC. NACP.
17. Harris, Sheldon H. *Factories of Death*. London: Routledge, 1994.
18. Ibid.
19. Top Secret Memorandum to MacArthur from the Joint Chiefs of Staff. March 20, 1947. War Department. NACP.
20. Ibid.
21. Report of Investigation Division, Legal Section, GHQ, SCAP. February 28, 1947. Norman S. Tracy. "Fukujiro Ishiyama et al." Inv. Div. No. 420. SCAP Legal Section Case Files. RG 331. NACP.
22. Ibid.
23. Ibid.
24. Ibid.
25. Ibid.
26. Ibid.
27. Ibid.
28. Ibid.
29. Memorandum for Record. May 6, 1947. NACP.
30. Report of Investigation Division, Legal Section, GHQ, SCAP. April 18, 1947. Neal R. Smith. "Motoji Yamaguchi et al." Inv. Div. No. 330. SCAP Legal Section Case Files. RG 331. NACP.

13. From Tokyo to Kyushu: April–June 1947

1. Report of Investigation Division, Legal Section, GHQ, SCAP. April 23, 1947. Norman S. Tracy. "Kajuro Aihara et al. (Western Army Atrocities and Murder of eight (8) POWs in Medical Experiments at Kyushu Imperial University)." SCAP Files. RG 331. NACP.
2. Ibid.
3. Ibid.
4. Ibid.
5. Ibid.

6. Ibid.
7. Ibid.
8. Ibid.
9. Ibid.
10. Report of Investigation Division, Legal Section, GHQ, SCAP. April 25, 1947. Neal R. Smith. "Noboru Ariyama et al." SCAP Files. RG 331. NACP.
11. Ibid.
12. Testimony of Tomoda Masanobu. May 14, 1947. SCAP Files. RG 331. NACP.
13. Ibid.
14. Ibid.
15. Ibid.
16. Handwritten notes by Robert Miller. May 15, 1947. SCAP Files. RG 331. NACP.
17. Ibid.
18. Ibid.
19. Ibid.
20. Ibid.
21. Ibid.
22. Ibid.
23. Report of Investigation Division, Legal Section, GHQ, SCAP. June 9, 1947. Neal R. Smith. "Kajuro Aihara et al." SCAP Files. RG 331. NACP.
24. Testimony of Jinnaka Seichi. May 15, 1947. SCAP Files. RG 331. NACP.
25. Ibid.
26. Ibid.
27. Testimony of Ohno Yukizo. May 16, 1947. SCAP Files. RG 331. NACP.
28. Ibid.
29. Ibid.
30. Testimony of Tsurumaru Hironaga. July 1, 1947. SCAP Files. RG 331. NACP.
31. Ibid.
32. Handwritten notes by Robert Miller.
33. Testimony of Goiyama Shinji. July 1, 1947. SCAP Files. RG 331. NACP.
34. Testimony of Makino Reichiro. June 26, 1947. SCAP Files. RG 331. NACP.
35. Testimony of Kishi Tatsuro. July 10, 1947. SCAP Files. RG 331. NACP.
36. Testimony of Matake Shichiro. June 18, 1947. SCAP Files. RG 331. NACP.

14. The Liver Case: July 1947–February 1948

1. Testimony of Tsurumaru Hironaga. July 1, 1947. SCAP Files. RG 331. NACP.
2. Account based on Tsurumaru's account of the luncheon at the Kaikosha Hospital dining room.
3. Testimony of Tsurumaru Hironaga. July 1, 1947.
4. Testimony of Kishi Tatsuro. July 10, 1947. SCAP Files. RG 331. NACP.
5. Testimony of Ito Akira. July 11, 1947.
6. Testimony of Matake Shichiro. July 14, 1947. SCAP Files. RG 331. NACP.
7. Testimony of Miyamoto Genso (July 23, 1947), Shinno Junjiro (July 17, 1947), Kamata Nasafusa (July 22, 1947), and Oda Tayuru (July 16, 1947).
8. Testimony of Tsurumaru Hironaga. July 1, 1947.
9. Testimony of Kishi Tatsuro. July 10, 1947.
10. Testimony of Oda Tayuro (defense). July 21, 1948. SCAP Files. RG 331. NACP.
11. Testimony of Tsurumaru Hironaga (defense). July 21, 1948. SCAP Files. RG 331. NACP.
12. Testimony of Oda Tayuro (defense). July 21, 1948.
13. Ibid.
14. Testimony of Kishi Tatsuro. July 10, 1947.

15. Closure: September 1947–March 1948

1. Civil Affairs Division Telecom. September 10, 1947. SCAP Files. RG 331. NACP.
2. Civil Affairs Division Telecom. September 14, 1947. SCAP Files. RG 331. NACP.
3. Report of Investigation Division, Legal Section, GHQ, SCAP. April 10, 1948. Robert E. Miller. "Case 712: Tokihiro Sato et al." SCAP Files. RG 331. NACP.
4. Ibid.
5. Ibid.
6. Ibid.
7. Ibid.
8. Ibid.
9. Ibid.
10. Report of Investigation Division, Legal Section, GHQ, SCAP. July 2, 1949. Robert E. Miller. "Kajuro Aihara et al." SCAP Files. RG 331. NACP.
11. Report of Investigation Division, Legal Section, GHQ, SCAP. April 10, 1948. Robert E. Miller. "Case 712: Tokihiro Sato et al."

12. Ibid.
13. Itinerary of Marvin Watkins. SCAP Files. RG 331. NACP.
14. Ibid.
15. Report of Investigation Division, Legal Section, GHQ, SCAP. April 10, 1948. Robert E. Miller. "Case 712: Tokihiro Sato et al."
16. Ibid.
17. Itinerary of Marvin Watkins.
18. Report of Investigation Division, Legal Section, GHQ, SCAP. April 10, 1948. Robert E. Miller. "Case 712: Tokihiro Sato et al."
19. Author interview with Beatrice Watkins. August 2002.
20. Ibid.
21. Report of Investigation Division, Legal Section, GHQ, SCAP. April 10, 1948. Robert E. Miller. "Case 712: Tokihiro Sato et al."
22. Ibid.
23. Ibid.

16. The Trial: 1948

1. Trial transcript. *U.S. v. Kajuro Aihara et al.* Case Docket 290. Record Group 153. NACP.
2. All dialogue from trial transcript.

17. Prosecution: 1948

1. Trial transcript. *U.S. v. Kajuro Aihara et al.* Case Docket 290. Record Group 153. NACP.
2. Scene is a reconstruction based on testimonies of Hirako, Mori, Torisu, Morimoto, Senba, and Miki.

18. Closing and Clemency: 1948–1950

1. Trial transcript. *U.S. v. Kajuro Aihara et al.* Case Docket 290. Record Group 153. NACP.
2. U.S. Department of State. *Foreign Relations of the U.S. Government.* 1950.

Index